*1. Unfolding the Mystery*

# Unfolding the Mystery
# of Religious Life

CONSECRATION AND SERVICE

Volume II

# unfolding the mystery of

## religious life

by
REV. ELIO GAMBARI, S.M.M.

*Translated and abridged by*
*Mary Magdalen Bellasis, O.S.U.*
*and others.*

ST. PAUL EDITIONS

Original title:
*Manuale della Vita Religiosa alla Luce del Vaticano II*
Vol. II: Svolgimento e pratica della vita religiosa

Centro Mariano Monfortano, Via Prenestina 1391, 00010 Salone, Roma, 1971.

*Nihil Obstat:*
   P. Patrizio Zuliani, Sup. Prov.
   Rome, July 2, 1970

*Imprimatur:*
   ✚ Pietro Severi, Vesc. di Palestrina
   Palestrina, July 16, 1970

*Library of Congress Catalog Card Number: 73-86210*

In filial homage to
THE FAITHFUL VIRGIN
Perfect image of religious life

TO HIS HOLINESS PAUL VI
Highest Superior of the Communities
of consecrated life

# CONTENTS

15

## Chapter II — **Chastity**

## Chapter III — **Poverty**

## Chapter IV — **Obedience**

## Chapter V—**The common life**

## Chapter VI—**The life of prayer in a praying community**

## Chapter VII—**Prophetic and apostolic dimension**

# Chapter VIII—**The life-style of religious**

# Chapter IX—**Religious meet and unite in the Church**

# Chapter X—**In union with the hierarchy**

# Chapter XI—**Principles underlying the structures of government**

## Chapter XII — **Authority in religious life**

## Chapter XIII — **The institute and its parts**

## Chapter XIV — **Organs of government and collaboration**

## Chapter XVII─**The religious vocation: fidelity**

## Abbreviations of the Council Documents
## used in this book

AA      *Apostolicam actuositatem*, Decree on the Apostolate of the Laity.

AG      *Ad gentes*, Decree on the Mission Activity of
the Church.

CD      *Christus Dominus*, Decree Concerning the Pastoral Office of Bishops in the Church.

DV      *Dei Verbum*, Dogmatic Constitution on Divine
Revelation.

DH      *Dignitatis humanae*, Declaration on Religious
Freedom.

GS      *Gaudium et spes*, Pastoral Constitution on the
Church in the Modern World.

GE      *Gravissimum educationis*, Declaration on Christian
Education.

IM      *Inter mirifica*, Decree on the Media of Social
Communication.

LG      *Lumen gentium*, Dogmatic Constitution on the
Church.

OT      *Optatam totius*, Decree on Priestly Training.

OE      *Orientalium Ecclesiarum*, Decree on the Catholic
Churches of the Eastern Rite.

PC      *Perfectae caritatis*, Decree on the Adaptation and
Renewal of Religious Life.

PO      *Presbyterorum ordinis*, Decree on the Ministry
and Life of Priests.

SC      *Sacrosanctum concilium*, Constitution on the
Sacred Liturgy.

UR      *Unitatis redintegratio*, Decree on Ecumenism.

## Other Documents

ES      *Ecclesiae Sanctae,* Motu Proprio of 8-6-66. Norms for the implementation of some conciliar documents.

ET      *Evangelica testificatio,* Apostolic Exhortation on the Renewal of the Religious Life According to the Teaching of the Second Vatican Council, Paul VI, 6-29-71.

RFIS      *Ratio fundamentalis institutionis sacerdotalis,* A Basic Scheme for Priestly Training, Sacred Congregation for Catholic Education, 1-6-70.

SCl      *Sacerdotalis caelibatus,* Priestly Celibacy, encyclical letter of Pope Paul VI, 6-24-67.

The above documents are available in pamphlet form from the *Daughters of St. Paul,* 50 St. Paul's Ave., Jamaica Plain, Boston, Ma. 02130.

# Chapter I
# Religious life—
# a covenant with God

## A life's program

The fulfillment of the mystery of religious life has its beginning in the mind and heart of God; it leads to the vital encounter between God and man, develops and ripens the divine life of charity in the person who responds generously to God's call, and finds its conclusion in the final meeting with God face to face for eternity.

The basis of it is the new covenant by which baptism incorporates man with Christ in the Church; the source and strength of it is love—predilection on the part of God, love whole and undivided in man's response, which will find expression in contemplation and zeal.

It is a whole program of life for the one who answers God's call by entering into the covenant, for he enters as an individual, with all that goes to make him a person, as a member of human society, as a Christian and as an apostle, pledged to make the Church actively present in the world, and he brings with him all his resources of nature and grace. Moved by the Holy Spirit and aided by the Church, he grows to the stature of the fullness of Christ in every dimension—liturgical and priestly, prophetic and regal, redemptive and apostolic—in the service of his brethren, until the end.

The Constitution *Lumen gentium* speaks of all these dimensions with reference to the People of God and the universal call to holiness (LG 10-13), with particular reference to priests (LG 18,1) and to priestly training (PO 13ff.).

A diagram in Volume I of this work (p. 27) shows religious life growing upwards from Christian life under the figure of a tree with trunk and brances, in which love circulates, permeating, vivifying and sanctifying all, recapitulating all in Christ. Grafted upon Christ, the religious lives with His life and shares in His fecundity as Priest, Prophet, Envoy of the Father and Servant of all until the final *"consummatum est."*

# 1. Preparation

The entry of a person into the mystery of religious life by profession in a particular institute is considered as a new covenant, renewing in some measure the covenant made by God with Abraham and the chosen people, who prefigure the Church and also those chosen by God to be His own people as religious. The oldest formula of profession known to us makes use of the term.[1]

The covenant has three stages; (1) vocation, by which religious life exists in the mind and will of God and is transmitted as a call; (2) formation, in which the one called works together with God in the discovery and development of his vocation, and is given the ability to fulfill it; (3) the acceptance of the call by free and spontaneous choice, sealed and made permanent by the act of religious profession.[2]

# 2. Meaning and content

Profession is the act in which a Christian pledges himself, by public vows of chastity, poverty and obedience, to follow Christ, virginal, poor and obedient; the Church makes the offering her own and presents it to God, who accepts it. Three wills are therefore joined in one: the will of God, the will of the Church and the will of the person who accepts the divine call in faith and in faith responds to it by the total gift of himself. The act of profession which marks the beginning of religious life contains within itself the vital energy required to make the whole of that life grow, flourish and mature. The whole mystery of religious life develops from this act of consecration to God in a religious institute, which gives the strength to practice the vows and strive for holiness in the common life and in accordance with the charism of the institute and its way of life.

The word "profession" thus has two meanings, the act of making the vows and the state of life which results from it. Profession includes the apostolate and service of the brethren according to the particular vocation of the institute to which the religious gives himself.[3] Because the vows are public, consecration to God and incorporation in the institute are inseparably joined by the Church, so that if the professed leaves the institute he is released from his vows.[4] Profession is a covenant with God and a mutual obligation between the religious and the institute in the Church. It is, above all, spiritual, ascetic and religious, though it has a social and juridical aspect which carries its own consequences.[5]

The entry into an institute by the act of profession may be compared to entering a family by birth or adoption.

## 3. Action of God, of the Church and of the one making profession

Of the three wills which join in the act of profession the emphasis was in past times laid chiefly on the will of God who calls and consecrates, setting the person apart for His service. More recently, greater emphasis has been placed on the act of the person and also on the act of the Church, which in the new rite places profession in the most suitable setting, the offertory of the Mass.[6]

# 4. Diversity of bonds

## Temporary and perpetual profession

As regards duration, vows may be temporary or perpetual.

It was can. 488,1 that introduced into religious law the important principle that temporary vows, to be renewed at their expiry, admit a person to the religious state. It is not a question of profession for a limited time; it is understood that normally the vows will be renewed.[7]

Ordinarily, temporary profession is considered as a stage in the preparation for perpetual vows, but in a few institutes, such as the Daughters of Charity, founded by St. Vincent de Paul, only temporary vows are made.

Between the limits of three and nine years, fixed by *Renovationis causam* 37,1, every institute is free to determine the duration of its temporary vows or promises. A number of institutes have fixed five years as the norm, major superiors having the power to shorten the time for individuals to three years or lengthen it up to nine.

As regards the dividing up of the time, some institutes prefer annual vows, some a longer period, others again, one single temporary profession for the whole time up to perpetual vows.

If the vows are annual, the year may be calculated otherwise than by the calendar, making it either longer or shorter than the chronological year.

For good reasons, temporary vows may be made for less than a year.[8]

A religious is not allowed to make an interruption in the period of temporary vows and yet remain a member of the institute.[9]

The act by which members of societies of common life or secular institutes undertake to observe the evangelical counsels, and which is called profession, consecration, oblation or something similar, follows in general the same practice as religious profession, except in what is specifically for religious.

## Renewal of vows

The renewal of vows at the expiry of temporary vows is, like profession itself, juridical as well as theological and spiritual in nature. Renewal made while vows are in force is an act of devotion intended to give fresh fervor and strengthen the resolution to be faithful. There is a liturgical rite of renewal in the new rite of profession which is not intended for merely devotional use, but may nonetheless be so used if desired, especially on certain anniversaries such as a silver or golden jubilee; there is a special Mass for the occasion.

It is an excellent practice to combine renewal of religious vows with the renewal of baptismal vows at the Easter Vigil, or the renewal of a priest's pledge to celibacy and obedience on Holy Thursday; it is an invitation to a review of one's life and one's responsibilities; St. Paul bids Timothy, "rekindle the grace of God that is within you" (2 Tm 1:6).[10]

# 5. Conditions required

The importance of profession in the life of a religious and of the Church explains the Church's interest in it and the conditions required.

The juridical requirements are set forth in canons 572-575 and clearly demand that superiors and candidates be satisfied that the latter are suited to the religious life, well prepared for it and possessed of the necessary psychological and affective maturity; the help of divine grace does not dispense from human effort but presupposes it.

## Age

The free choice of a new state of life, to be made with understanding and responsibility, obviously calls for an adequate novitiate and a minimum age; sixteen years is the minimum for first vows and twenty-one for perpetual.

The tendency in our day to raise the minimum age in practice is a right one, for experience has shown that mental and affective maturity is reached somewhat later than in former times. Modern conditions and the changes in religious life call for really responsible persons with a mind of their own.

Nonetheless, profession should not be put off too long. The grace of God is there, and a person who is in condition to do so has a right to give himself to God.[11]

## Novitiate and period of temporary vows

The importance of the novitiate as a preparation for profession is clearly shown by the fact that a valid novitiate is an indispensable condition for a valid profession; the same is true of the period of at least three years of temporary vows before perpetual profession (can. 572; Instr. *Renovationis causam*).[12]

The Church assumes that during these periods of preparation the necessary maturity has been reached, and great variety of length is now allowed, so that persons may be dealt with as they require.

Stability in religious life is obviously the chief aim and purpose of all periods of preparation.

The minimum bond involved in the three-year period is that of observing the constitutions of the institute.[13]

At the end of the period of temporary vows, the religious must either make perpetual vows or return to the world.[14]

For a reasonable cause, superiors may advance the date of renewal of temporary vows, but not by more than a month.[15]

## Freedom

By its very nature, and by the terms of canon law, profession is invalid unless it is freely made, without coercion, grave fear or deception. This freedom of choice is more than once declared by the candidate in the rite of profession.

In past times it was thought necessary for women to be interviewed and questioned in private by the bishop or his representative to ensure this absence of coercion and make sure they understood what they were undertaking. The practice became unnecessary with the emancipation of woman and has been stopped; indeed, a contrary abuse is far more probable; means are used to induce girls to stay in the world and not enter a convent.

## Admission

Since by profession a person becomes a member of a religious family, he must be accepted by a superior who represents the institute and hence, the Church (can. 572 § 1). Admission is therefore the act of the superior who authorizes the taking of vows implying incorporation into the institute, and thereby implicitly expresses a favorable judgment on the suitability of the candidate, on his vocation and his acceptance by the institute.[16] It is an act of great importance and responsibility toward the subject and the community, and may be compared to the call to ordination given by a bishop. Admission by the superior is distinct from and presupposed by the acceptance of the vows by the institute in the rite of profession.

Can. 543 attributes the right to admit a person to profession to major superiors with the vote of their respective councils; the vote is deliberative for the first profession, consultative for the perpetual.[17] The constitutions can decide whether it is the superior general or the provincial who admits. The tendency now is to decentralization, in view of the closer knowledge of persons and circumstances by those on the spot. Some women's institutes require ratification by the superior general. The opinion and even the decisive vote of the local council may also be required, which is a return to the practice of former times and has certain advantages; those who actually live with a person are the best judges of her suitability for life in the institute. However, there is the advantage of greater objectivity in the decision of a council less closely concerned, though local opinion can and should be given due weight in the matter.

Canon law requires an eight-day retreat before the first profession — now reducible to five[18] — to give the candidate the best opportunity to make such an important act with the best dispositions.

# 6. Pronouncement of the vows

## Acceptance

The nature of religious profession demands that the lawful superior receive the vows in the name of the institute and of the Church, and hence in the name of God.[19] The lawful superior is the one designated in the constitutions; it may be the superior general, the provincial, or the one highest in rank present at the ceremony, and the vows may be received personally or by delegation; delegation may be provided for in the constitutions or given personally by the competent superior.[20]

The usual formula says the vows are made into the hands of the person receiving them[21]; the gesture of placing the hands between those of the superior goes back to feudal times and is included in some rites of profession, followed by a declaration of acceptance or of reception into the family made by the superior.[22]

## Profession must be expressed and recorded

By can. 572 § 1 it is laid down that profession must be made by an act or declaration expressing the intention of binding oneself by the vows of religion; tacit profession is not valid in law.

The three vows need not be explicitly mentioned if the Rule or constitutions make it clear that all three are included. Benedictines and Dominicans make no mention of poverty or chastity. The general praxis is to express the three vows.

A written record of the vows drawn up in legal form must be signed and kept in the archives of the institute.[23]

The formula of vows used in an institute must be composed with the care that befits so important an act, and approved by the Holy See.[24] The new rite furnishes an example or model that can be used as a basis.[25]

## Place

Canon law formerly made it obligatory for first profession to be made in the novitiate house, but *Renovationis causam* authorizes major superiors to have it made elsewhere, as, for instance, in a cathedral or parish church (see Rite 45, 50). Since profession is a public act concerning the whole Church, it is quite natural to link it with the diocese or the parish.

Several different institutes may join in such a ceremony, the vows of each person being received by his own superior (Rite 46).

## Rite

In accordance with the Council directive (SC 80,2) the Congregation for Divine Worship has promulgated the *Rite of religious profession* prepared by the Consilium for the Liturgy.[26]

It sets out some theological, liturgical and pastoral principles, and then gives rites for entry into religious life, temporary profession, perpetual profession and renewal of vows (Part I for men and Part II for women). An appendix gives an example of a formula for profession and texts for the Mass.

The rite concerns only profession during Mass, which is strongly recommended by the Council (SC 80,3). If it is to take place at some other time, each institute must draw up its own rite.

So many possibilities are offered by the rubrics, ceremonies and texts, that institutes can use them to compose a rite really corresponding to their own particular nature, end and spirit. It must be presented for approval to the S. C. for Divine Worship.[27] Care must be taken to distinguish what is obligatory in the rite from what is only suggested or recommended, and from what is left entirely to the choice of the institute.[28]

# 7. The effects of profession

## A new state of life

Profession, even temporary, places a person in a new state of life (see also Volume I, ch. XX) which binds him in a special way to God, the Church and the institute, with the obligation to strive for the perfection of charity in fidelity to the Gospel, the manner of life and the charism of the Order or Congregation. The giving of the book of the constitutions during the profession ceremony signifies that the religious pledges himself to live according to those rules.

In apostolic institutes, profession makes the apostolate a right and a duty, and confers, at least implicitly, the *missio canonica*, which is an official mandate; the religious gives himself to the Church and the institute, and in a certain measure the Church and the institute give themselves and their own personality to the religious.

## Incorporation into the institute

The bond arising from profession links a religious to the institute not only juridically but theologically and spiritually, since the charism of the institute marks out his path to union with God; the link is permanent, mutual and unreserved.

The constitutions are like the tables of the law of the new covenant and are specifically mentioned in can. 593; profession is bound up with the observance of them.

## Particular effects

The professed religious shares in the graces and spiritual privileges of the institute (can. 578,1); any previous vows made by him are suspended; because his offering is an act of perfect charity, it is considered to blot out both guilt and penalty of all wrongful acts.[29]

Juridically he falls under the canon law for religious as regards both rights and duties, unless on specific points his constitutions determine otherwise.

Solemn vows make acts contrary to them not only illicit but invalid, e.g., marriage; perpetual vows, whether solemn or simple, remove a priest from his diocese and incorporate him in the institute[30]; clerics cease to hold offices, parochial benefices becoming vacant one year after profession, others after three years (can. 584).

According to can. 578,3 professed of temporary vows have neither active nor passive voice unless the constitutions decide otherwise. Active voice is frequently given.

## 8. Convalidation

If a religious profession is discovered to be invalid, either through lack of a right intention and will on the part of the person or from external causes, it can be convalidated; in the first case, it suffices for the religious to express his wish for it, provided the institute agrees; in the second case, a sanation must be obtained from the Holy See or the act of profession repeated after removal of the obstacle.

## 9. Consecration of virgins

The consecration of virgins was the ancient form of profession for women and included a pledge to observe perpetual virginity, and an act of consecration by the Church.[31] It was adopted by the Benedictine nuns who gradually took the place of the consecrated virgins, and by a few other monasteries; but other nuns and religious women used the rite of religious profession, which included a vow of perpetual virginity or perfect chastity. Hence there were two distinct rites for women.

The consecration of virgins was made use of by some who wished to remain in the world, but in 1927, this was forbidden,[32] and in 1950, the Constitution *Sponsa Christi* reserved the use of the rite to strictly enclosed monasteries, at the same time authorizing those who had used it in former times to revert to it.

On May 31, 1970, the S. C. for Divine Worship published the new rite for Consecration of Virgins.[33] It is intended for women living in the world who wish to consecrate their virginity to Christ, for monasteries where it was already in use, and for women's institutes duly authorized to use it.

The religious who use it must already have made perpetual vows or must make them in the course of the ceremony, so that profession and consecration of virgins are combined.[34]

1. It comes from the monastery of Atribe in Egypt, directed by the Abbot Shenoudi about the middle of the 5th century.

2. Here we speak only of profession, hoping to write later on about vocation and the formation of religious.

3. In early times a distinction was made between the vows made to God and the gift of himself made by the religious to the institute.

4. See can. 648 and the Decree of the S. C. of Religious of 11-27-69 (AAS 61, 1969) by which a religious under temporary vows dismissed from the institute is by that very fact released from his vows and reduced to the lay state.

5. Religious profession must not be equated with a civil contract; a person who leaves the institute or is dismissed has no right to claim payment for the services he has rendered to it.

6. The new rite contains a long and solemn blessing or consecration used for a man or for a woman; in perpetual profession the consecration is definitive. A. Colorado writes at length of profession as a sacramental and dwells upon the part played in it by the Church (*Los Cosejos Evangelicos,*[Salamanca: Ediciones Sigueme,1965], pp. 375-385).

7. When temporary profession was first introduced into men's Orders it was looked upon as permanent on the part of the religious but temporary on the part of the institute, and it is still so considered by the Jesuits.

After a certain number of years, temporary profession has the same effect as perpetual profession as regards dismissal from the institute or promotion to Holy Orders (Statutes for the application of *Sedes sapientiae*, 1956, Art. 8 § 1).

8. E. Gambari, *Updating of Religious Formation* (Boston: St. Paul Editions, 1969), p. 129. *Renovationis causam* 38, allows for a temporary separation from the institute in order to ensure that preparation is sufficient.

9. Can. 575 § 1; 577 § 1; *Renovationis causam* 37, 1.

10. Cf. Circular Letter from the S. C. for the Clergy of 11-4-69.

11. *Cf. Renovationis causam* 4, 3 and 5, and the comment in E. Gambari, *Updating of Religious Formation* (Boston: St. Paul Editions, 1969), pp. 70-71.

12. Cf. Encyclical *Neminem latet* of 3-19-1857, for men's orders, and the Decree *Perpensis* of 5-3-02 for nuns.

13. Some would wish to abolish the period of temporary vows and substitute a prolongation of the novitiate when necessary; consecration, according to them, is of its nature permanent.

14. Can. 575 § 1; an interruption would not, however, invalidate the profession made subsequently.

15. Can. 577 § 2. For a serious reason, renewal might be anticipated by more than a month, provided the three-year period was not diminished.

16. The institute does not give the vocation but only recognizes its existence.

17. No vote of the council is required by canon law for renewal of vows.

18. Cf. Decree of 6-4-70, art. 5.

19. Since in the act of profession the Church is represented by the superior, it is fitting that he or she occupy a suitable place in the sanctuary, and the new rite provides for this.

20. All possibilities should be provided for, so that whatever happens, someone present is authorized to receive the vows.

21. Cf. *Ordo professionis religiosae,* p. 111.

22. In some Orders and Congregations the superior makes the following or a similar declaration:

*I, by the faculty granted to me, receive in the name of the Church*
*the vows you have made,*
*and earnestly recommend you to God*
*that you may perfect your offering*
*in union with the Eucharistic sacrifice.*

The superior sometimes also welcomes the newly professed into the religious family.

23. The new rite recommends that the document be placed on the altar and, if possible, signed on the altar itself.

24. Some institutes have been authorized to try the experiment of allowing each one who makes vows to draw up a personal formula.

This, however, only applies to the time of experimentation; at the end of it, every institute will have to obtain approval for the formula adopted.

25. The following is the formula of the new rite:
*For the honor of God*
*and moved by a firm resolve to consecrate myself more fully to him*
*and to follow Christ more closely in my whole life,*
*here and now in the presence of (N. N.)°*
*I (N. N.) vow perpetual°° chastity, poverty and obedience*
*according to the (rule and) constitutions of N.°°°*
*I give myself with my whole heart*
*to this religious community,*
*so that by the grace of the Holy Spirit*
*and the help of the Blessed Virgin Mary*
*I may seek perfect charity*
*in the service of God and the Church.*

° name and office of the one receiving the profession
°° or the period of temporary profession
°°° name of the religious community

26. The Latin text which is the original is published by the Vatican Polyglot Press, 1970. The episcopal conferences in the different countries are responsible for the translation of it into their own language, in agreement with the Unions of Religious Superiors.

27. Cf. Decree of promulgation and art. 14 of the preliminary instructions. The new rite does not suppress forms that institutes legitimately possess, but there should be a revision of existing rituals to bring them into line with the new directives.

28. The rite is concerned solely with the liturgical function. On its theological, spiritual and personal content, see M. Calabuig, O.S.M., "Note sulla teologia e spiritualità della vita religiosa alla luce dell'Ordo Professionis," *Per una presenza viva dei Religiosi nella Chiesa e nel mondo*, pp. 933-975.

29. Cf. *Constitution* of Paul V of May 31, 1606.

Aguilar, in *La vida de perfección en la Iglesia*, discusses at length the traditional view that religious profession is equivalent to a second baptism and agrees with Dom Leclercq in concluding that
— there is no question of an equivalent to baptism
— nor of a second baptism
— nor of a renewal of baptism.

It is simply a bringing of baptismal grace to perfection and maturity *(op. cit.,* p. 210); whereas in matrimony there is a sacrament, in religious profession the sacrament is baptism as nuptial union with Christ and a prelude to the time when sacraments will cease and God will be all in all (1 Cor 15:28).

30. This is the law now in force; for a religious the institute takes the place of the diocese.

31. The consecration of virgins is one of the most ancient and significant rites. Cf. R. Metz, "La consécration des vierges," *Vie Consacrée*, 41st year (1969), pp. 5-25.

32. Decision of 3-25-27 (AAS XIX, 1927), p. 138.

33. *Ordo Consecrationis Virginum* (Vatican: Polyglot Press, 1970), p. 65.

34. Although combined, the two acts are distinct (cf. Preliminary notes to the new rite, 7).

As regards the adoption of the rite by institutes with simple vows, the bulletin *Notitiae* of the S. C. for Divine Worship of March, 1971, says, in reply to a question, that this modification of the present rule would appear right and reasonable and may be hoped for. In other words, women's institutes with simple vows might apply for permission to use the rite of consecration of virgins.

# Chapter II
# Chastity[1]

## 1. Interest and concern of the Church

The Council, after recalling that Christ chose a virginal life for Himself, a life which had also been chosen by His Mother, the Blessed Virgin Mary (LG 46,2), declares that the holiness of the Church is expressed and fostered by the observance of the counsels, among which the counsel of virginity stands out pre-eminently (LG 42,3) and is therefore not only preserved and safeguarded by the Church but proposed and praised to priests, religious and the laity[2] (LG 43; PO 16; OT 10; PC 12).

Among the evangelical counsels, perfect chastity was the one that chiefly drew the Council's attention; all that was said of priestly celibacy applies equally to religious. In addition to the Council texts the Church's esteem for virginity is expressed in Pius XII's *Sacra virginitas* (March 25, 1954),[3] Paul VI's *Sacerdotalis coelibatus* (June 24, 1967)[4] and his *Evangelica testificatio* (June 29, 1971) in John XXIII's allocution to the Roman Synod and in various allocutions of Paul VI.[5]

The Synod of Bishops in October, 1971, led to deeper study of the significance of celibacy.

Chastity may be said to be the heart of religious life; it is inseparable from the holiness of the Church. Perfect continence for the sake of the Kingdom of heaven has always been held in particular honor in the Church (LG 42, 3).[6]

## 2. Chastity named first

We have always been accustomed to hearing the classical triad named as poverty, chastity and obedience, but *Lumen gentium* and *Perfectae caritatis* name chastity first.

The reason for this change was that chastity was the counsel most explicitly proposed by Christ (Mt 19:12), most praised by St. Paul (1 Cor 7:32-35) and first recognized as a form of life (Acts 21:9).

The Church has always provided with particular care for virgins, giving them from very early times a special rite of consecration. The profession of chastity appears as a luminous sign of the new covenant and the special consecration of religious men and women to Christ and the Church[7]; it involves the whole personality and characterizes a way of life.

## 3. What chastity is

### Terminology

Various terms are used in the Council documents referring to this counsel: chastity, celibacy, perfect chastity, virginity, continence, a virginal way of life. With reference to religious, the term most frequently used is chastity, as in the past (can. 487), but virginity and a virginal life are also spoken of both for religious and for men who are bound to celibacy.[8]

Celibacy, which denotes a special state of life, is the word most commonly used for priests; some people would like to use celibacy, or celibate chastity, for religious, since chastity is a virtue obligatory for all Christians. The term used is not of itself of primary importance if we have exact ideas of the precise realities referred to.

### Scope of the counsel

The decree *Optatam totius* speaks of priestly celibacy as a state in which clerics "renounce the companionship of marriage for the sake of the kingdom of heaven (cf. Mt 19:12)" and give an undivided love to God; it bids them recognize "the surpassing excellence of virginity consecrated to Christ," which is a complete gift of body and soul (OT 10,2).

Vowed chastity is not simply a matter of renouncing physical acts which give pleasure; it is far more than that. It means giving up, for the love of God, all the human hopes and joys that go with the founding of a family, the joy of fatherhood and motherhood. And that is, strictly speaking, not chastity but celibacy.

The virtue of chastity — a form of the virtue of temperance — imposes control of the sexual instinct both outside marriage and within it; the counsel has its origin in the desire to belong to God alone. Celibacy for the sake of the kingdom means "the choice of a more intimate and complete relation to the mystery of Christ and the Church, for the benefit of all mankind."[9] Love, therefore, is the source of it, and the result of it is deep and close friendship with Christ, Spouse and Friend.

## The vow

The vow of chastity binds to the observance of the counsel with the added force of the virtue of religion. As commonly expressed in the constitutions of religious institutes, it is a promise to abstain from marriage and from all acts forbidden by the sixth and ninth commandments; this is its material object; its formal object, i.e. its motive or purpose, is the love of God and neighbor — the kingdom of heaven. Our Lord's invitation seems to imply a permanent state, most fully expressed by perpetual vows.[10]

Perfect chastity implies a vow of virginity, but the vow obviously concerns the future, not necessarily the past, for it can be taken, e.g., by a widow. Virginity is physical integrity, but the value of it lies in the inward attitude.

A vow must be so expressed that it is clear when it is broken; therefore the form is negative, "abstaining from," but the positive aspect of total and undivided love of God is what claims our enthusiasm. Abstention is a means to an end[11]; it is the end that gives it its value and opens the way to the measureless joy of union with God, and that end is the kingdom of heaven (Mt 5:8). Such joy is a witness, and a witness with great attractive power.

## The kingdom of heaven

The kingdom of heaven, for the sake of which the counsel of chastity is observed, has its beginning in this world but has also a dimension which transcends the limits of time. When there is no more "marrying nor giving in marriage," human love will be sublimated, and this eschatological dimension of the counsel is seen among us already in the love of others which grows and develops from the love of God.[12] The human heart given wholly to God loves with the love of God Himself; it is widened to take in all mankind in a love that is supernatural but also intensely human. The vow of chastity breaks down natural barriers and throws the heart open to universal love. John XXIII, speaking to religious women on July 2, 1962, said, "You show by your example that your hearts are not closed in sterile selfishness; you have chosen the condition that necessarily opens them to the needs of your neighbor."

## 4. Chastity is a gift of God [13]

Even more than the other counsels, chastity must be the result of a free choice and a preferential love, but it is first of all a gift. It is indeed one of God's most precious gifts, adorning Our Lady and the Church.

Christ indicated its charismatic character when He said, speaking of those who choose continence for the kingdom of heaven, "not all men understand my words but only those to whom it is given" (Mt 19:11-12). There is a call which enlightens and a driving force which impels to a kind of life that can only be lived with the special help of the Holy Spirit.[14]

God Himself chooses the person and gives him the grace to respond by choosing God (1 Jn 4:19) as the sole object of his love.[15] Chastity is received as a gift before it can be brought as an offering. A vocation includes the grace to understand the gift, appreciate it, accept it as implying a duty, and live by it.[16]

# 5. Celibacy or matrimony?

Marriage is spoken of by St. Paul as a mystery symbolizing the union of Christ and the Church (Eph 5:23-32) and this text is quoted by the Council in the directions given to seminarians: "Students ought rightly to acknowledge the duties and dignity of Christian matrimony, which is a sign of the love between Christ and the Church" (OT 10, 2). He also speaks, in 2 Cor 11:2-3, of presenting all the faithful to Christ as betrothed to Him.[17] But St. Paul emphasizes the freedom of the virgin to give her whole mind and heart to God, and states clearly that if he who marries does well, he who refrains from marriage does better (2 Cor 7:34, 38). The passage from *Optatam totius* continues: "Let them recognize, however, the surpassing excellence of virginity consecrated to Christ, so that with a maturely deliberate choice they may consecrate themselves to the Lord by a complete gift of body and soul."

We know that the Council of Trent solemnly declared the pre-eminence of virginity over matrimony, and Pius XII treats the subject at length in *Sacra virginitas*. In his allocution of September 5, 1952, he referred to those — both priests and lay people — who have not a word of praise for virginity but maintain that only in marriage can a human personality find full development and self-fulfillment.

The exaggerated importance given to natural values by a great many people in our day is largely a reaction against lack of recognition of them in the past; and like many reactions, it goes much too far. It is unthinkable that the recognition of a personal call from God and the response of total love for Him should cramp the personality or hinder its self-expression.

The state of virginity "for the kingdom" is indeed esteemed and admired by many who, without understanding it, see its beauty in contrast to a world dominated by the senses and a prey to eroticism. They have no idea, however, of what the Council means when it speaks of consecrated celibacy as contributing to the richness of the whole personality of man and woman alike.

The demands of love extend beyond measure the horizon of the priest, deepen his sense of responsibility and give him a delicacy of feeling arising out of a higher and wider fatherhood.

The religious Sister will bring her feminine qualities to the task of building up the kingdom of God in herself and in others; that task will bring out all the resources of her womanliness.

Intimacy with Christ, truly lived, cannot but develop all human values.

## 6. The vital energy of chastity

All three counsels have a twofold action, freeing man from all that is not of God in order to serve God exclusively. *Perfectae caritatis* says, "Chastity frees the heart of man (cf. 1 Cor 7:32-35) so as to set it on fire with love for God and neighbor."[18]

To have its true value, chastity must be the result of a free and deliberate choice, personal, exclusive and definitive, made in full knowledge of what it involves.

The choice of God loved above all will bring with it availability to others in a new relationship[19]; it will not be a mediation of creatures leading men to God, but communion with God that leads them to creatures.[20]

Participation by sacrifice in Christ's passion and death will mean participation in His resurrection to share His life and to love as He loves.[21]

## 7. The counsel of chastity is Christ-centered

The celibate consecrated to Christ participates in His priesthood and in His mission as Mediator between the

Father and the human race (PO 16,3); he shares in Christ's total dedication to the service of God and man (SCl 21), and from this participation flows the liturgical, apostolic and ecclesial content of consecrated chastity, seen also as prophetic and eschatological.

The vow of chastity is a sublime act of worship, placing the one who makes it at the entire disposal of God as supremely worthy of love, and this links it naturally and appropriately with the priesthood. The encyclical *Sacerdotalis coelibatus* points this out, saying that by celibacy the priest brings fuller unity and harmony into his priestly life.

It is likewise a prophetic witness to faith in the supernatural values and the life to come, an eschatological sign reminding the world that the People of God is moving toward its fulfillment in Christ.[22] In PO 16,2 it is called a "living sign of the world to come, by faith and charity already made present, in which the children of the resurrection neither marry nor take wives." OT 10 speaks of witness to the resurrection and to the world to come, and of example and encouragement in the mastery of soul and body to which all Christians are bound.

The public profession of virginity expresses among the faithful the nuptial mystery of Christ and the Church, and this emphasizes its ecclesial aspect. *Sacra virginitas* speaks of "living images of that perfect integrity by which the Church is united to her divine Spouse."[23] Chastity, "in its preferential love for the Lord, symbolizes the union of the bride with her eternal Bridegroom" (ET 13). Again, consecrated virginity manifests "the love of Christ for the Church and the virginal and supernatural fecundity by which the children of God are born, not of flesh and blood, but of God (Jn 1:13)" (PO 16,2); in Christ, those who have given up the right to found a human family will have a life of abundant fulfillment because, like Him and in Him, they love and give themselves to all the children of God (SCl 26, 30).[24]

*Perfectae caritatis* points out that chastity, "by which religious dedicate themselves with undivided heart to the service of God," gives special efficacy to the apostolate. Celibacy widens the heart and increases its power of loving, for the love of God above all things expresses itself in the love of mankind and the building up of the Church. It is a crying need of the world today, when the very word "love" is debased to signify self-seeking and pleasure. Its true meaning must be learned anew, without falling into the opposite error of giving the first place to man and forgetting that love of man must flow from love of God. We are at the service of others in all friendliness and sociability, because the love of God drives out selfishness and self-seeking. This apostolic aspect of celibacy is emphasized in PO 16, PC 6, LG 42,3 and ET 15. The last-named article speaks also of the Marian basis of consecrated chastity; as always, we find in Mary the type and symbol of the Church, virgin and mother.

## 8. The practice of the counsel

The attitude of those who have made the vow may be summed up in a few words; it should be one of gratitude, trustful faith, eager responsiveness and firm determination to persevere; it is not enough to take back nothing; we must continually strive to perfect the gift.

Fidelity to a promise, fidelity to a vow, is nowadays thought little of by too many people, because fidelity means effort. Let God, at least, find fidelity among those vowed to Him.

To ensure fidelity we must first of all and obviously avoid what may endanger it, but we must above all deepen and increase our love — our love of God in Himself, and our love for those around us, loved in Him and drawn to Him by us; the loneliness which lies in wait for the celibate is then no danger for us; the human need to love and be loved is more than satisfied by the friendship of God, who is always faithful to His promises. At the same time a relationship to others grows up which draws them as it were into the family of those who are called *Brother* and *Sister*, and who care especially for those most in need of it. The joys and sorrows of the world are felt in a religious community.[25]

Within the community the bond of brotherly love is a defense against selfishness and self-centeredness and may develop into true Christ-centered friendship. In community, as in the individual, all that contributes to a sound and healthy condition, physical and mental, is a safeguard for chastity; and this includes a healthy attitude of mind, which understands that dangers exist but that a continent life can be perfectly happy and normal.

Supernaturally, the traditional safeguards always remain the same and must not be neglected, for "we carry our wealth in frail vessels" and for some there may be moments when nature tries to reassert itself. A passing impression of loneliness and the lack of a human family will then be overcome by a renewal of fervor in prayer, the sacraments, a deep interior life, devotion to Our Lady, perseverance in faith, hope and charity. The best safeguard will always be not so much a negative attitude of defense against danger as a positive aim to grow in the love of God, for any emptiness in the human heart is filled to over-flowing when possessed by Him.[26]

# 9. Formation

In *Perfectae caritatis* we read: "The practice of complete continence touches on deep-rooted human instincts, and for this reason, before a candidate is allowed to make profession of it he must have undergone an adequate period of probation and have reached the necessary psychological and emotional maturity." This life is not for all, but only for those who are called, and the Decree reminds superiors of their grave responsibility as regards admission; young people should only be accepted if they have given sufficient proof of suitability, and this responsibility is shared by all who can form an opinion on it: parents, teachers, the spiritual director and others.

In this area the psychological and affective maturity aimed at involves many factors. There should be an equilibrium between one's sexual life and one's other tendencies. There ought to be a tranquillity of spirit in different life situations, a delicate open manner of dealing with people, and a mastery of one's senses. At the same time there should be a strength of spirit born of the capacity to give oneself for the love of the Lord, and of constancy in this self-giving. In a word, mastery of self should be combined with the capacity to give and to devote oneself without *looking* for or *seeking* reciprocity in the human forms proper to conjugal love. All of this is an aspect of general maturity which presupposes a deep unity of life centered on the gift of self to God and the commitment to give God to others.[27]

## Education

Formation to chastity, is first of all preparation for maturity. As such it is the fruit of intellectual instruction and of will-training which initiate the candidate into a life centered directly and totally on God. This education should be positive rather than negative. The students should indeed know the scope and significance of the renunciations required of them, as well as the dangers and difficulties they will encounter; but above all they ought to explore in depth the positive content of celibacy, its relevance in the mystery of Christ and the Church, and the contribution which it can make to the good of one's neighbor. The necessary preparation for perfect chastity, then, is made up of many elements. There must be correct teaching, which not only points out the falsity or inexactness of some current theorizing, but which opens the mind to the richness of this gift. There must likewise be an education of the will and affections to an openness to more-than-ordinary ideals, and to an unlimited disposition to give oneself without expectation of reward.

## Integration of the person

The celibate has a particular need to be able to direct toward the affirmation and integration of his person every resource of nature and of grace which God has given to a man or to a woman. This is why *Perfectae caritatis* (12,3) asked that religious should be educated so as to embrace their consecrated celibacy as a good for the integral development of their own personalities. The student must therefore be in a position to understand and to live his total gift of himself to the Lord and to the Church, and to see it as a continuous source of fulfillment and satisfaction that will exclude any justified feeling of frustration. This means that every one of his powers, on the physiological, psychological, intellectual, affective, and volitional levels, as these are elevated by the supernatural gifts, ought to be employed to the greatest advantage in the practice of a chastity which is a total and universal gift to God and neighbor. It is in this way that the celibate for the sake of the kingdom of heaven will, like Jesus and Mary, enrich even his human nature.

# 10. Renewal in chastity

The world of today still responds to the language of consecrated chastity even though it is far removed from its practice. It is perhaps just because of this distance at the level of actuality that there is still esteem for those who reserve themselves exclusively to the love of God. Such a consecrated life is a reminder of heavenly reality. It awakens admiration and perhaps even a sense of nostalgia for a life not dominated by the senses. This is why religious have been invited to renewal in chastity, that this virtue may be more evident in their conduct and that it may give no cause for unfounded criticism on account of outdated attitudes or customs.

In the matter of chastity, a constant return to the sources of religious life will be translated into a full appreciation of the dynamic and positive content of this vow, which is much more an enrichment of life, of joy, of serenity, of equilibrium, and of devotion than a process of simple renunciation. With this perspective we can see new value in true and healthy friendships among members of a religious institute. The same is true, under proper conditions, of friendship with persons outside the community. The abuses and the unauthentic relationships which can arise here call for vigilance and prudence, but this need does not take away the value and strength of genuine friendship, which is not just a kind of compensation or turning back on self, or even a studied choice of some persons for exclusive affection. Genuine friendship is charity; it is love.[28]

A renewed chastity will also know how to inspire a human warmth in all our relations, whether with men or with women, and this because these relations will be animated with the love of Christ, whose own divine love has assumed a human countenance. In a special way religious women, who are called to express the love and care of the Church for her neediest children, ought to exhibit a really maternal kind of charity.

Another requirement of renewal in chastity among religious can be more information about problems of life and sex. This is a need for sisters committed to service apostolates, and perhaps for all sisters, because of new circumstances in the environment, in the general culture, and in the apostolate. The ideas currently in vogue, the dangers to be encountered, the advice for which they are asked, the confidences·they receive, the mass media to which they are exposed, and even the problems discussed in Church documents, require a much broader formation than what could suffice for the past.

Finally, it should be noted that for the sake of adaptation in this area we are seeing an elimination of rules and customs which are no longer understood and which, instead of favoring serenity in the practice of chastity, can today even present obstacles to it. It should be superfluous, however, to point out that adaptation cannot become occasion and pretext for introducing experiences and innovations that will endanger chastity or diminish its witness. The delicacy of this subject matter and the fact that our natural inclinations remain with us, ought to make us cautious and prudent. What is truly necessary for the apostolate should be welcomed with serenity, but pseudo-needs should not be yielded to. This, of course, is particularly true for the period of formation.

1. In connection with this chapter and the two following, it may be found helpful to reread what is said in Volume I on consecration and the counsels.

2. AA 4,7. The Council also spoke of conjugal chastity (cf. GS 49,51).

3. AAS 46 (1954), pp. 161-191.

4. AAS 59 (1967), pp. 657-697.

5. Paul VI, *Il Sacerdozio* (Ancora, 1970).

6. The words of St. Cyprian quoted in *Sacra virginitas* are very significant: "Virginity is a flower that blossoms in the Church and beautifies spiritual grace; it is the joy of nature, a masterpiece of praise and glory, an image reflecting the holiness of the Lord, the chosen portion of Christ's flock. The Church rejoices to see her own fecundity flourish in it; the greater the number of virgins, the greater the Mother's joy."

7. It has been said that although marriage is a sign of the new covenant, and a "sign of the fruitful union of Christ with the Church" (Denz. 2238), virginity is the sign of the "perfect integrity of the union of the Church with her divine Spouse" (AAS 46 [1954] 173; *Sacra virginitas*).

8. Concerning the counsel of chastity, a very interesting paper was read by J. Moreno de la Helguera at the International Congress of Secular Institutes at Rome, Sept. 20-26, 1970. He called attention to the new points of view put forward in our day by psychology regarding sexuality, with particular reference to chastity.

The link between physical union and conjugal love is much emphasized nowadays, but sexuality is also considered in a much wider aspect, as a psychosomatic phenomenon reaching its climax in matrimony but also including all the relationships between man and woman for their mutual enrichment. Chastity is an inward attitude that should characterize all such relationships and safeguard them from the prevalent tendency to think too much of the physical side, which can easily become unbalanced and self-seeking.

9. Paul VI, *Sacerdotalis coelibatus*.

10. Pius XII, *Sacra virginitas*, AAS (1954), pp. 164, 165.

11. Abstention from marriage can be for a human ideal good in itself, e.g. to dedicate oneself to scientific research, politics or art; it can also be from selfishness, fear of sacrifice, personal preference for a single life; none of these reasons enter into the observance of the evangelical counsel.

We may use a modern simile: to get into the orbit round God (the end) man frees himself from the attraction of the earth (the means). In practice, means and end are inseparable.

12. The motive of the counsel of chastity is the close relation between virginity and the perfection of Christian charity. Cf. *Sacerdotalis coelibatus*, 27.

13. Cf. Lucien Legrand, *The Biblical Doctrine of Virginity* (London: Geoffrey Chapman, 1965).

14. A very instructive article is the one by Sr. Jeanne d'Arc, O.P., "La chasteté et la virginité consacrée dans l'Ancien et le Nouveau Testament," *La Chasteté* (2nd Ed. du Cerf, 1953), pp. 11-35.

15. Cf. Instruction of the S. C. of Religious of 2-2-61, art. 22. The encyclical *Sacra virginitas* stresses the necessity of a special vocation.

16. The encyclical *Sacerdotalis coelibatus*, which refers to celibacy as a free response to a special vocation and charism, replies in art. 7 and 15, to those who distinguish between the charism of a priestly vocation and the charism of the choice of celibacy as a state of consecrated life.

17. In this sense all the faithful belong to Christ through baptism and are totally consecrated to Him, but not all are called to express this "virginity" in the same way. Married people express it in their mutual help to live for Christ; celibates "for the kingdom of heaven" in their direct union with God in Christ.

18. At the Council someone wished to say "can free" instead of "frees," but the proposal was rejected.

19. It is sometimes said that the unmarried have more time to give to others; this may or may not be true, but it is beside the question.

20. St. Angela Merici says of virginity (Rule, Chapter X) that it "keeps the flame of charity burning in our hearts"; love must keep us from doing anything that can offend or displease others.

21. Virginity for the kingdom is like a resurrection, prefiguring the meeting of Christ with His Father, to whom He refers all things. As His whole existence is relative to His Father, the Church is wholly relative to Christ and the clearest manifestation of this is to be found in consecrated virginity, which is therefore compared to mystical espousals.

22. A full bibliography on this aspect of chastity is given by P. Perrault, O.P., *L'Adaptation et la Rénovation de la vie religieuse*, (Ed. du Cerf), p. 400, no. 37.

23. Consecrated chastity is like a nuptial gift from Christ to His spouse for her adornment. Cf. *Lumen gentium* 43.

24. It is a most valuable and consoling thought that virginity makes a person share in the maternal fruitfulness of the Church. Here the religious woman finds the satisfaction of her desire to give and to commit herself. In this way the nature of woman becomes a positive factor in the building up of the kingdom of God. Far from experiencing frustration, the religious experiences self-fulfillment that is in a certain way greater and more continuous than that which she would enjoy in the condition of spouse and mother according to nature.

25. Celibacy for him who is called to it is in no way harmful to human development (PC 12, 2) and does not require, for human equilibrium, any other natural substitute or affective integration at the human level. Nevertheless, precisely because it reinforces the capacity for love, it involves an education to an adult affectivity. True love is the soul of human relations (cf. Tullo Goffi, *L'integrazione affectiva del sacerdote*, Queriniana, Brescia, p. 136).

26. It is a sobering thought that a religious might live without ever breaking the vow of chastity and yet miss the whole point of it by leading a selfish and self-centered life.

27. Cf. P. Brocardo, "Formazione alla maturità umana e alla disciplina," *Il Decreto sulla formazione sacerdotale* (Elle Di Ci), pp. 359-376.

28. In the past, the word "friendship" was avoided because of its traditional use for the kind of egoistic self-seeking known as "particular friendship," which was and is in opposition to Christ-centered love.

# Chapter III
# Poverty

## 1. Poverty and renewal in religious life

### The Council's interest centered on poverty

The Council rediscovered poverty as a distinctive mark in the mystery of the Church, so characteristic as to justify calling it "the Church of the poor."[1]

In the Old Testament the poor occupy a very special place and were looked upon as particularly dear to God[2]; Christ was sent to preach the Gospel to the poor and chose poverty for Himself in His birth, life and death.[3]

The world of today, torn by economic strife and suffering from the plague of poverty which afflicts the greater part of the human race, was in need of a message addressed to rich and poor alike concerning the true value and function of material possessions.

Poverty has been and still is one of the most pressing problems inside the Church and outside it, and the Council did not disappoint those who expected it to be plainly spoken of. Religious are reminded that poverty is today looked upon as an essential feature of the following of Christ, and exhorted to practice it assiduously (cf. PC 13,1; ES 23). In *Evangelica testificatio*, Paul VI lays great stress on "the cry of the poor that must find an echo in the lives of religious," and on the response it should find (Arts. 17-22).

## Poverty in religious life

The practice of poverty has always held an important place in religious life, not only because it forms an essential part of religious consecration, but because it has often been the starting-point of a vocation,[4] and it has always been a wall of defense and the sign of a true religious life. Movements of reform in religious Orders have usually begun by restoring the practice of poverty to rectify the decadence that had followed upon its neglect.

In the eyes of the Church and of the world, poverty places religious in a special position and confers upon them an indispensable mission for the good of the Church and of society.

The veritable renewal of religious institutes will come about when they seriously and perseveringly set themselves, as communities and as individuals, to renew their practice of poverty.

## How poverty should be envisaged

Article 13 of *Perfectae caritatis* may be taken as a model for the treatment of poverty in the constitutions and also for the period of formation. It will have greater power to attract people and rouse their fervor if it is given in all its fullness, with its doctrinal and spiritual content, combined with the pastoral and apostolic as well as the juridical, in the practical intention of reviving it in the Church and in religious life in all its splendor.

*Perfectae caritatis* shows concern for genuineness and the interior attitude; it is not enough to talk about poverty or even make some outward show of it; it must be in the heart and be shown by deeds — *re et spiritu*. It must also adapt itself to present-day circumstances, to the needs and the customs of the day, and against the background of world-poverty, which cries out for a Church that is truly the Church of the poor.

Religious poverty should admit no half-measures, no calculating between the demands of the vow and the virtue,[5] but permeate the whole life with its spirit and make its aim the beatitude of the poor.

# 2. Religious poverty in general

## Christ as its source and its end

It is by fixing our eyes on Christ,[6] who chose to be poor, that we shall best understand the mystery of poverty and the demands which sharing His poverty will make on us. No elaborate definition could be so striking as the simple words, "the following of Christ, who though He was rich, yet for your sake became poor, so that by His poverty you might become rich" (cf. 2 Cor 8:9; Mt 8:20; PC 1,1).

The Council shows Christ living as a poor man; the Master Himself said to the rich young man, "If you would be perfect, go, sell what you possess and give to the poor, and come, follow me" (Mt 19:21); He declared that He had come for the poor and that the poor in spirit are blessed (cf. Lk 6:20; Mt 5:3, 19:27; 2 Cor 8:3).

For love of us the Lord of all things had not a place to lay His head; the poor were His friends and He considers as done to Himself what is done to one of them. He and His virgin Mother chose a lowly form of life and carried out the work of redemption in poverty (cf. LG 8,3; 46,2).

The counsel of poverty is expressed in Christ's words to the rich young man quoted above; it is clear from them that it is an invitation—*if* you would be perfect—and not a command; all must live in a spirit of detachment, but not all are called to set limits to their right to possess and make use of material things.

In the practice of poverty learned from Christ, the religious will find a way of life that makes them more Christ-like, as did St. Francis of Assisi.

## What poverty is

### The attitude of the poor

From Christ we learn that the basic attitude of religious poverty is a turning away from material wealth toward heavenly things; it leads to a style of life which uses earthly things with moderation, according to need, as God intended them to be used, and to voluntary limitation of the right to possess and dispose of them.

This attitude is primarily spiritual and can be possessed by the rich; but, human nature being what it is (Lk 18:24), it is more easily acquired by the actual giving up of property together with the free use of it.

Pius XII, speaking to the general Congregation of the Jesuits on September 10, 1957, said, "For the living of a life with Christ crucified, the faithful observance of poverty will be a great help..., not only the poverty of dependence...but particularly that which consists in the moderate use of temporal things and the giving up of many conveniences which seculars may legitimately make use of."

The very least that religious poverty can demand as regards temporal goods is a limitation of the free use of them, whether it be by permission, accountability or in some other way. But *Perfectae caritatis* tells us that "it is not enough for a religious to be subject to his superiors in the use of property; he must himself be really poor in spirit too, having his treasure in heaven (cf. Mt 6:20)" (PC 13).

Religious poverty is not poverty in the common sense of the word. The poor are those who lack what they need — housing, clothing, food and other things required to live a normal life — but these things are not lacking to religious, though they should be used with moderation, to satisfy genuine needs.

This fact seems scandalous to some people, and they would wish to see religious leading lives of real privation; others would drop the use of the word "poverty" and substitute "community of goods" or some other term.[7]

The idea that religious poverty means free choice of a situation implying detachment from earthly possessions is certainly a little difficult for ordinary people to grasp. But although the word is ambiguous, it seems preferable to keep to it. It at least reminds religious that they should try, in some measure, to live like the poor, whereas "community of goods" might apply to an extremely comfortable and even luxurious life.[8]

The important point is that if religious do not wish to be accused of hypocrisy, their life-style must bear some resemblance to the life of Christ.

## The object of religious poverty

The object of religious poverty is material possessions, anything that can be valued in terms of money; also, in a broad sense, whatever the world offers that gives power over others, influence and prestige.[9]

The evangelical counsel concerns a personal attitude toward material things which goes beyond the detachment required in every Christian and calls for a particular style of life with specific demands.

## The vow of poverty

To ensure the concrete and permanent observance of the counsel, the need was felt to express it in the form of a vow. The vow, however, is necessarily limited to certain clearly defined acts; it cannot cover the whole scope of the counsel, but it is a starting-point and a stimulus.[10]

The content of the vow of poverty may vary from a maximum of giving up all rights to a patrimony, to a minimum of not disposing of one's own property without the intervention of others.[11]

The solemn vow makes a religious incapable of possessing or acquiring property; the simple vow forbids the free disposal or usage of any material goods, including one's own (can. 580 §1; 582).

In all religious Orders or Congregations, the vow of poverty imposes dependence by requiring the permission of superiors for disposing of any objects having a money value.[12] Since this is required by a simple vow, it is obviously obligatory when a solemn vow has taken away the right of disposal by the radical means of taking away the property.[13]

The question may arise of how dependence is to be put into practice. Must permission be asked each time? should it be asked previously and specifically, or may it be general and habitual? is it enough to render account of how things have been used or disposed of?[14]

Dependence on authority should always be real; the vow must not be emptied of its meaning. The superior must therefore be in a position to approve or disapprove what has been done.

Provided this is ensured, institutes are free to adapt their practice to their particular circumstances, the modern way of life and the tasks assigned to the religious. Some have chosen to allow a small sum to each religious for daily needs, especially those whose work entails going out. The abuses which arose in the past from the *peculium* (which might be spent without permission or accountability) must not be allowed to recur; the sum allowed should be used for specified purposes, and an account of its expenditure should be regularly made.[15]

The vow of poverty, whether solemn or simple, is defined and regulated at least in part by canon law; solemn vows are the same for all,[16] but the content of simple vows may be decided by the institute within certain limits.[17]

One who makes a simple vow retains the ownership of his property and the right to acquire more (cf. can. 580,1) but must hand over to others the administration of it and decide upon the use and usufruct (can. 569). The constitutions may go further and require use and usufruct to be given up[18]; they may also limit the right to acquire other property. Such limitation may apply to the nature of the property, e.g. only by inheritance, or only from close relations. Can. 569 §3 obliges religious who make simple vows in a Congregation to make a will before profession[19]; the Decree of June 4, 1970, by way of experiment, postpones this obligation until the time before final profession.

## Renunciation of patrimony [20]

The text of can. 580 §1 admits in general terms that constitutions may limit the capacity to acquire property and even withhold it, as also the right to possess property.

Actually, however, the Holy See has not admitted the suppression or limitation of the right to possess; can. 583 forbids those who have made simple vows to turn over their property gratuitously to others.[21]

In recent years there has been an increasing desire to bring the poverty of simple vows nearer to the Gospel, and the Church met this wish by art. 6 of the papal rescript *Cum admotae* of November 6, 1964,[22] for pontifical clerical institutes and by the Decree *Religionum laicalium* for lay institutes two years later.[23] The Council was favorable also, and in connection with renewal, spoke of new forms of poverty; *Perfectae caritatis* 13,4 says: "Religious Congregations, by their constitutions, can permit members to renounce inheritances they may have received or may be due to receive." *Ecclesiae sanctae* II (4) enters into details: "It belongs to the institutes of simple vows in their general chapters to define whether renunciation of inheritances – those which religious already possess and those which may come to them later – should be entered in the constitutions; and, if so, whether this renunciation should be compulsory or left to choice. They should state when such renunciation should take place, whether before the perpetual vows or after some years." [24]

The above directions concern only Congregations, that is, institutes of simple vows (cf. can. 488,2). Permission is not given for their members to make a solemn vow of poverty instead of a simple one, but to make an act which adds to the simple vow most of the effects of a solemn one. It belongs to the special general chapter to determine the precise degree and manner in which it may be done.

We have seen that the Council speaks of two kinds of property that may be given up, what is possessed at the time of profession [25] and what will come or may come after profession. By a solemn vow, what is actually possessed is given up, and also the capacity to receive any property in the future; anything received in the future becomes the property of the Order (can. 582). When the vow is simple, it may be decided that renunciation will be made when new property is received.

If renunciation is compulsory, it will only bind those who enter the institute after the rule is made, not those already professed. [26] If it is optional, no change in practice is introduced, since superiors general have the power to authorize it.

An act of renunciation must be made in all freedom, not from interested motives on the part of the institute. [27] The giving up of one's patrimony may be one of the new forms of poverty mentioned in PC 13 and ES 23.

## The virtue of poverty

The vow is as it were the first step toward a life of detachment from earthly things, leaving them behind in order to get into orbit round the kingdom of heaven.

Poverty recognizes in earthly possessions their true function of serving as instruments and means for reaching higher values, and leads man not to allow himself to be dominated by them but to dominate them by freeing himself as much as possible from the bonds which they create. The religious, by choosing to observe the evangelical counsel, tends toward the spirit of the beatitude of poverty.

The vow concerns the negative aspect of poverty; the virtue and the spirit turn toward the practice of it shown so clearly and so beautifully in the life of our Lord—love of heavenly things, love of the poor, faith in the loving providence of God.

## Common life

The counsel of poverty takes concrete form in the vow and in common life.

From the earliest times, those who wished to follow Christ, poor, chaste and obedient, found their inspiration in the attitude of the first Christians, who expressed their membership in the ecclesial community not only by the breaking of bread and praying together but by putting their property in common to be distributed to all according to their needs (Acts 3:42-47). The Church in Jerusalem was taken as a model by the cenobites and subsequent religious families, who made poverty more effectively felt than it could be by the solitaries.

Since man has need of material things, he cannot live without them; the nearest he can get to having nothing is to live in dependence on a community and whoever represents it, hand over to it whatever he earns and receive from it what he needs, irrespective of what he may earn.[28]

The three important elements in common life as regulated by canon law are the putting in common of all that is earned, receiving from the community all that one needs and contenting oneself with what is provided for all alike (can. 594).

Community of goods is so much appreciated today that some would identify it with the vow of poverty. It should be interpreted in a broad sense, so that everything received by a religious, including gifts, becomes community property; this sharing should bear witness to the spiritual union among its members (ET 21).

Dependence is not the whole of poverty, but it is an important part of it. The fact of having to ask for what one needs and depending on authority or on the community for the disposal of one's own property makes detachment a real and concrete thing.

Acceptance of what is given to other members of the community in similar circumstances means that the use of material things is regulated with preciseness.

Renewal means fidelity to the common life, which has a theological, spiritual and ecclesial content as well as juridical.

# 3. The practice of poverty

## A sense of detachment and moderation

Renunciation and actual detachment from possessions is considered as a liberation; the state of powerlessness of a poor man is considered as wealth, since it brings communion with Christ and gives us Christ Himself.[29]

Religious are indeed obliged to make use of material things, but it should be in a spirit of detachment, giving proof, even externally, of authentic poverty (ET 18).

Instead of earthly possessions they seek heavenly things and place their riches where neither moth nor rust consumes and where thieves do not break in and steal (Mt 6:19).

Detachment is shown in practice by moderation; the measure is limited to what is needed for the life and work of the institute and its members; material things are used in accordance with their function as means necessary to the purpose of the institute and the life and work of the religious.[30] *Perfectae caritatis* says that institutes have the right to possess everything necessary for their daily life and work, but must avoid any form of luxury, immoderate profit and accumulation of property. The Council thus warns us against even the appearance of being swayed by a desire for wealth or display.

This last directive concerns the possessions of the institute as such, but it applies equally to the poverty of the individual, who is told that it is not enough for him to be subject to his superiors in the use of property; he must be really poor in spirit and in fact, using only what is necessary or really useful and avoiding all luxury and superfluity.[31] It is the religious themselves who must ask only for what they need for themselves or for their apostolate.

Necessity will be estimated objectively, taking into account the circumstances of time and place and the aim and character of the institute.[32]

Before asking permission to get such things as books, working equipment, etc., a religious should ask himself whether it comes within the limits allowed by poverty.[33]

Moderation in the use of things will be inspired by the style of life common to the poor, or at least to those of humble condition, in the region where the religious live. The thought of the great numbers who lack even the necessities of life or can only procure bare necessities ought to encourage the religious to understand and observe poverty.

The same thing applies to superiors. In the first schema of the Council commission (23, 3) we read: "With prudence and in accordance with their constitutions, superiors will willingly give their own subjects what is necessary or useful to them, but will not give permissions contrary to poverty or not in keeping with it. They must be the first to give the example of poverty."

Paul VI warns us against the temptations that threaten poverty: the uncurbed seeking for ease, allowing oneself without discernment everything that is offered; the enticement of the alluring security of possessions, knowledge and power (ET 19), and a certain affectation or vanity (ET 22).

## Trust in Providence

Trust in God's Providence goes with poverty. This does not mean carelessness and neglect in administration; on the contrary, it calls for it, as also for care in the use of things; but it feels that the future is secure because God in His providence will send all that is necessary (PC 13,3). The saints who had a special love for poverty dared and accomplished great things, because they counted on their heavenly Father (cf. Mt 6:28; Lk 12:27).

## Subjection to the law of work

The Council rightly reminded religious that the law of work is an expression of poverty and brings them nearer to the lives of the poor. It is by work that they provide for their own needs and those of others, that is, of the poor, placing themselves on a level not only with the poor but with the other people of our time.

The Council gives us to understand that this form of poverty belongs to our day, whereas other forms, such as begging, are unfavorable.[34] Begging has not been abolished, but it has been regulated in such a way that it can be accepted.[35]

Another example is the system of benefices or dowries for either institutes or persons; work is substituted as a means of livelihood in place of an income from investments.

It is as a new form of poverty[36] that work is envisaged, not merely as a penance or a hobby; this is a consequence of the social and economic changes that have taken place; present attitudes differ from the past. But the attitude of the religious is not simply that of his fellow workers in the world. His aim is not to make money, nor to put away enough to ensure a future free from anxiety. Religious are called upon to show forth in their lives the human value and purpose of work as a means of support and of service. The emphasis placed on it must not lead to forgetfulness of religious values or to neglect of the specific tasks of the institute; it must not lead to secularity (ET 20).

## Concern for the community

The poverty he professes will make the religious feel responsible for his community, as a poor man for his household. He will contribute to its maintenance, be careful to avoid waste, take proper care of whatever is given him for his use and be prudent in administration if he is entrusted with it.

This is an attitude which is part of the common life and enters into co-responsibility. Some institutes have decided to keep their members better informed of the economic situation and problems of the community and to ask their co-operation in the more important affairs.

## Love for the poor

The poverty of the Church is expressed also in love for the poor and in doing what is possible for their relief, continuing thus the poverty of Christ. Its most eloquent manifestation is found in the religious, who act as ministers of the Church's charity.

Religious, who are at the service of the Church, should feel a special obligation toward her weakest members, the poor.

In all the temporal and spiritual works of mercy which they undertake they must keep in mind that they represent the Church; their action can therefore never be simply philanthropic or social — still less, merely economic or political.

This by no means signifies that the Church and the religious take no interest in the social or economic situation; the first act of charity is to help the poor to free themselves from poverty and claim their rights. The social action of the Church and those who act in its name have their own methods of work, not spectacular, but awakening the conscience of those who can put an end to unjust and intolerable situations in the social and economic sphere. By their example and their words, religious should aim at creating in all around them a sense of responsibility for combating poverty and social injustice by non-violent but efficacious means. In whatever kind of apostolate they undertake, their love for the poor should be shown by their own social attitude, their sympathy in word and deed, their choice of a way of life resembling the poor.[37] Religious choose poverty so as to enrich others,[38] and many religious families were founded to help the poor. Paul VI stresses the importance of their work in the spheres of charity, assistance and social justice (ET 16-17).

## 4. New forms of poverty

The Council wished poverty to be practiced with initiative and diligence (PC 13,1), finding, if necessary, new ways of expressing itself so as to be understood by modern man. *Ecclesiae sanctae* is more detailed and says that religious institutes must with diligence and in concrete form, promote the spirit and practice of poverty, devising and putting into effect, in keeping with the character of each institute, new forms which may render more effective the practice and witness of poverty today (ES 23). In other words, love for the poor should give rise to creative ingenuity and inventiveness in this matter.

The note of urgency in these documents corresponds to a strong desire for authentic poverty and shows what we should think of the requests, not infrequent, to mitigate the practice of poverty and especially of dependence, on the pretext that respect is due to persons and their natural right to possess property.

*Ecclesiae sanctae* rightly speaks of acting in accordance with the character of each institute. Not all religious can give outward witness to poverty in the same way, but certain innovations are compatible with the nature of all institutes.[39]

For one thing, the content of the vow can move from the minimum mentioned above—the cession of the administration and disposal of use and usufruct—to the renunciation of use and usufruct, and further still, to the renunciation of patrimony, present and future.[40]

Another form proposed by the Council is the greater emphasis placed on work as a means of self-support and of help given to the Church and the poor.

There are some who would wish to adopt a form of poverty which consists in accepting a salaried work. It is maintained that in this way religious could participate in the life, the anxieties, and the problems peculiar to workers. This proposal to work for others is advanced in order to do away with the appearance or the reality of the power which religious enjoy when they work in their own institutions. We will return to this question when treating of collective poverty. Suffice it to remark here that the nature of the institute must be taken into account, and the purpose for which it was founded; what is possible for the Little Brothers of Jesus will not be possible to all.[41]

Some institutes will feel urged to begin or to resume work for the poor in the educational or social field or in nursing the sick. The novelty would not consist in the work itself, which would continue to demand professional competence, respect for those receiving help and delicacy in the manner of giving it, but in the fact that the recipients would be the poor.[42]

A fair number of proposals are made for living in surroundings more like those of the poor, which would involve reducing the size of communities so as to live in smaller houses, like those all around them.

Somewhat similar is the proposal to have fewer colleges, schools and hospitals and to let the religious work in state or private institutions. A further suggestion is to separate the living quarters of the religious from the buildings where their work is carried on, and let them be poorer and less spacious. Others again propose to turn over to the use of the poor certain of their existing works and buildings (ET 18).

It should be observed here, however, that it is quite another matter when reasons of poverty are given as a pretext for really opposing the institutional apostolate as such, and the much greater demands of time and devotion which it makes on religious. It seems to be a fact that some of the alternatives to the institutional apostolate are not themselves apostolic at all, but constitute simply a choosing of a secular life style with its accompanying freedoms.

An innovation which is a return to the past consists in giving free of charge to the poor the services which others pay for. There is indeed a strong feeling in the Church against the acceptance of stipends or fees for any form of ministry, when it is possible.[43]

The basis of all such changes must be the interior attitude of the religious, rejecting all idea of working for gain. All charitable or educational work is a form of sacred ministry (cf. PC 8) and should not be carried out for the sake of profit.

It is for each institute to examine the pros and cons of such proposals; it is a wide and interesting field of experiment open to the fervor of the religious. However, discussion must not remain theoretical, but come down to the actual and concrete situations and see whether the action proposed will really make poverty more meaningful in the eyes of both believers and unbelievers.

It must be borne in mind that innovations prejudicial to the common life as envisaged by the Church and the founders cannot lead to true poverty (cf. can. 594). Changes may be made in the form of it but not in the substance.

# 5. The wealth of poverty

Religious poverty is, in reality, richer than all the wealth of the world; it is sovereignly independent of earthly things and its rights of possession extend to heavenly things: "How happy are you who are poor: the kingdom of God is yours" (Lk 6:20).

## Theological content

Before all else the counsel of poverty has a theological and theocentric content rather than an economic or social function, though the latter also exists; it recalls the true value of material things and their purpose in view of the end.

Poverty is connected particularly with the theological virtue of hope, since it places all its trust in God and counts on Him for everything. It is connected also with faith and charity, since it rests on the word of God, lives by Him and for Him and has in Him its treasure; the giving up of possessions is an act of faith and love in view of which the hundredfold is promised (Mk 10:29). One who is truly poor is not anxious for the future nor desirous of the protection of the rich.

## Salvation content

Poverty for Christ's sake is a share in His redemptive action; He expiates the sins of cupidity and the misuse of riches and enriches His brethren with heavenly possessions. Poverty also places the religious at the service of his fellow men. "Just as Christ carried out the work of redemption in poverty and persecution, so the Church is called to follow the same route that it might communicate the fruits of salvation to men" (LG 8,3).

## Ecclesial content

The Acts of the Apostles, describing the life of the primitive and apostolic Church (Acts 4:32-36) stresses the putting in common of property and consequent disappropriation; no one called anything his own but looked upon everything as belonging to the ecclesial community.

Belonging to the Church, when expressed in the living of full community life, leads logically to community of goods and personal property. Property is a source of divisions and distinctions and often of quarrels; and the members of a body will obviously be more fully and deeply united if no such cause of differences and strife exists among them.

Further, since the Church by its nature requires detachment and the moderate use of earthly things as well as love for the poor, it is clear that religious poverty expresses the poverty of the Church in all these dimensions. *Gaudium et spes*, 88,1, declares that the spirit of poverty and of charity are the glory and witness of the Church of Christ.

## Liturgical content

The Church has made the offering of goods a liturgical act, an act of worship; the offertory forms part of the Eucharistic celebration; the collection of alms to supply the needs of the church and its indigent members is a sign of ecclesial communion that dates back to the earliest days of the Church. Religious poverty takes on a liturgical value because it is the object of a vow; it places the property of institutes at the service of the Church to relieve the necessities of its members.

## Prophetic and eschatological content

The Constitutions *Gaudium et spes* (38) and *Lumen gentium* (31), speaking of the mystery of Christ, tell us that He is now at work in the hearts of men through the energy of His Holy Spirit, not only arousing a desire for the age to come but purifying and strengthening the longing to make the lives of their fellow men more human; they speak of members of the Church whose charism is "to give clear witness to the desire for a heavenly home and to keep that desire alive among the human family," and say that by their state in life "religious give splendid and striking testimony that the world cannot be transformed and offered to God without the spirit of the beatitudes."

## Social content

Religious who are faithful to poverty render a social service also, by reminding all men of the true function of property and placing themselves at the service of others with their own property and that of their institute.

The world sometimes grumbles at what it calls the wealth of religious institutes, forgetting that what they have is used for the benefit of their fellow men in apostolic and missionary activity and works of charity.[44] And poverty is the glorification of work. St. Benedict's motto was *Ora et labora*.[45]

More than ever today those who profess poverty have an urgent duty to respond to the cry of the poor by never compromising with any form of social injustice, by arousing men's consciences to the present tragedy of destitution and doing all they can to change existing mentalities and attitudes (ET 17-18).

## Apostolic content

It is easy to see how poverty helps the apostolate by eliminating every suggestion of interest or profit.

The truly poor man whose treasure is in God feels freer in his apostolate, and this gives special efficacy to his action.[46]

# 6. The poverty of the institute

## Collective witness

The Council asks from institutes a testimony that may be called collective. Not only individuals but the institutes themselves are called upon to practice religious poverty; the surroundings and the atmosphere in which the religious lead their lives must be poor.

In the history of religious life, and especially in apostolic institutes, we find tension between radical spiritual detachment and the measure of actual outward renunciation, both in persons and in institutes.

## The institute and the ownership of property

### The right to possess

Not only every institute but every province and every house is capable of acquiring and possessing the property needed for their life and their works (can. 531).

The Council stresses the condition which justifies possession: the property must be necessary. If an institute possesses more than is required for the existence of itself, its members and its works, whatever is not needed should be used for other purposes or given away. A just and reasonable amount may, however, be kept in reserve as dictated by prudence.

The right to possess includes movable goods and real estate, and no limit is laid down deriving from the nature of the goods or the manner of keeping them or turning them to profit.[47] Limitations may be imposed by the Rules and constitutions of an Order or a Congregation, as, for example, the Friars Minor and the Capuchins. The Mendicant Orders have no right to possess except within limitations.[48] By canon law as at present in force, the property of the strictly Mendicant Orders is vested in the Holy See (cf. can. 582).

Other institutes which disallow or limit the right of possession are so organized that ownership and administration are in the hands of some other body or organization; a typical example is the community of the *Piccola Casa* of St. Joseph Benedict Cottolengo; another is the Society of Assistants of the Seraphic Work of Charity in Switzerland.[49] This system seems more practical than vesting ownership in the Holy See.[50]

## Possession of a fixed income

The question has been raised whether the possession of property bringing in a fixed income, either for immediate needs or as a provision for sickness and old age, is not contrary to the spirit of poverty and even to poverty itself.

Some institutes forbid the possession of capital and wish to prove their trust in Providence by refusing the security of a fixed income. It does not seem possible to lay down rules in the matter; each institute must bear witness to poverty in its own way. St. Ignatius allowed colleges to have an income because the work of education would be difficult without it.

The taking out of insurance policies may be counseled by prudence without signifying a lack of trust in Providence.[51]

## Ownership of property and the exercise of the apostolate

There is a strong tendency today in some countries to get rid of property as far as possible, especially of large and complex buildings such as hospitals, colleges and schools. It is said that the possession of these is contrary to the witness of poverty.

It cannot be denied that the sight of such buildings gives rise to doubts and criticism; the administration they involve is very much like the management of a commercial enterprise, with its accompanying sense of power and prestige.

This problem, however, must be approached realistically. The basis for such realism is the apostolic purpose for which the institute is founded and the consequent necessity of being able to dispose of economic means for the carrying out of this purpose. In inviting the institutes to search out new forms of poverty, *Perfectae caritatis* 13 asserts that account must be taken of the character of a given institute and hence of the apostolate proper to it, and the group should do this without letting itself be carried away by a passing enthusiasm or some supposedly charismatic impulse.

At the same time, account should be taken of the demands of poverty in the particular environment where the work is done.

There are many examples, past and present, of apostolic activities of religious that have been carried out without the possession of property in hospitals, schools, or other edifices. Obviously whenever it is possible to carry on an apostolic work equally well without the encumbrance of large patrimonies, it is in principle preferable to do so. In concrete cases, thought can even be given to the possibility and suitability of passing from one system to another. It is understood that in a case of cession of property all the ecclesiastical requirements will be observed. Sometimes the handing over of the goods or property connected with a given work could be required by the actual poverty of a religious institute which is not in a position to meet the expenses and other needs of the work itself. In this case the cession can be of such a kind that the work's nature is no longer ecclesiastical or religious. At times, however, this kind of change permits a work to receive subsidies or aid from the state or from other bodies which would not otherwise be granted.

In all of this, however, it should be recognized that no general norm can be laid down. In concrete cases, the property which serves a given apostolate is a presupposition and condition for the efficacious exercise of the apostolate itself. If religious work in their own houses, they can enjoy apostolic facilities which they would not otherwise have. This whole problem of the possible separation between the possession of goods which serve an apostolate and the actual exercise of the apostolate itself has to be looked at from a supernatural, ecclesial, and apostolic point of view, while taking concrete circumstances into account. The issue is by no means simple, and could even call for the intervention of church authority.

## Poverty in the conditions of modern life

The right of possession must be exercised in such a way that it does not clash with the demands and conditions of modern life; in other words, religious must not be expected to behave in a way that seems unfitting and causes surprise in the milieu in which they live and work.

The practice of poverty for institutes is the same as for individuals, calling for detachment and the use of material things only as means to an end; but the end has to be attained in existing conditions and circumstances. Institutes which undertake nursing and teaching must be provided with what their work requires by modern standards; their hospitals and schools must not be inferior to those of the state or other bodies; they must therefore have the conditions and equipment possessed by others. The efficacy of their apostolate will depend partly on their possession of the labor-saving devices in common use nowadays and up-to-date methods.

## The practice of poverty

The practice of poverty by individuals and by the institute will run parallel and indeed in conjunction. Authentic personal poverty creates an atmosphere which influences the whole community. The common life implies a mentality and an attitude toward material things which ought to be shared by all the members of the group and therefore expressed in the community as such. Institutes as well as individuals are asked by the Council to avoid all that contradicts the witness of poverty, "any form of luxury, immoderate profit and accumulation of property" (PC 13,6).

Luxury is a display of wealth in the possession and use of costly things, and even the superfluous may be called luxury if it is used with ostentation and from the pleasure of possessing.

Immoderate profit indicates greed of gain, which often results in the asking of very high prices and also in accumulating property. Moderate profit allows of keeping a prudent amount in reserve, but poverty forbids an exaggerated wish to gain and to save money, to increase one's capital and heap up riches.

## Charity and the distribution of goods

An eloquent testimony to collective poverty is the setting aside of part of the institute's property for the other needs of the Church and the poor. The Council invites the extension of the bond between the religious and the Church to the economic sphere and the inclusion in it of all Church organisms, dioceses, parishes, missions, etc., so that whatever Providence sends is shared with them.[52]

Whatever the institute uses for its own ends serves the needs of the Church, since the institute is the Church and everything in it is ordered to the good of the Church; this is implied by the words of PC 13,4: "they must be willing to make contributions from their own resources to meet *other* needs of the Church." The bond uniting religious to the Church puts them and all they possess at the disposal of the Church through the Holy See, so that they form part of the Church's patrimony.[53]

This is the basis of the Council's suggestion that temporal goods be shared with other Church organisms that are in need. It does not refer to what an institute has to spare over and above its own needs, but to a sharing that will entail real sacrifice. The measure of it will depend on many things, on the necessary expenditure of the institute on its own work, on the urgency of the appeal for help,[54] and on its readiness to give without receiving anything in return. Some institutes have a fixed sum in their annual budget for aid to the Church and the poor.

The duty of sharing in this way is obviously in proportion to the institute's capacity to give, and falls more urgently on those which possess property beyond their immediate needs. Economic collaboration between institutes might well be extended, and would be very desirable.[55]

## Aid to the poor

It is taken for granted that religious institutes utilize their poverty for the benefit of the poor. Many of them were indeed founded for that very purpose.

Love for the poor, deeply felt and clearly expressed, is the necessary basis, founded upon the teaching of the New Testament; the poor are to be loved with the heart of Christ Himself; but love must be expressed in act and in material help. The Council speaks of "other needs of the Church and the support of the needy" in the same breath.

Individual religious feel the sacrifice of being unable to give personally to the poor. It is true that sometimes those religious who actually come in contact with them are allowed something to give away as alms; but for the most part almsgiving is the affair of the community, and it is important for the community to feel and put into practice the desire to give. It might be a profitable subject for discussion at a community meeting.

## Mutual help within the institute

Life in community includes its economic aspect and calls for a sharing of goods and a certain equality in the style of life in a religious family, and therefore between provinces and the different houses in a province, due allowance being made for the standards of living which vary from country to country and region to region.

*Perfectae caritatis* speaks of this under the heading of poverty (13,5), saying that "provinces or houses ought to share their temporal goods with one another; those which are better off must give assistance to those in straitened circumstances." As remarked above, the same principle applies to institutes, some being well off and others not. As their tasks in the Church are complementary, so let it be with their temporal possessions, one supplying what may be lacking to another.

1. "Just as Christ carried out the work of redemption in poverty and persecution, so the Church is called to follow the same pattern, that it may communicate the fruits of salvation to men" (LG 8, 3).

Paul VI, *Lo spirito di povertà gloria e segno della Chiesa di Cristo;* cf. allocution of October 2, 1968; discourse of June 24, 1970, on the poverty required of Christians in general and of the Church in particular (*Osservatore Romano*, June 25, 1970).

2. We can trace an evolution of the concept of poverty in the Old and New Testaments. At first the poor man was simply the beggar, destitute, dependent and easily oppressed (Dt 24:14-15); but dependence on fellow men, who were often inclined to tyranny, gradually became dependence on God; material penury became spiritual detachment, trust in God's Providence, lowliness (cf. Mt 5:5; Lk 1:52).

Cf. "Povertà," A. Pery in *Vocabulaire Biblique*, by Von Allmen (Neuchâte: Delachaux et niestle, 1964).

A. Gelin, *Les pauvres de Jahvé* (Paris: ed. du Cerf, 1962).

"Povertà," M. Stenzel, ed. Benes, *Dizionario di teologia biblica* (Brescia: Morcelliana, 1967).

J. Dupont, *Les Béatitudes*, Vol. II (Paris: Gabalda, 1969), pp. 19-34.

3. Christ declared that He was sent to preach the Gospel to the poor and chose poverty for Himself.

Cf. SC 5,1; LG 8,3; AG 3,2; 5,3; GS 88; John XXIII, discourse in Sept. 1962.

Cf. also LG 41,1; 46,2.

4. For example, St. Anthony Abbot and St. Francis of Assisi.

5. The Council preferred to treat of poverty as a whole, since vow, virtue and spirit are all contained in the counsel. In this it goes back to the early Rules which made no distinction between vow and virtue.

6. The Incarnate Word of God entered into contact with earthly realities and taught us the attitude we should take up toward them. Remember the answers that He gave to the tempter in the wilderness.

7. St. Francis long ago used the expression "to live without owning."

8. Religious life, though it rejects the theories of communists and socialists, puts some of their ideas into practice.

P. Voillaume, in the retreat which he preached at the Vatican in 1968, speaks of poverty as *privation* and declares it a hateful condition; poverty as *detachment* is required by Christ as a condition of entering the kingdom of heaven; poverty as *vowed* by religious adds to the need for detachment a minimum of material and effective poverty. Cf. *Retraite au Vatican* (Paris: Fayard, 1969).

9. St. Angela Merici in Chapter XI of her Rule has a very broad concept of poverty, saying that it leaves itself wholly in the hands of God, trusting in His Providence.

Paul VI, speaking to Franciscan tertiaries (5-19-71), dwelt on the meaning of poverty as a seeking of the kingdom of heaven.

10. Undue rigidity should be avoided; rigorous poverty imposed on all is not desirable, but neither is a reduction of poverty solely to a spiritual attitude. True interior detachment leads to outward forms of effective poverty. Cf. A. Colorado, *op. cit.*, pp. 201; 213-215.

11. This is certain for religious; secular institutes usually require accountability for ordinary expenses and previous permission for the extraordinary.

12. The Norms of 1901 say: By the simple vow of poverty the Sisters give up the right of disposing licitly of any temporal thing without permission from legitimate Superiors.

A text used by the S. Congregation says: By the simple vow of poverty the religious give up the right of using or licitly disposing of any material thing possessing a money value without permission from legitimate Superiors. They may therefore not give, transfer, buy, sell, receive, keep or get others to keep, borrow, lend, exchange, make an act of ownership or administration, or use material things without the aforesaid permission. Cf. PC 13,2.

13. The formula of the solemn vow may vary, but the meaning is always the same. Religious must know exactly to what the vow of poverty obliges them in conscience.

14. In secular institutes accountability is sufficient as regards acts of habitual use and disposal.

15. This sum must not in any way contradict or take from the common life. Cf. can. 594.

16. Cf. can. 583,2; 582; 579.

17. Cf. can. 580; 583; 579; 569.

18. This formula was called "bizzarian" from the name of Card. Bizzari who introduced it when he was for twenty years Secretary of the Congregation of Bishops and Regulars.

19. Powers have been given to superiors general to authorize a change of will. Cf. the rescript *Cum admotae* 17, and the Decree *Re-*

*ligionum laicalium,* art. 6. The obligation of making a will exists if the religious fulfills the conditions laid down by civil law for the making of a valid will.

20. Cf. "Rinunzia ai beni e voto solenne di povertà," C.I.S.M. *Notiziario* (April-May 1968).

21. Many reasons — historical, juridical, social and economic — led the Church toward the beginning of the last century to authorize only simple vows and disallow a form of poverty equivalent to a solemn vow.

22. "To grant, with the consent of their Council, to their subjects who have made simple vows, when they ask it for a reasonable motive, authorization to renounce their patrimony for a just cause and in accordance with the rules of prudence. This faculty may, with the consent of their Council, be subdelegated to other major superiors, who, however, may make use of it only with the consent of their Council." Cf. AAS 59, p. 377, and a comment by the present writer in *Facoltà speciali dei Superiori Generali* (Milan: Ancora, 1965), pp. 91-96.

23. "To grant, with the consent of their Council, to their subjects who have made perpetual simple vows and who ask for it, authorization to renounce their patrimony for a just cause and in accordance with the rules of prudence. With the consent of their Council they may subdelegate this faculty to other major superiors, who, however, may not make use of it without the consent of their Council." Cf. AAS 59 (1967), p. 363.

A comparison of the two documents shows a tendency to less strictness in the wording.

24. It could not possibly be allowed earlier than just before taking perpetual vows, and it will come into effect only when the perpetual vows have been taken, as is said in can. 581 §1, for those who make solemn vows.

25. Property possessed at the time of profession may include not only what is actually in the possession of the subject but also anything due to come to him in the future, e.g. a debt to be repaid, a share in the family property, etc.

26. Renunciation of property is a matter for individuals; it cannot be imposed on one who made his vows before the obligation existed.

27. Cf. can. 181,1; 569,3. Each one should remember, however, that the institute may be included among the poor to whom property is distributed (Mt 19:21). One form of renunciation might be to constitute a dowry with the property; in the case of leaving the institute it would be given back.

28. Cf. can. 580 §2: "Whatever the religious acquires by his own industry or in respect of his institute belongs to the institute."

Can. 594,1: "In every religious institute all must carefully observe the common life, even in matters of food, clothing and furniture."

All that a religious acquires, even superiors, according to can. 580,2 and can. 582,1, immediately becomes part of the property of the house, province or institute; money and title-deeds must be put in the common fund.

29. The religious can say like Peter, "I have no silver or gold but I give you what I have; in the name of Jesus Christ of Nazareth, walk" (Acts 3:6).

30. Showing the true function of material things is a particularly valuable testimony in the world of today.

31. The word "superfluity" reminds us that the counsel goes beyond the precept; religious give up things that would not necessarily be superfluous to the state of the layman.

32. A Franciscan institute would have stricter rules than others.

33. It is better that the religious should put the question to himself than that the superior be obliged to do so. In the first schema of the Council commission it was said explicitly: "The religious themselves, without any desire for temporal possessions, should ask their superiors only for what they need for themselves or for their apostolate." Necessity may be judged more broadly for apostolic work than for personal needs, but there is sometimes real difficulty in deciding when and how far greater efficiency justifies further expenditure.

34. St. Paul himself said he worked for his living so as not to be a burden on others (cf. 1 Cor 4:12; 2 Thes 3:8).

35. *Ecclesiae sanctae* 27, says that the episcopal conferences in each country will, after consulting the superiors of the religious institutes concerned, lay down rules for the collection of alms, to be observed by all Orders and Congregations, including those known as Mendicants who do in fact live on alms and are not to be deprived of the right to beg.

It adds that money is not to be collected by public subscription without the permission of the bishop in whose diocese it is done.

The Italian Episcopal Conference gave rules on May 15, 1968. Cf. *Commentarium pro religiosis* (1968), pp. 372-373.

36. Some institutes chose to base their plan of renewal on a new concept of the law of work for religious; work and religious poverty are linked together. *Sponsa Christi* for November 21, 1950, contains the following passage: "Work, manual or intellectual, is an obligation for all, not excepting men and women dedicated to the contemplative life. It is not only a natural law but a duty of penance and satisfaction. Besides this, work preserves from many dangers and raises the mind to higher things; it is the means by which we, as in duty bound, make an offering to divine Providence in the natural and in the supernatural order, and carry out charitable works. Lastly, work is the fundamental rule and law of religious life and has been so from its origin: 'Work and pray.' Beyond doubt, the disciplinary rules of monastic life were in great part drawn up with a view to ordering, organizing and carrying out work."

37. A way of life resembling that of the poor (cf. Mt 8:20) is a witness in their favor and an apostolate, helping them to sanctify their condition and reminding everyone that "the new command of love is the basic law of human perfection and hence of the world's transformation" (GS 38).

38. The following of Christ is linked with giving to the poor (Mt 19:21) and this must be remembered when patrimony is renounced.

39. The character of an institute should not serve as a pretext to blocking anything new.

40. This form of poverty may be new to the institute but is not new in the Church.

41. The Little Brothers give their testimony by being present among others in a great diversity of dwelling-places and occupations.

42. The state has taken over a great many services that used to be given free to the poor, and established systems of social ʾsecurity by which these services are paid for. Nonetheless, love for the poor will be ingenious in finding ways of expressing itself.

43. This is a much discussed question, not easy to solve. It must be remembered that religious have to live on what they can earn and therefore have a right to take payment from those who can afford it.

44. As remarked in note 8 above, some of the ideas of communists are put into practice in religious life; it is the bases of them that are totally different.

45. Serious students of history have no difficulty in tracing the benefits brought to society by the religious Orders, beginning with St. Benedict. The civilization of Europe was almost entirely in their hands for a considerable time, and the Council makes mention of it when dealing with monasticism.

46. On condition that there is no self-seeking, personal or collective.

47. There may be some methods that are unsuitable for religious; local conditions play an important part here.

48. Some of them can possess the house and garden or orchard, but nothing else that can be turned to profit. Others disallow the possession of any kind of capital that gives an income. In addition to the Mendicants, some other Orders, including the Passionists, have imposed similar restrictions on themselves.

49. This Society is profoundly Franciscan in spirit. Its constitutions allow of ownership but only in circumstances when the apostolate would be impossible without it.

50. During the present period of renewal the system of ownership in the strictly Mendicant Orders is under examination.

51. Cf. Brovetto, "Povertà e realtà," *Vita religiosa,* 4 (1968), pp. 589-592.

52. The property of religious institutes is Church property (cf. can. 1497). Institutes which are in a position to help the diocese in which they live, especially when they draw advantages from it, should do so.

Contribution to the financial needs of the Church is one form of expressing union (cf. PC 2c).

53. Cf. E. Gambari, *For Me To Live Is the Church* (Boston: St. Paul Editions, 1970), p. 180.

54. One can scarcely imagine that religious would not give financial help in certain public calamities or when works of the Church were in difficulties.

55. Something has been done in this direction, but much more could be done if the sense of fraternity were stronger; much wastefulness might be avoided and more work undertaken. Obviously, it would call for scrupulous honesty and mutual straightforwardness.

# Chapter IV
# Obedience

## 1. Concern and interest of the Church

### A central question with its problems

There are few subjects within the Church and religious institutes, so much studied, discussed and disagreed about as obedience and authority.

This situation is due to a number of things, principally the following: a spirit of criticism, the sense of personal dignity and responsibility, a new outlook on the values of the world, the spread of democracy, the process of socialization and secularization, exaggerated humanism, naturalism, and above all, a weakened sense of faith — all these combine to bring it about.[1]

Obedience and authority are closely linked as different aspects of one reality and the means of attaining one and the same end (cf. PC 14).

The solution of the problem depends partly on the way obedience is presented. When looked at theologically and spiritually, as the Council presents it, obedience — and also authority — will be seen to harmonize with man's rightful tendencies and aspirations; its apostolic dimension points in the same direction; obedience will be the expression of an inward attitude making it both active and responsible.

There must, however, be a juridical structure defining and limiting the exercise of obedience and authority, which would otherwise have a blurred outline satisfactory to no one; it is linked with the social, juridical and hierarchical structure of the Church as well as with that of the religious institute.[2]

Without its theological basis, however, the juridical structure would be a body without a soul. Rights and duties must be seen in the light of the total meaning of obedience, a special participation in the mystery of the Redemption; Christ redeemed us by loving obedience to His Father's will, voluntary, not enforced; religious obedience seen in that light is both inspiring and light-giving.

This twofold aspect of obedience is brought out in the Council documents and in various discourses of Paul VI, particularly on January 12, 1967, to the major superiors of Italy. *Perfectae caritatis,* 14, speaks of obedience and authority as an expression of love[3]; *Lumen gentium,* of Christ's redemptive obedience (3, 36, 37, 41) and of Our Lady's co-operation in it (56, 61); we may also mention AG 5, 23, 24 and PO 7, but for an exhaustive list of references recourse must be had to the Index of Council words.[4]

Religious life is indeed inconceivable without the pledge to follow Christ in His self-offering[5]; it includes the other counsels and is the only one vowed by Benedictines and Dominicans.[6] It is evident that renewal in religious life cannot but depend largely on a new and deeper understanding of what obedience truly means. The practice of it will vary according to the nature of the institute, as will the exercise of authority, but both must be the fruit of long and careful training.[7]

# 2. The royal road of obedience

## The whole reality

As with the other counsels, *Perfectae caritatis* treats of obedience as a whole, not dividing it into vow, counsel and virtue nor distinguishing between the theological aspect and the juridical. It emphasizes what should lead to renewal and adaptation in the practice of it.

Art. 14 is a description rather than a definition,[8] pointing out its *object*, the dedication of one's own will; its *motive*, the sacrifice of self offered to God; its *strength* and *value*, greater stability and security in union with God's salvific will; its *example*, Jesus Christ; its *expression*, submission to superiors as showing us the will of God; its *social dimension*, the service of others; its *ecclesial* dimension, a stricter obligation to serve the Church; and lastly its *end* and *aim,* to attain to the stature of the fullness of Christ (cf. Eph 4:13).[9]

Since religious obedience consists in the offering of one's own will, that is, one's very self, as a sacrifice in order to be more surely united to God's will, it brings us more decisively and securely into His plan for mankind, in communion with Christ and in the service of the Church, and it is normal that it should sometimes lead to the cross (ET 23, 29). It is a death that brings forth life. Our fragile and inconstant wills, which so often make wrong choices, are raised up to the level of God's will. To choose this path is an excellent use of our freedom. Nothing expresses strength of will and liberty better than to voluntarily make a vow of obedience.

Obedience in itself is based on our creaturehood; religious obedience — a higher development of baptismal obedience — is ultimately based on the divine Sonship of Christ and His perfect love for the Father.[10] The first text of the Council commission, 25, 2, said that the Gospel origin of the counsel of obedience was to be found in the universal and loving submission of Christ to His Father, whose will was His food (Jn 4:34) and His obedience unto death, even death on a cross (Phil 2:8).

As, in the life of Christ, obedience appears as the basic element and unifying principle, so does it appear in His Body the Church, which is subject to Christ as Christ is to the Father. St. John quotes His words: "I and the Father are one" and His prayer that all Christians might be one in Him (Jn 10:30; 17:22). Obedience was the expression of His love for the Father and His response to the Father's love for Him. So with us. "If you love me, you will keep my commandments. And the word which you hear is not mine, but the Father's who sent me" (Jn 14:15, 24).

Religious obedience appears as a sacrificial oblation to God imitating that of Christ, who in submission to His Father gave His life as a ransom for many (Mt 10:28; cf. PC 14).

## The counsel

Obedience sums up the whole of Christian life, but it may flower into an obedience that goes beyond what is commanded for the various states of life, and pledges itself to do the will of someone who acts as mediator by making the will of God known to us.[11] *Lumen gentium* says in art. 42, 4, that the Church rejoices at finding within her bosom men and women who follow their Savior very closely and become subject of their own accord to another man...to become more fully like the obedient Christ.[12]

The counsel, then, consists in giving up the right of self-determination and voluntarily accepting the guidance of one whose decisions are taken as expressing God's will, in order to be more sure of it and enter with greater security into His plan.

The one who acts as guide must be in a position to make God's will known with due authority. Now the superior may have a particular relationship with God by the gifts of knowledge, prudence and holiness, bestowing a charism for the guidance of others. But even when he has such a charism and therefore interprets rather exactly the will of God, the decisive force of his order does not come from this charism. It comes from the fact that he is the legitimate representative of God, carrying out a mission conferred by Christ on His Church. When the Church gives a measure of authority, then, to a religious superior, we may be sure that in spite of possible weaknesses and errors, if he uses all the means at his disposal to find out the will of God and make it known, his guidance offers the best guarantee to the subject. Obviously, the "superior" must exercise some true ecclesial authority.

## Its origin in the Gospel

It would be difficult to find in Christ's words as given in the Gospel any formal statement or instruction on the counsel of obedience as it is understood by religious. The nearest we get to it is the text in Mt 16:24, which says, "If any man would come after me, let him deny himself"; and the statement given in all four Gospels that death to self is a source of life: "He that loses his life for my sake will find it."

What we find in the Gospel is far stronger than any specific words or teaching; it is the whole life of Christ shown as filial and religious obedience to the Father, from the first moment when He said, "I have come to do your will, O God" (Heb 10:9) to the last triumphant cry that all was accomplished (Jn 19:30). Obedience was His life-program, so that He could say, "My food is to do the will of him who sent me" (Jn 4:34).[13]

To His disciples He said when He called them, "Follow me." We have considered chastity and poverty as inspired by this call, but the following of Christ finds no truer interpretation than the imitation of His attitude and the sharing of His life — obedience as the most perfect expression of love.

## Our Lady's example[14]

Total obedience was the life embraced by Mary (LG 46,2) and for this reason she was represented as a model to priests (cf. PO 18).

By her obedience she gave her unique co-operation to the work of redemption. Her immediate response to the will of God is seen in her reply to the angel's message: "Behold, I am the handmaid of the Lord, let it be done to me according to your word" (Lk 1:38). Thus Our Lady, with no weight of sin to impede her, gave wholehearted acceptance to God's salvific will and dedicated herself as the handmaid of the Lord to the person and work of His Son, co-operating under Him and with Him in the mystery of the redemption, by the grace of God Almighty.

The Fathers of the Church were of the opinion that Mary was no merely passive instrument in God's hands but gave her free co-operation by faith and obedience. St. Irenaeus says that "being obedient, she became the cause of salvation for herself and the whole human race," [15] and her collaboration was intelligent, active and responsible. [16] "By her belief and obedience,....as the new Eve she brought forth on earth the very Son of the Father" (LG 63,1).

Like the Church and with the Church every religious looks toward Mary and strives to become more and more like her, "seeking and doing the will of God in all things" (cf. LG 56; 58; 65,1). [17]

# 3. The basis and support of obedience

## Imitation of Christ

The characteristic mark of religious obedience is that it is voluntary; a situation of dependence not simply accepted, still less submitted to, but chosen. And it is chosen in imitation of Christ, of His loving and redemptive obedience.

All obedience is an imitation of Christ, but for the religious it is not a passing act but the basis of a state; it is connected with humility and poverty; St. Paul calls it a self-emptying (Phil 2:7).

Natural reason would call for someone to exercise authority in a community for the sake of order, harmony and efficiency; when people work together there must be co-ordination and therefore direction. In apostolic work there is a further reason: because it is a participation in the mission of Christ, it calls for an apostolic mandate from authority.

Religious obedience recognizes the truth and reasonableness of all this, but is not based upon it. Its basis and support lie deeper. Its motive is the following of Christ.

## The rights of God

Supernatural obedience involves not only a person's activities but the person himself. Dependence might be accepted from various motives: to co-ordinate work with that of others; through recognition of a person's weakness or incapacity to manage his own affairs; through fear of responsibility. The religious, however, gives his superior the right to dispose of him as a person. It is not the obedience of children to parents, pupils to teachers, citizens to the civil authorities or workmen to employers; it is in the line of the obedience to which Christians are obliged by Baptism and is indeed a development of it. It is not even the obedience of a priest, which is required by his ministry and limited to it, though that also is based on Christ's obedience and normally leads to a certain practice of the counsel.

The religious chooses to express by his obedience his entire dependence on God, and the filial adherence to His will of the One who was "obedient unto death, even the death of the cross" (Phil 2:8).

## Faith and love

*Perfectae caritatis* tells religious that they must be obedient to superiors in a spirit of faith and of love for God's will, as to persons who hold the place of God.[18]

Co-operation with God's designs does not depend upon the reasons for choosing a particular person to act as His representative, that is, his prudence and experience, nor upon that person's way of acting, but solely upon the belief that his authority is conferred by God and the love that makes us respond gladly to God's will, even when it involves sacrifice and suffering. Humanly speaking, submission to another is painful, and may be made harder by the weaknesses and limitations of the one called to exercise authority; faith and love will raise us to a higher level, from which we see clearly that the only thing of vital importance is God's salvific plan in which we are called to collaborate.[19]

## The basis of authority

Holding a post of authority does not change the nature of a man or remove his weaknesses; nor does it depend upon his prudence and holiness. What is bestowed on him is the right to give orders and hence the right to be obeyed.[20] The obligation to obey does not depend on either the thing commanded or on the qualities of the person commanding, but on God's will that what is decided by a lawful superior be done. That alone is what gives power to authority and makes of it a sacrament uniting religious with the will of God. God may not indeed will the action but He wills the obedience (see note 12 above) and that is what gives strength and courage to the religious who is given an order difficult to carry out. He accepts the order and brings the best of himself to its execution, actively and responsibly, knowing that thus he enters into God's plan.

Superiors are bound to seek the will of God in order to make it known; and for this they receive special grace, so that by study, reflection, consultation and dialogue they may reach a decision that seems to be in accordance with God's designs.

It is not for the subject, however, to decide whether this is so. He obeys because the order is given by lawful authority, not because it appears to him to be reasonable; otherwise every order would be subject to appraisal, weighing the reasons for and against; one religious would be for, another against, and in the end the order would be obeyed — if it was obeyed — on its own merits and not because it came from authority. And that is not obedience.

God, let it be repeated, knows quite well that orders will seldom be perfect, but He wishes them obeyed nonetheless, because order and the common good require it. Religious obedience and authority must be looked at in the context of community and communion in an institution which has a social and hierarchical structure. The religious can and should try to enlighten the superior, but if the latter persists in his decision, God undoubtedly wishes the religious to obey. God does not withdraw His authority from one who exercises it with many errors and faults.

There is a certain analogy with the administration of the sacraments, which are valid even if badly administered; when God has given power to a man He does not withdraw it even if it is not exercised as He would wish. We cannot make a similar analogy with the teaching of doctrine by a master; a doctrine is not true because the master teaches it; but an order is to be obeyed when and because a lawful authority gives it.

It has been remarked that obedience is connected with humility and poverty, and this is self-evident. To set aside one's own way of thinking in order to obey shows humility and increases it. It can also be a source of redemptive suffering, if the will of God is such as to arouse natural repugnance and feelings of revolt, only to be overcome by a hard struggle. Here again we come to the imitation of Christ, who, "Son though he was, learned obedience through the things he suffered" (Heb 5:8). And all His sufferings were the sign and proof of His perfect obedience.

## Can obedience contradict conscience?

If a religious is told to do something to which his conscience objects, he should explain his difficulty to his superior and be willing to believe that one who holds authority from God is in a position to form correct judgments. Anyone who enters an institute pledges himself to a covenant with God and the community, which includes accepting the guidance of the one at the head of it and giving up personal views and preferences not in accordance with his. The exception has always been an act which is manifestly a sin. On all other points opinions may differ as to where the greatest good lies; but the common good requires that the superior be obeyed.[21]

# 4. The binding force of religious obedience

## The will of God

Obedience unites and binds the religious to the will of God in whatever way it may be expressed; for the religious, as for others, He reveals His will in circumstances,

events and the signs of the times; but we are here concerned more directly with the practice of the counsel.

In religious life God expresses His will through superiors at every level, and the laws and rules by which they
govern; it is commonly found that obedience is given
more readily to a superior than to a subordinate or delegate,
and yet in each case it is God who is obeyed.[22]

The community also can act as mediator in making
God's will known. In certain cases it is an authority in the
full sense, when the local chapter has decisions to make;
but even apart from that, it plays an important part in the
life of all, superiors and members alike. Considered simply
as a group of persons gathered together in the love of Christ,
it is normal that its discussions should throw light on the
problems that concern it and that due weight be given
to the contribution each can make. The Spirit speaks
through the brethren, even the least important (cf. Rule
of St. Benedict). All can thus help to find the will of God,
but the seal of authenticity must be given by authority.

## The vow of obedience

The binding force of obedience is both clarified and
strengthened by the vow, which is an act of worship in-
fluencing one's whole life.

Obedience to an authority conferred by the Church is
ecclesial in character, and to that fact it owes its spiritual
and apostolic content and its juridical effects.

Over the centuries the pledge to obey superiors has
taken various forms, and it still differs from one institute to
another.

In recent years the Holy See has given preference to
a formula by which the obligation of the vow is limited to
clear and precise commands given by duly qualified
superiors in accordance with the constitutions. This wording has the advantage of being concrete in its definition,
and of bringing the vow more frequently into effect without giving cause for hesitation or scruples when an order
is not clear. According to circumstances the obligation may
be grave or not.

There are some who would wish—as for poverty—to make no distinction between vow and virtue; it appears to them to impoverish the counsel.

It must be remembered, however, that the Church and the founders of institutes did not act in this matter without due consideration. It was felt that the life of obedience needed a clear and solid basis; the vow was seen as a starting-point, and since it obliges the conscience before God it must be precise and give no cause for anxiety. Obedience is an ideal to be pursued with one's whole strength; it cannot be vowed in that form, but the vow is a help and a stimulus.[23] In the constitutions this must be made clear and the ideal set forth, together with the extent, matter and manner of the obligation[24]; the vow is therefore taken to obey "in accordance with the constitutions," which should open the minds and hearts of the religious to the whole horizon and demands of the counsel.

## Duly qualified superiors

"All religious are subject to the Roman Pontiff as to their highest superior" (can. 499 § 1)[25]; after him come the superiors within the institute as named in the constitutions.

The nature and end of the vow of obedience make it normal that all superiors may, within their competence, give orders in force of the vow; this would apply to chapters, the superior general, the provincial or his equivalent, the local superior and his delegates.

Constitutions approved before Vatican II often exclude the local superior but with the present tendency to broaden the scope of the vow, it would seem regrettable to do this; it is right that local superiors should not give an order in force of the vow unless in grave and exceptional circumstances,[26] and constitutions commonly emphasize this (cf. Norms of 1901, art. 137), but it is good that possession of the right should strengthen and uplift obedience to the one who presides over the life of the community.

Obviously, no civil authority can give orders in virtue of the vow, nor can ecclesiastical authorities unless canon law or the constitutions say otherwise; the virtue of obedience, however, obliges religious to obey the law of the land and the just demands of civil authorities or of others under whom they have agreed to work (cf. GS 74,4).

## The virtue

The Decree *Presbyterorum ordinis* 15,2 says that obedience is the gift of one's own will in the service of God and one's fellow men, receiving and carrying out in a great spirit of faith whatever orders may be given by superiors. Superiors here include all those who are invested with authority; the virtue of obedience also binds religious to observe the laws of the Church, their constitutions and all rules that are in force in their institute; it requires the practice of dependence upon those who, though not invested with authority in the strict sense, have a duty of direction; such would be the novice master or mistress, the principal of a school, the superintendent in a hospital.

Nor is obedience limited to those who form part of the institute; it is extremely important in the relations of religious with bishops and their representatives, particularly in what concerns the apostolate. *Lumen gentium* points out that bishops have pastoral authority in their dioceses, and that there must be unity and harmony in the apostolate (45,2). For this reason, religious obedience merges into apostolic obedience where the apostolate is concerned.[27]

We have remarked above that the practice of obedience may and does vary in manner and degree in different institutes; nonetheless, it remains true that fundamentally the relations between subject and superior are always of the same nature; the function of a religious superior is to guide those under his care to holiness, and also to help them to carry out their duties toward other authorities.[28] Since its end and aim arise from the very nature of a religious vocation, with its total consecration to God, it would be possible and helpful to draw up a doctrine and theory of obedience applicable to all religious regardless of their form of government and the specific purpose of their institute.

# 5. The sphere of religious obedience

## According to Rules and constitutions

Since the vow of obedience is made "according to the Rule and constitutions," that phrase indicates the field within which orders may be given (cf. PC 14,2). All the members of an institute are included in the plan derived from the charism or inspiration which gave origin to it, sketched out and defined as a way of life approved by the Holy See or other competent authority. The particular vocation and mission of an institute is God's will for it, and the constitutions declare that what touches its life directly or indirectly falls within the sphere of religious obedience. Such matters include appointment to various offices, formation, the assignment of religious to apostolic activities.

It must not be deduced from this that certain sectors of life lie completely outside the competence of the superior, as, for example, professional matters, questions of health, relations with other people. It is true that a superior cannot carry out the duties of a technician or a doctor; true also that personal relationships, especially family matters and those arising from the ministry, are to a certain extent considered private; tact is called for in dealing with them. However, in another sense everything concerning a religious is a community question. Community life, the availability of the individual and his share in common interests bring all that concerns him within the sphere where the superior can, if not command, at least guide and advise. Every institute must work out its own plan of relationship between subject and superior, and then leave the application of it to circumstances and persons.

Authority is given with a view to the end and aim of the institute and to carry out God's purpose for it; subjects and superiors alike are bound to work together for it in a common effort and to tread the path traced out for them by the Lord and described in the institute's code of life.[29]

A religious who works outside the religious house is not dispensed from obedience; neither is one who is a specialist in some particular field, or who works in a group which has its own regulations. In all cases the work undertaken must conform with the institute's vocation; the two spheres ought to be clearly marked off, and it must be possible to pass from external activity to the demands of common life (ET 26).

## 6. The vital energy of obedience

Obedience is a liberating[30] and unifying force. It frees us from egoism, self-seeking, weaknesses and illusions, from love of power and to a large extent from being dominated by our own passions; the commitment to obey is an act of full freedom used in the noblest way (cf. ET 27). The religious does not obey through coercion but because he has chosen to do so.

It was through obedience that Christ freed mankind from the slavery of sin, and opened the way to union with God, for union with God's will is union with God Himself; in this sense obedience can be called a sacrament, and holds the place of first importance among the vows.[31]

Human nature, restored to wholeness by Christ, is brought to maturity by this liberating and unifying force; its natural resources can be put to the fullest use and the personality of each one developed in all freedom to become what God in His wisdom and love intended it to be[32]; it can give of its best to the building up of the Body of Christ, for personality is not weakened but strengthened by obedience properly understood. In the measure of his obedience, a man attains greatness and dignity by participating in the Sonship of Christ.[33]

The vertical dimension of obedience is combined with a horizontal dimension which puts the religious at the service of the Church[34] and all its members, particularly in the field of the apostolate; his covenant with God becomes a covenant with all men, his availability to God, an availability to all, especially to those who share the same charism, for obedience to authority is a source of cohesion and therefore of strength in the community.

## 7. Dimensions and practice of obedience

Obedience is, as we have seen, God-centered and Christ-centered. It is a living out day by day of the prayer "Thy will be done" and by it the only thing we really possess as our own, our liberty, is offered to God so that our will may merge with His. It is a personal link between man and God whereby His sovereignty is acknowledged, unconditional service offered, and true friendship formed in faith and love.

Christ-centered it is in its origin, its motive, its end and aim: to attain to the stature of the fullness of Christ (cf. Eph 4:13); and the confirming of it by vow unites it to the religious and priestly character of Christ's obedience to the Father. "Through Him, with Him and in Him," we obey.

It is through the action of the Holy Spirit, the Spirit of love proceeding from the Father and the Son, that obedience is actually practiced[35]; it is through Him that the exercise of obedience and authority becomes the exercise of love — the love of God for man in authority, the love of man for God in obedience; God is thus its beginning and its end.

The sacrificial aspect of obedience is sometimes so much stressed that people seem to forget that it can bring joy, both natural and supernatural. It is true that we follow the cross-bearing Christ and each has his own cross to carry, but the happiness and usefulness of a normal religious life will increase in proportion as it carries out God's will and fulfills His purpose.

Since the purpose of obedience is the building up of the Body of Christ according to God's plan, dependence on the hierarchy emphasizes the close bond between religious and the Church[36] and ensures collaboration at the place and in the manner willed by God (AA 12,2; PO 15,2; PC 14).[37] *Perfectae caritatis* bids them honor and love their pastors. But the service of the Church is expressed in a more detailed and intimate manner when it is the service of the institute and the community[38] to which the religious belongs. The apostolate undertaken in obedience to the Church takes a specific form in institute and community,[39] and this is implied in the vow itself.

The honor and love due to pastors is owed to superiors; and the practice of obedience must be filial, the relationship, one of mutual confidence. Two extremes are to be avoided: "infantilism" or flight from responsibility, and an independent attitude that neglects to ask permission or render account.[40] On the part of the superior, active and responsible obedience should be expected and a spirit of initiative encouraged; if there is proper understanding of subsidiarity and co-responsibility, a good margin of choice may be left with regard to details. Obedience no more consists solely in receiving orders and carrying them out than poverty consists solely in asking and receiving permission.[41] Although decisions and orders are necessary, obedience has been defined as a relationship of dependence rather than an act, and, as remarked above, a relationship which implies mutual confidence based on oneness of mind and heart; in true dialogue[42] each one speaks with simplicity and openness, either as person to person or with a group or the whole community. It may sometimes end in a general consensus, but obedience must not be lost sight of; it is not a question of a majority vote as in politics. The decision rests with the superior, whose aim is the good of the community and the loving fulfillment of God's designs.

1. The permanent Committee of Religious in France edited, in 1966, a study of the interior and exterior factors affecting obedience. *Essai de réflexion de prospective* (Paris: U.S.M.F., 1968), pp. 11-27.

2. In some of the constitutions drawn up by special chapters there is a lack of basic juridical elements or norms.

A new vision of the Church as the People of God should give a new vision also of obedience and authority.

3. The history of the text can be found in an article by P. Tillard in *L'Adaptation et Rénovation de la vie religieuse*, pp. 391-398.

4. *Index verborum Concilii Vaticani II*, under the headings *oboediens, oboedientia*, and *oboedio*.

5. The whole Gospel is a message of obedience: "Go and teach all men...to observe all that I have commanded" (Mt 28:18).

6. Cf. Rule of St. Benedict, ch. 58. St. Augustine in *The City of God* calls obedience the mother and guardian of all the virtues (Book 14, ch. XII).

7. Cf. Card. Garrone, *L'obéissance et la formation à l'obéissance,* (Vatican Polyglot Press), p. 22; G. Corallo, "L'educazione all'obbedienza," *Seminarium,* July-Sept. 1967, 603-624.

8. The first text of the Council commission was more like a typical classic definition: "Religious obedience consists in the submission by which the subject, freely offering to God the holocaust of his own will, renders humble deference for the love of Christ to the superiors who hold the place of God, in all that is commanded according to the Rules and constitutions" (Art. 26, *Schema constitutionis de statibus perfectionis adquirendae,* 1963).

9. The chief source of this description is Paul VI's allocution to a group of General Chapters, May 23, 1964.

10. "Truly, truly I say to you, the Son can do nothing of his own accord, but only what he sees the Father doing" (Jn 5:19); "I have come to do your will, O God" (Heb 10:9).

11. The superior's function is not to be understood as if he were a loud-speaker relaying God's commands and as if his every order were an order emanating from God; his orders are simply given on the strength of authority conferred on him by God.

12. Not all the commands which Christ obeyed were willed by God, but God willed that He should obey them.

13. The Decree *Perfectae caritatis* gives some references to Gospel texts. Some new constitutions quote other appropriate texts.
Cf. K. Rahner, S.J., "Christus ut exemplar oboedientiae clericalis," *Seminarium,* July-Sept. 1967, pp. 465-479; on pp. 569-571, he refers to New Testament texts on Christ's obedience.

14. Cf. E. Gambari, *For Me To Live Is the Church* (Boston: St. Paul Editions, 1970), pp. 314-318. M.J. Nicolas, O.P., "L'obéissance de Marie," *Seminarium,* July-Aug. 1967, pp. 491-499.

15. Hence the comparison between Mary and Eve and the parallel drawn Jesus-Adam: Mary-Eve.

16. Paul VI, November 21, 1964.

17. Mary is the prototype of the obedience described in PC 14.

18. The theological basis of obedience is summarized in PC 14, as the salvific will of God, imitation of Christ, inspiration of the Holy Spirit, a spirit of faith and love, service of our fellow men in Christ.

19. Difficulties with regard to obedience often arise from a lack of faith and love on the part of superior or subject.

20. By placing a mediator between Himself and men, God responds to a deeply ingrained need in human nature to have a guide close at hand.

21. The Holy Spirit cannot contradict Himself. If the superior is deaf to a suggestion coming from Him, he will answer for it to God. If, on the other hand, a religious seems genuinely called to a line of action not in keeping with the charism of the institute, it may be that God calls him elsewhere (cf. Decree 280 of the 31st General Congregation of the Jesuits).

22. Decree 270 of the same General Congregation emphasized that it is always to God that religious obedience is addressed.

23. Cf. Volume I of the present work, ch. XI, on the vows in general.

24. Approbation of the constitutions falls within the Church's duty to interpret and regulate the practice of the counsels.

25. The Roman Pontiff is distinct from the College of Bishops.

26. It seems unnecessary to require the presence of two witnesses or a written command, as in the canonical admonitions of can. 2309 §2.

27. The need for this is more felt than in the past. In some cases, particularly in lay clerical institutes, there was a wish to include dependence on the bishop in the vow of obedience. For apostolic institutes, dependence on the local hierarchy is essential.

28. Religious obedience is a unifying principle in life, and is not excluded from the professional sphere. It is with the permission of his superior that a religious engages in any professional activity or ministry under another authority; and the superior, without attempting to direct the work itself must in a general manner follow up the religious in the way he lives.

29. Not even a general chapter can change the nature of an institute as it was willed by God and accepted by those who entered it. The Lord's design includes the institute as a whole and each member of it.

30. Paul VI, in his allocution of Jan. 28, 1970, speaks of the liberating force of obedience. Cf. present work, Volume I, ch. XXI, on the richness, efficacy and power of religious life.

31. The union of espousal with Christ is achieved by obedience even more than by consecrated chastity. The two vows are closely united by their unitive force.

32. For this, it is essential that superiors have a clear view of the relationship between authority and obedience and a deep sense of their own responsibility. T. Goffi in ch. 4 of *Obbedienza e autonomia personale* (Ancora, 1967), speaks of governing in function of the subject's self-determination, and one of the superior's duties is to teach the individual how to use his freedom. This was recently pointed out in the general chapter of a women's institute.

33. See S. Lyonnet, "Liberté chrétienne et la loi selon l'Esprit" in the volume I de la Potterie and S. Lyonnet, *La vie selon l'Esprit condition du chrétien* (Paris: Ed. du Cerf, 1965). B. Gingras, *Obéissance religieuse et personnalisme* (Montreal: Editions Paulines, 1966).

On the whole question of religious obedience there is a useful chapter in L. Örsy, *Open to the Spirit* (Chapman, 1968).

34. Cf. E. Gambari, *op. cit.*

35. From the Gospels we learn of Christ's obedience to the impulse of the Spirit; e.g., Mt 3:16; 4:1; Lk 4:1, 14, 18.

36. The religious who obeys superiors whose authority derives from the Church becomes thereby an envoy of the Church.

Even outside the strictly apostolic field, the obedience of the religious builds up the Church and the kingdom of God.

37. The Dominicans in their revised constitutions show union with Christ and the Church as the fruit of obedience; the Jesuits state that obedience makes them instruments in the hands of the Church (cf. 269). Cf. E. Gambari, *op. cit.*

38. Both Dominicans and Jesuits give obedience as the principle of unity in a community, and the Special Chapter of Discalced Carmelites says that "authority and obedience should be a source of fraternal communion so that all the brethren cultivate and enjoy a family spirit."

The juridical aspect of obedience merges in the theological, and all members meet in the accomplishment of the salvific will of God.

39. The service of the community is carried out through the superior who regulates it; therefore, even if the community has a share in decision-making, obedience is formally promised to the superior and not to the community.

Cf. E. Gambari, *For Me To Live Is the Church* (Boston: St. Paul Editions, 1970), p. 195.

40. It may happen that from one extreme a person passes to the other.

41. The Council speaks of dialogue between bishops and laymen (LG 37), between bishops and priests (CD 28,2; PO 15,2; ES Introduction), and between priests and laymen (AA 25,2; 19,3).

42. I. Hausherr, S.J., *L'obéissance religieuse* (Toulouse: Prière et Vie, 1966), pp. 91-110, treats of the necessity and the limits of dialogue. Cf. *Renovationis causam* 32. Paul VI, Jan. 12, 1967.

It may happen that the superior and the community come to an agreement about the action to be taken; in that case the agreement on the superior's part is equivalent to a permission.

In a person-to-person discussion, the superior as educator may lead the religious to come to a decision himself.

# Chapter V
# The common life

## 1. Its place and importance in religious life

One of the signs of the times which finds an echo in religious life is the recognition that man cannot live and develop fully without other men; the human person by his very nature stands in need of social life. One of the salient features of the modern world is the growing interdependence of men on one another, very largely promoted by modern technical advances.

It is in God that man finds the origin of his relationship of brotherhood and equality with other men; the bonds linking them together bind them all to God, who is the goal for one and all (GS 23-25).

Universal brotherhood, the social dimension of man, has a very strong appeal today, especially to the young, even when—as is too often the case—they do not know that their meeting-place is in God.[1]

*Lumen gentium,* in the very titles of its second and fifth chapters—"the People of God" and "the universal call to holiness"—calls to mind and lays down the principle that God's plan is not to sanctify and save men isolated one from another but by building them into a people, a people "made one with the unity of the Father, the Son and the Holy Spirit."

The Church is shown as "the visible sacrament of this saving unity," "a sign and instrument of a closely knit union with God and of the unity of the whole human race"; its inward reality is shown as communion and its outward and visible structure as community, including the hierarchical structure; its members, equal in their dignity as children of God and members of the Body of Christ, each and all called to holiness, have different parts to play according to their particular vocation and mission in the building up of the Body of Christ, which is the Church.

Paul VI frequently speaks of the Church as a community based upon communion, in which the collegiality of bishops and the various services or functions of ecclesiastical authority find their natural place.[2] In *Evangelica testificatio* 33-39, he develops the same concept as applied to the religious life.

The deeper feeling for community and communion is perceptible in all Orders and Congregations in our time. Some, like the Franciscans, make the idea of fraternity the central nucleus of their specific religious life, thus going back to their origins; in others, it is the common life in one aspect or another that is seen as essential to renewal — a genuine commonness which both recalls and expresses the meeting of all in Christ. *Perfectae caritatis* 15 lays great stress upon it, upon its theological and spiritual basis, which is at the same time profoundly human, rather than upon the juridical and structural aspect; the latter is taken for granted (can. 487, 488,1).[3]

When given its full significance, the common life gives to the practice of the evangelical counsels the characteristic mark that distinguishes the religious from the secular institute; it is a constitutive element in religious life and has been recognized as such for hundreds of years. The practice of the counsels assumed a more concrete form, at once more demanding and more stable, when lived in inward and outward communion with others and presided over by one as the representative of Christ. Monastic and religious tradition in general has modeled itself on the group of disciples gathered round the Master and on the first Christians living in community in Jerusalem in the time of the apostles.

Life in community has been the thread running through the web of religious life, giving concrete shape to the practice of the evangelical counsels, and it is an indispensable feature of renewal for individuals as for communities.[4] The far-reaching changes in the society of today, with its new political and economic structures, are reflected in the life of religious institutes and the groups that compose them; everywhere we find the sense of solidarity and common destiny of all men, the need for participation, for openness to others, and at the same time consideration for individuals, who must not be submerged by or in the community, but find in it the means of life and growth. The common life must not be limited, as it was in the past, to material things or juridical rules; its value is essentially theological and spiritual.

# 2. Meaning and implications of the common life

The following terms are used in Council documents:
"a true family gathered together in the name of the Lord" (PC 15,1).

"fraternal association in the militia of Christ" (LG 43,1)

"the bond of brotherly love" (PC 15,2)

"unity of the brethren" (PC 15,1)

*Ecclesiae Sanctae* speaks of "fraternal life in common, as a family united in Christ" (25).

A complete definition or description might be given thus: a permanent group of persons gathered together as in a true family in the name of the Lord, sharing the same charism, inspired by charity, strengthened by the presence of Christ, linked together by the Church and pledged to put all things in common for the service of the whole group and the building up of the Body of Christ.

Putting all things in common means making a plan of life and carrying it out together, each one feeling responsible for himself and for the group and contributing all that he has to give, naturally and supernaturally, so that his life merges with the life of the others. The result is a wonderful and most fruitful unity, in which the material aspect of the common life is caught up into the living reality of community life with the specific end to which it is directed.

The theological basis of community life needs to be brought out more than it has yet been. It will show that the genuine friendship and brotherhood within the group grows out of the sharing of the inspiration or charism and helps it to develop as a spiritual and apostolic force; every religious community is by its nature a charismatic group.

Its members, like the early Christians spoken of in Acts 4:32, are of one heart and soul, and this, whatever the outward structure of the community may be; for, like the Church, the community united in Christ and the Holy Spirit has outward forms and structures and a juridical organization.

In the first place and above all, its basis is a permanent spiritual attitude of readiness to share with others and move with them toward the same spiritual goal (cf. *Pacem in terris,* art. 36),[5] but since it is human as well as divine, it must be seen as concrete and social. The inner reality expresses itself in the outer forms which sustain and protect it.

In a community, because of its small size, these outward structures can be far more complete than in the Church of today; they can, in fact, resemble those of primitive times.

Canonical common life follows precise rules on such matters as residence, apostolate, finances, and so forth. In general, its organization requires that the members of the group live, pray and work together. In some institutes what is done in common occupies a great part of the day, but on this point there is great variety. Apostolic institutes often reduce common acts to a minimum, but this does not affect community life or its theological and spiritual basis.[6] A minimum there must be, but not necessarily in a monastic framework. *Ecclesiae Sanctae,* though it emphasizes the importance of community life, remarks that in apostolic institutes it will often happen that the order of the day cannot be identical in all the houses, or even sometimes for all the religious in the same house (25, 26).

Canon 594 deals with the consequences of the common life as regards the use of material things. Whatever is acquired by the religious, even by his personal work, belongs to the institute (cf. can. 580); it cannot be kept by individuals. Superiors, like everyone else, must put it into the common fund. The community must provide food, clothing and other necessities for each one according to the rules of the common life, that is to say, treating all alike and giving to each what he needs, without distinction or consideration of persons (cf. can. 594 §1). The history of religious life shows that institutes flourish when the common life is observed as regards material things, with due regard to poverty; circumstances may call for adaptations, but possession in common and equal treatment for all must be faithfully observed.

The outward framework which supports the spiritual reality joins with it in giving its complete meaning to the common life. From every point of view—theological, anthropological, psychological and spiritual—each member not only belongs outwardly to the group but is really incorporated into it, so that his whole life merges into the life he shares with others.

# 3. Basis and unifying factors of the common life

The basis of the common life is both natural and supernatural. God, who created man with an innate tendency and need to seek his fellow men and live in their society, finds in him a certain predisposition to answer the call to live in a religious community. More deeply than in membership in the Mystical Body, man will find there a brotherhood rooted in the unity of the Three Divine Persons. More deeply than the ecclesial community is the religious community, "a community of believers united in the same faith, the same hope, the same charity, a community that lives with a life given and maintained by Christ Himself."[7] The *koinonia* or fellowship of the first

Christians, constantly united in prayer and the Eucharistic celebration, is an ideal picture of those who share in the same charism.

At the center of the religious community is Christ, with a group of followers. Their life in common takes its immediate origin from religious profession; and a number of people wish to see this expressed in the formula used, emphasizing its horizontal dimension, for it is not only a covenant with God, but with the brethren.[8]

But the presence and action of Christ surpass all other unifying factors. The Constitution on the Liturgy speaks in art. 7 of His presence in the liturgy, in the Eucharist, in Scripture and in prayer. The Eucharist is first and foremost as a means and an expression of unity; the words communion and concelebration say it plainly; we meet God *with* our fellow Christians, in no transitory way but in a unity of life which is mysterious but permanent and real.

Christ is found also in the Liturgy of the Word and in prayer. "Reading and meditating daily on Holy Writ" is enjoined upon religious by *Perfectae caritatis* (6), and great importance is now attached to reading and commenting on it in common; when this is well done, it is a real meeting-point in Christ. As for prayer, there is a familiar saying, "The family that prays together stays together," and it may be applied to a religious family. Christ, who said "Where two or three are gathered together in my name, there am I in the midst of them," takes the prayer of the community and makes it His own.

From and through Christ the group is unified by the spirit of fraternity or brotherhood,[9] which is built up day by day through the personal effort of each member. The bond that links members together is a community of mind and heart which is not something imposed from without but rather the result of daily and mutual self-giving. The necessary minimum of structure that provides for someone to preside in the community is there for the purpose of ensuring yet another form of the presence of Christ.[10]

# 4. Components of the common life

In general, every community has its origin in the will of the Father, who calls and gathers together for a common purpose a group of persons, each of whom responds by giving himself, with all his resources of nature and grace, to carry out a specific end and aim by active and responsible collaboration.

Like all the People of God, but more intensely, the community shares in Christ's priestly and prophetic office, in His apostolic office and in His ministry (cf. LG 11-13; 17).

We have just spoken of the presence of Christ in liturgy, Eucharist and prayer. The community's prophetic office consists in its witness to values not measured by the world's standards nor limited to this life.[11] Many people declare that all men are brothers, but not many live up to that ideal. The religious community puts that belief into practice, showing that it is based on belief in God, and that only belief in God will draw men into a life of true cohesion and unification.

The value of collective work in an apostolate assumed by the institute as such is too obvious to need emphasizing. It is true that there is a certain tendency today to minimize that value in favor of individual apostolic tasks. The truth is that modern conditions offer opportunities for individual work that did not exist in the past, but nothing alters the fact that a religious working outside his community works in its name and under its responsibility and guidance. From the community he receives strength and encouragement as well as the ecclesial character of his apostolate.

Certain kinds of apostolic work demand a large community—and also, perhaps, large buildings where this is required by the specific end of the institute. Other apostolates call for work in small houses and small groups. It is not the size of the group, however, that gives value to its work but the spirit of unity in its aim—one of mutual appreciation and encouragement, and of readiness to collaborate in the common task.

A community spirit extends beyond its own group to include other houses, the province and the whole institute in its readiness to serve and to share, its interest and its sense of co-responsibility.[12] The relatively new name brought into use is *collegiality*,[13] which implies a share in decision-making. More importantly it implies the bond of solidarity by which each member is responsible for each and all of the others. This is always to be reconciled with the responsibility of Superiors. *Perfectae caritatis* 4 and 14 lay stress upon the need for all the members of an institute to be concerned and consulted in what concerns it. Logically also it implies equality between members and the unification of classes if differences still exist.[14]

The unification of classes is a spirit expressing itself in a structure, but community life is more than a spirit and a structure; it is made up of actions and attitudes that add up to a life-style, and in our time young people want its dimensions to be, as they say, "more human." Twenty years ago Pope Pius XII told a group of women superiors general to do away with outdated customs. The recommendation was more important than at first sight it appears, for community life is lived daily, and it is largely out of customs that daily life is built.

## 5. The value and vital energy of the common life

Early in the life of the Church it was discovered that the evangelical counsels were better practiced in common than in solitude. The advantages of mutual support and help are too clear to need setting out in detail; we may mention in passing the means for formation and the safeguard against inconstancy, but others spring to the mind at once; many of them are commented upon in *Evangelica testificatio* 33-39.[15] Life in common provides surroundings and a rhythm of regularity which direct and unify the efforts made to advance in the spiritual life (cf. LG 43,1).

Religious life in common is largely based on the same principles as family life and social life, and expressly applies those principles by, in and through the practice

THE COMMON LIFE    109

of charity. Love for God and man is its meaning and its motive, and hence the source of its vital energy.

"Through his dealings with others," says *Gaudium et spes*, speaking of the human community, "through reciprocal duties, and through fraternal dialogue, man develops all his gifts and is able to rise to his destiny." Let us add that the more a man rises above self-seeking, the more perfectly he fulfills his destiny.

The religious community is a living example of what the human community ought to be, and a moving contrast to what it too often is. A true religious family is a stimulus and an encouragement to the unity, charity, availability and self-forgetfulness that must go into the building up of human society.

# 6. The practice of the common life[16]

The very word "community" indicates that its life is a life of interpersonal relationships; persons who have everything in common and share most of their activities are closely connected, and no one can or should wish to cut himself off and live in isolation. From the beginning of his formation the religious must learn that a community is an existential reality based on love and that love brings with it openness and trust; self-giving is mutual and the spirit of brotherhood which grows with the daily exchange of kindnesses, reaches out beyond the group to others and to the whole world. Sharing is seen as desirable and desired; it will include shouldering a part of the burden for the common good.

## Relations with the institute

To his own institute the religious is bound by love, esteem, a spirit of service and of devotion to its interests, even material. He will avoid needless or wasteful expense, take care of the things he uses and expect to contribute by his work to the common fund. To do otherwise would be mere selfishness.[17] It would recoil on him, for the community can only give its members what it receives from them, materially or spiritually, and yet it exists for the purpose of giving.

Religious life is not a form of totalitarianism in which the individual exists solely for the benefit of the group. The community, even if engaged in apostolic work, is reponsible for its members from every point of view[18] and may not sacrifice the true welfare of the person to the demands of the work.

Here, however, we must emphasize that it is the real good of the person that is implied. The Council documents speak of respect for the person and for his personal vocation and capacity (PC 14; GS 26, 29, 35, 73, 91). The emphasis suggests that in the past these were often set aside for the sake of the institute, its needs and its work, without a sufficiently serious attempt to reconcile such exigencies with the real abilities and needs of the person. But we must remember that the real good of the person sometimes includes sacrifice; and if the person is a community member his fulfillment includes team work, with all the unselfishness that this implies. The person should continually gain in value all his life long from every point of view; this is his real good and this is what lifelong formation means.[19]

## Relations with his fellow religious

The spontaneous tendency today to form groups for every kind of action shows that we live in a period of groping for brotherhood; it is strongly felt in religious life, and a certain restlessness and dissatisfaction will result if a true family spirit is lacking. It depends largely on the superior, but much more on the individuals who build up — or fail to build up — the community.[20]

A community is based on love, or it fails of its purpose, for it must be in the world a witness to love. Cordiality, then, the acceptance of others as they are, friendliness to all without exception and real readiness to collaborate must be seen in action; it is not enough to have these dispositions at the bottom of one's heart. Each one, if he feels that he is loved, will be happy among his brothers and glad to return after an absence. St. Paul's picture of charity (translated as "love" in modern versions) in 1 Cor 13 might have been quoted by *Perfectae caritatis* instead of Rom 12, "Love each other as brothers should" and Gal 6:2, "Bear one another's burdens"; it is our love for one another that bears witness to our faith in God's love for us (1 Jn 4:16) and gives concrete proof of the possibility and the fruitfulness of such a life as we here describe.

It must include in its basis the human virtues highly prized today: justice, honesty and sincerity—especially, perhaps, sincerity. Less value is commonly attached to self-control; one even hears it criticized as contrary to sincerity, and that is nonsense.[21] Self-control is obviously basic to mutual relations in charity; to lack it is a sign of immaturity. It is required in all contacts with others, whether individually or in groups, for recreation or for serious discussion, simply because we differ from one another and difference must not be allowed to become friction.

Where there is a true family spirit it should be easy for one to make suggestions to another even about his personal conduct, not in any carping spirit but in all friendliness and simplicity, as between mature and well-balanced people who have the good of the community at heart. However, we must remember that life in community means frequent giving up of personal tastes and preferences and—to speak colloquially—putting up with other people's ways that are not to our liking. This is the penitential side of community life, and no one must be too quick to decide that what is not to his liking is contrary to the good of the community.

An important practice in communities and elsewhere today is what is called revision of life. It originated in Catholic action groups as a method of learning how to "see, judge and act." In religious life it consists in a meeting of the community at which all examine their own life and conduct, the life and conduct of the group, and events or problems concerning it, judging and evaluating them in the light of the Gospel and the teaching of Christ, so as to decide what each one and the group as a whole should do or avoid in order to carry out God's will at that particular time and place. The point of view is spiritual, not administrative, and it needs careful preparation. Remarks should not be made in a way that might hurt anyone.[22]

There will also be occasions when religious who wish to do so can make public reparation by asking pardon of the community for particular faults.

Serious discussion is an important part of renewal. It is commonly called dialogue and can be extremely valuable both between individuals and among a group large or small. It consists in setting out reasons for or against some suggestion or point of view, and it is not easy to carry on successfully. The first necessity for a true dialogue is to be able and willing to listen to what others have to say, to see what is good in it and how we might make use of it, even if it contradicts our previous ideas; a complete obstacle to dialogue arises when someone goes to it with his mind already made up and bent only on persuading others to agree with him. This kind of conversation is quite legitimate on occasion, but it is not dialogue. To be bent on getting a certain thing done may be in view of a real advantage or benefit for the community; it should nonetheless be discussed in a spirit of courtesy and of readiness to listen to others. Courtesy tends to be neglected nowadays, which is a pity, for it has great value.

In a community truly based on love, friendship will flourish if it is true friendship[23] "in Christ," as St. Paul says, using similarity of tastes and views for mutual help and encouragement, with a special sharing of joys, sorrows and difficulties, but merged in the love of the community and not shutting anyone out; it has nothing in common with an attachment which excludes all others, and calls itself friendship, but does not merit the name.

Another factor of the common life is work undertaken in common, much of which would be impossible to individuals or even to groups of seculars, because the latter would not have the same guarantee of continuity and fecundity. It is not impossible that more religious will be asked to take up individual tasks outside the group's work, but even then, as we observed above, they labor in the name of the community and from it they gather strength and encouragement.[24] The same applies to those whose work frequently takes them away. It is all important that communication be regular, and that those absent can count on the interest and if necessary the help of the brothers or sisters who have answered the same call and form with them one family in Christ.

1. Men have perhaps never felt as strongly as they do today that they are close to one another. Cf. Paul VI's *Message* for 1971, "Every man is my brother."

2. Allocution of January 28, 1970.

3. Can. 594 §1 enjoins the exact observance of the common life; can. 587 §2 requires it in houses of formation as a condition of the admission of students to ordination.

Even a rapid glance shows the difference of approach between the Code of canon law and the teaching of the Council. The stress, to be remarked, in PC 15 was explicitly desired by the commission. Cf. Report by Msgr. Compagnone, which was read to the Council Fathers (1965).

4. Cf. XXXI General Congregation of the Jesuits, art. 315.

5. God made man in His image, and God is Three, wholly relative, wholly interdependent, and yet distinct.

6. The substantial content of the common life is distinct from and does not depend on the frequency or amount of the means and ways by which it is expressed.

7. Allocution of May 28, 1970.

8. The Rule and the constitutions trace out its terms.

9. Cf. T. Ratzinger, "Fraternité," *Dictionnaire de Spiritualité*, col. 1141-1167.

10. The common life was sometimes looked upon as a form of penance, no doubt because of its rigid rules and their strict application. St. John Berchmans said indeed that it was his greatest penance. In our time the rigidity has been relaxed and the emphasis is laid upon community of life as a means of union with God, mystical rather than ascetic.

11. Cf. Volume I, *Consecration and Service* (Boston: St. Paul Editions, 1973), ch. XVI. Paul VI, May 23, 1964.

12. We are now speaking of co-responsibility from the fraternal point of view; later on, in treating of government, the term will be further examined.

13. The institute is a collegiate moral person (cf. can. 99) with a moral and juridical spiritual unity.

14. Cf. Chapters XXXIII and XXXV of Volume I, *Consecration and Service* (Boston: St. Paul Editions, 1973).

15. Cf. G. Dho, S.D.B., "La formazione del religioso realizzata attraverso la convivenza fraterna e la maturazione della comunità," *Presenza viva dei Religiosi nella Chiesa e nel mondo*, pp. 817-842.

16. Cf. Sr. Marie Beha, *The Dynamics of Community* (New York: Corpus Books) which treats at length of community and the way of building it.

17. Religious used to be accused of thinking too much of the interests of the house or the institute; the tendency now is to be too careless about them.

18. In this they differ from groups of seculars engaged in apostolic work.

19. Here the question arises of providing for religious who feel out of place in the institute and not fully made use of. It is a difficult one, especially during the time of experimentation. The institute must keep in view the good of the whole Church and recognize that certain persons may possess special charisms. Discernment of spirits, under the guidance of the Holy Spirit, will help to distinguish between true and false charisms and combine the good of the person with the good of the institute and the Church. In the attempt to combine both goods it is well to remember that the ideal of the "full use" of an individual, if misunderstood, without regard for the sacrifices and adjustments demanded by any kind of team work, could constitute a dangerous and actually unattainable ideal. The impossibility of fulfilling *all* of one's human potentialities is part of the human condition.

20. The greater responsibility now given to the members of a community calls for greater care in the choice of them and in their training, which should be not only spiritual and apostolic but human and psychological, not brief but prolonged.

21. Self-control would indeed be insincere if it were merely external, hiding but not combating an inward attitude contrary to charity.

22. For the history, functions and methods of the revision of life see J. Bonduelle, *La révision de vie, situation actuelle* (Ed. du Cerf, 1964). C. Perani, *La revisione di vita strumento di evangelizzazione* (Torino-Leumann, L.D.C., 1968).

23. Allocution of February 7, 1968.

24. The dangers of working in isolation without this support were shown in the first experiment of priest-workers.

# Chapter VI
## The life of prayer in a praying community[1]


## 1. Religious life is a life of prayer

The above statement refers to religious life as a whole, or, if you prefer it, the whole of religious life; the very word "religious" shows it. Prayer is not only something that plays an important part in it; it compenetrates everything. A life given up to the following of Christ as "the one thing necessary" and seeking God alone, finds Him in contemplation and in the apostolate which is another form of prayer (cf. PC 5,3 and 4).

In the catacomb of Priscilla is a representation of the *velatio virginis* and opposite to it an *orante* — the Church, and the one who prays. Every religious is by profession an *orante*. All his actions become in a certain sense spiritual sacrifices pleasing to God through Christ (1 Pt 2:5) and offered to the Father with Christ's own offering, just as his own profession was blended with the offering of the Mass.

The life of the religious is a sharing in the paschal mystery in its vertical dimension and in the horizontal; as in the Church, liturgy or prayer is the end toward which every action tends and the source from which all power flows (cf. SC 10,1). It is true for the contemplative; it is true for the apostolic laborer; all are exhorted by the Council to cultivate the spirit of prayer.[2] Rules and constitutions

115

emphasize it.[3] Paul VI calls it a basic necessity for religious, and says that faithfulness to prayer or its abandonment is the test of the vitality or the decadence of the religious life.[4]

Until recently, a monastic observance of silence was prescribed for practically all religious. In apostolic institutes silence during the day is now largely left to the discretion of individuals, more room being allowed for the requirements of the work itself and for courtesy and charity; it remains true, however, that restraint in talking is not only an important form of self-control in general, but essential to that readiness to listen to God which is part of the spirit of prayer.

If their whole lives are to be an offering, religious must set aside sufficient time for direct meeting with God in mutual self-giving. They owe to men, especially the young, a testimony that will help them to find the contemplative dimension of their own being and see that man's dignity comes from being called to communion with God (GS 19,1).

Prayer is a personal meeting with God in filial dialogue, and as in every dialogue, there is listening and response, a listening to God's inspirations and a response giving Him honor, praise and self-offering. The dialogue becomes communion; God comes down, gives Himself and His gifts to man and admits him to His intimacy; man rises up, opening his heart to the greatness of God, speaks to Him freely, gives his whole self to Him. It may take many forms, but essentially prayer is intercommunion.

Personal relations with God cover the whole of life, which all becomes prayer in a broad sense; to live in the spirit of prayer has no other meaning than this.[5] But there are times of closer relation through the word of God in Scripture, His action in the sacraments and in the Church, and especially through the liturgy and prayer in the strict sense (ET 43; PC 15,1).

Vatican II gives all these as means for priests to grow in union with Christ (PO 18)[6] and says that those in training for the priesthood should learn to live in intimate union with the Father through His Son Jesus Christ in the Holy Spirit (OT 8).

To religious are given in special measure the attributes of priesthood that belong through baptism to all the People of God, and they pray in the name of the Church.[7] The whole world is caught up into the prayer of the contemplative with its "mysterious fecundity" (PC 7) and into the prayer of the apostle who is God's instrument.[8] The apostolic worker finds God in his very work; it is a continuation of the Eucharistic encounter, and furnishes endless subjects for petition, thanksgiving and praise; at the same time man is encountered, and the Holy Spirit gives the grace to discover the image of the Lord in the hearts of men (PC 7). There is a vast downward and upward movement by which God gives Himself to man through man, and man — through man — rises up to God.[9]

Man's meeting with God is always personal, sometimes individual, sometimes as member of a group. For a religious community, prayer in common has particular significance and efficacy; it is a source and manifestation of unity, deepening the sense of having been chosen by God for a special vocation. In actual practice it smooths the way to mutual understanding and, when it is called for, mutual forgiveness. Together, in the intimate familiarity of prayer, the community grows in the faith, hope and love on which all religious life is based, and therefore grows in holiness. One can scarcely imagine a religious community without some measure of prayer in common.[10]

This prayer in common is not a substitute for the individual prayer in which each religious seeks God for a personal encounter and spontaneous interchange, but it may well provide matter for it; private prayer and public prayer will influence and help each other.

Mental prayer — usually called meditation in English — holds a very important place in the daily life of every religious. The time allotted to it may be as little as half-an-hour; frequently it is an hour, either unbroken or divided between morning and evening; among the ideas put forward for re-thinking religious life, no one seems as yet to have suggested that this individual prayer could be dispensed with; its necessity is too obvious. Paul VI expressed the fear that if personal prayer were neglected, the liturgy would be impoverished and would become a body without a soul. "Each one," he said, "must learn to pray within himself and by himself."[11]

The liturgy which calls for this interior effort is declared by the Council to be the summit toward which the activity of the Church is directed and the source from which all its power flows (SC 10).[12] The religious, the Church's *orante,* is specially pledged to take part in it and live a life imbued with its spirit. The whole of the Constitution on the Liturgy has for him a depth of meaning and a light which are all his own, and religious houses everywhere show that this is not lost upon them; the liturgical revival now taking place proves that its importance has been grasped, and in many places with real success. Vocal prayers have been reduced and more time allotted to personal prayer (ES II, 21). Many institutions have adopted the recitation of the divine office in whole or in part, substituting it for the prayers formerly said morning and evening; by this very fact the Church's liturgical seasons are followed. This movement has come about partly in response to the Council's appeal (PC 3,1) but largely because that appeal expresses a widespread desire. The general feeling today is in favor of more interior and personal prayer and closer participation in the liturgy.

The spirit of the liturgy must be applied also to non-liturgical devotions and prayers, but the Council in no way wishes to limit prayer in common to the liturgy only. It says in Art. 13 of *Sacrosanctum concilium* that popular devotions of the Christian people are to be highly commended, provided they accord with the laws and norms of the Church, especially such as are approved by the Holy See and encouraged or prescribed by the bishops. The Instruction on the Liturgy adds that they should take into account the seasons of the liturgical year.[13]

Prayers prescribed by the constitutions of religious institutes are by that fact approved by the Church, and the approbation confers on them something of the character of public prayer made in the name of the Church.[14] *Ecclesiae Sanctae,* while it recommends a reduction of too numerous vocal prayers to allow time for mental prayer, asks that those commonly in use in the Church be kept. The rosary, for instance, and the stations of the cross

form part of the Church's spiritual patrimony and bridge
the gap between private prayer and the liturgy. In certain
countries especially, these forms of prayer express the
profound and spontaneous devotion of the faithful and
are of great value. The rosary, in particular,[15] has been
encouraged by the Popes throughout the years and recommended to clerics and religious.

The use of particular devotions in a religious institute may
express its family spirit. A congregation which specially honors
the Sacred Heart or Our Lady will make itself known by the
prayers in use in its communities; they form a part of its "sound
traditions" and fidelity to its own character requires that they
be maintained.

In a word, to do away with all special and characteristic devotions would be an impoverishment of the Church.[16]

The whole movement of revision and updating of prayer
and the manner of praying is beset with dangers and difficulties.

To begin with, there is a general tendency to lessen the time
given to prayer; apostolic activity, it is said, is the form of prayer
essential to this age, and it is in our brother that we find God. But
the emphasis placed on the value of man must not make us forget
that prayer is not only horizontal in dimension but also and first of
all vertical. In addition, the whole atmosphere of life today makes
concentration difficult and the tendency is to ceaseless activity
if not agitation (cf. ET 35).[17] Some will tire themselves in seeking new forms of prayer and end by a distaste for all forms and
for prayer itself.

The claim heard on all sides is for greater freedom of choice
in the content, the manner and frequency of prayers and religious
practices in general. The question is how much should be given.

The liturgical reform seems to encourage it in the sense that
much is left open to choice — the Eucharistic prayers, Scripture
readings, etc. According to canon law the prayers of religious
must include an annual retreat, daily assistance at Mass, if possible, and whatever else their constitutions prescribe. It is taken
for granted that some prayer and spiritual practices will be prescribed. Mental prayer is prescribed by can. 592 together with a
visit to the Blessed Sacrament, the rosary and examination of
conscience.[18]

A number of institutes have, in their special chapters, decided in favor of greater flexibility; nonetheless, a minimum of
daily prayer in common and in private seems essential; not everything should be left to the choice and the sense of responsibility

of the individual. It should be made clear, however, that the obligation arises out of the nature of religious life and is not simply imposed by authority.[19]

Some institutes have given the individual religious the right to work out what they call a personal rhythm of prayer with certain times of greater length or intensity. More frequently this freedom is given to communities. The general movement is certainly in favor of prayer that is more personal, more interior and more authentic.

The updating of methods of prayer is a field of renewal which is not only extremely interesting but a very hopeful sign. In their genuine desire for prayer and their search for new light, religious seem to be repeating the plea of the apostles, "Lord, teach us to pray" (Lk 11:1).

## 2. The Eucharist

The Eucharist, the very presence of our Lord Jesus Christ, is the focal point of the Church's prayer and therefore of her whole life. Every Christian community must be founded and held together by the celebration of the Eucharist, and the Council documents naturally emphasize the fact, e.g., in SC 10,2; 47; LG 3; 11; 26; CD 30; PO 5,6.

Obviously, the Eucharist is the focal point of the religious community[20] and whenever possible should be celebrated by the whole community; it is the strongest of all means of establishing the union of all in faith, hope and charity. God's word is heard; Christ Himself is received; by participation in the Mass the religious learns to offer himself; "through Christ the Mediator he should be drawn day by day into ever more perfect union with God and with others, so that finally God may be all in all" (SC 48).

Full participation, needless to say, includes communion,[21] by which we are assimilated into Christ and intimately united with one another.[22] It is the response to an invitation: the celebrant's comment is "Happy are they who are called to His supper."[23]

The Instruction of May 25, 1967, suggests that small communities of Brothers or Sisters, especially those engaged in parish work, should go to the parish Mass on Sundays and feasts; their active participation in union with all the faithful will be a sign and example of unity.[24] Paul VI, speaking to the Sisters of Charity on February 8, 1967, asked them, as parish workers by vocation, to be at the heart of the parish community and set the example of attendance at Mass together.

And surely there can be no better way of spreading the Christian spirit through the world and being witnesses to Christ.

It is not only at Mass, however, that we witness to our belief in Christ's word. It is to be man's friend and companion that He stays on earth in the Eucharist, housed in magnificent surroundings or in the humblest oratory. It is as a personal friend that He is visited and adored in the intimate familiarity of faith, hope and charity, whether in private visits or in public exposition and adoration (cf. ET 48).[25]

A change of emphasis may be noted here. In former times, prayers and devotions to the Blessed Sacrament apart from Mass filled many books; attendance at Mass was often subconsciously linked with the idea of obligation for Sundays, and much less stressed as a bond of community and a personal and common participation in Christ's worship of the Father.

Nonetheless, the greater importance attached to participation in the Mass should not lead to neglect of the practice of adoration. It is noteworthy that in the new form of apostolate of the Little Brothers and Little Sisters of Jesus, the daily hour of adoration is a fundamental obligation. This is understandable. It is their way of ensuring that a life totally immersed in the living conditions of those around them shall not be a hindrance to their person-to-person relationship with Christ.

# 3. Holy Scripture

Vatican II brought the Church back to more frequent contact with the living word of God, which it calls the sup-

port and energy of the Church, the food of the soul, the pure
and everlasting source of spiritual life (DV 21).[26]

The Gospel is the first and ultimate norm of renewal
for religious. It means a constant return to Christ, a continual and authentic return to the Gospel in all its fullness,
with its radical and exacting demands.[27] The Council therefore bids them read and meditate upon it daily (PC 6,2).

It is at the table of the Word and the Eucharist that the
faithful are fed.[28] The word of God points the way and provides food for the journey. Twofold provision is made.[29]
"As the life of the Church is strengthened through more
frequent celebration of the Eucharistic mystery, similarly
we may hope for a new stimulus for the life of the Spirit
through a growing reverence for the word of God which
lasts for ever" (Is 40:8; 1 Pt 1:23-25; DV 26).

Among religious, the traditional *lectio divina* or meditative
scriptural reading which merges into prayer, has returned to its
place of honor.[30] Scripture must not only be read; it must receive
the homage of faith; intelligence and will must bring man's life
into conformity with it. The greatest praise Our Lord gave His
Mother was that she had "heard the word of God and kept it"
(Lk 11:28).[31]

When the sower went forth to sow, the seed was the
word of God, and religious must be the good soil that yields
a hundredfold (Lk 8:8-15). In some communities a passage
of Scripture is read in common with an exchange of comments and questions, relating the text to current events and
the needs of community life.

Whatever the method employed, religious, who have
left all things for the sake of Christ, must "listen to his
words" (Lk 10:39) so as to follow Him ever more closely.


## 4. Divine office

When we come to speak of the divine office we see
that what has been said of prayer and what has been said of
Scripture can be said also of the office, which is composed
almost entirely of psalms and readings taken from the Bible.

Religious institutes have responded to the Council's invitation to make their prayer-life more liturgical by adopting the divine office in whole or in part.[32] Some content themselves with Lauds in the morning and Vespers in the evening, and these are indeed the two hinges of the liturgical day; to that extent they return to the ancient tradition which linked religious closely with the liturgical life of the Church (ES II, 20; SC 99,1). They were and are deputed to join in the prayer which Christ Himself, together with His body, addresses to the Father.

Devised so that the whole course of the day and night is sanctified, the Hours of the office, said as nearly as possible at the appropriate times, are a powerful help in cultivating the spirit of prayer which should make our whole lives prayerful. Study of the meaning of the psalms and readings will be a particular aspect of the study of the scriptures referred to above (SC 90).

Office may be said in choir, in common or in private. Office in choir, including the conventual Mass, is an obligation for certain Orders and is strictly regulated by the Church; for the solemnly professed members of these Orders destined to choral office, it includes the obligation to say it in private if prevented from attendance in choir.[33]

The office is public prayer in the name of the Church when said by persons deputed by the Church, that is, priests and deacons, alone or with the faithful, and members of religious or secular institutes which prescribe it in their constitutions, even in a duly approved shortened form (SC 84; 98).[34]

The shorter office most widely used in the past was the Little Office of Our Lady, but other short offices were also in existence. The desire to come closer to the divine office led to the publication in the United States in 1962, of the *Short Breviary for Religious and the Laity;* and this, as its title shows, brings us to the momentous change brought about by the Council when recitation in Latin was no longer compulsory. Since the publication of the Interim Breviaries in England and the United States, these have been adopted by religious communities as a means of participating in the general prayer of the Church. It is to be anticipated that this trend will continue.

The introduction of the vernacular into the liturgy[35] and especially into the celebration of Mass was not done at one stroke — nor equally appreciated by all — but as regards the office, the Instruction of the S. Congregation for Worship simplified the matter on February 2, 1971, by declaring in a general formula that it might be said in the vernacular, while leaving freedom for another language to be used for some parts if desired. Many institutes thus saw their twofold desire fulfilled: to take part in the official prayer of the Church by using its actual text, and to do this in a language that they understood.

## 5. Penance and penitence: metanoia

One of the immediate results of a personal encounter with God is a profound sense of unworthiness. The first preaching of Christ was, like John the Baptist's, a call to repentance — *metanoia,* a change of heart — and by those who truly respond, it is felt to express the need they themselves feel, the need of turning away from the past to make a fresh beginning. "Repentance is a condition of true joy, of a ready and vigorous heart on the road to being. It is the mark of a youthful spirit, of joyfulness and the ability to be transformed."[36]

The sacrament of penance is given us in the first place to reconcile with God and the Church someone who has cut himself off by serious sin. But sorrow for sin is not felt only or chiefly by such people. On the contrary, those who have chosen to follow Christ more closely and never, by His grace, offend Him seriously, have far more light on their need for the forgiveness and the grace of "continual conversion" which the sacrament brings. Confession is an essential part of their spiritual life.

By a Decree of December 8, 1970, the Church revised the existing laws concerning confession for religious men and women, bringing them into line with the movement which relies upon inward conviction and a sense of responsibility rather than obedience to imposed rules.[37] The Decree begins by recalling the theological, spiritual and pastoral aspects of the sacrament[38];

it is a sacrament of the love and friendship of God, pictured in the "mercy parables," a paschal gift to the Church, closely linked in its effects with baptism, by which we pass from death to life. It is also linked with the Eucharist[39]; Mass begins with a public penitential act.

Religious men and women—the difference formerly made between men and women is done away with—are free to go to confession to any priest of their choice; the Decree adds that confession should be frequent, that is, twice a month. This last point is directive; a directive is not a law or a command, but it is more than a suggestion or a counsel; it tells us what the Church considers a right way of acting for those who seriously wish to make progress in the spiritual life.[40]

In order to remove possible difficulties, superiors are told—and this time it is an obligation—to provide opportunity for confession at least twice a month, and weekly for those who wish it. For religious, it is not only a great practical convenience to have a confessor available in the house every week; it also tends to unity of spirit by ensuring that the whole community is guided in the same direction, by a priest with prudence, knowledge of the spiritual and religious life, and other necessary qualities. The Decree therefore provides for the appointment of an ordinary confessor in contemplative monasteries, houses of formation and large communities[41]; smaller communities may have one if they wish, and if a priest is available. All appointments of confessors are made by the bishop,[42] and the Decree directs him to find out the wishes of the community before making a decision. The influence of the confessor on the community is considerable and a right choice therefore very important.

The public penitential act, including a brief examination of conscience, by which Mass and the evening Hour of the office still begin, expresses what is more strongly felt than formerly among the faithful and among religious, that is to say, the communal nature and results of sin. The group as a whole feels the need of continual renewal and purification. Some go so far as to wish to substitute communal penitential acts for individual confession. This is manifestly an exaggeration. The benefits of individual confession have no need to be stressed,[43] and it is indeed included as a part of some forms of penance service. Penitential celebrations with readings, singing and prayers have great value, however, as a part of parish or community life. They concentrate thought on our general sinfulness rather than on a list of trivial faults which may make weekly confession a matter of routine.

The sorrow for sin thus emphasized, coupled with a desire to follow Our Lord closely and share His lot, cannot but lead further and draw us toward a penitential life.[44] What form it should take is a highly controversial question, but Christ's words are clear: "If any man would come after me, let him deny himself and take up his cross daily and follow me" (Mt 16:24); and this kind of following enters necessarily into the spiritual life of a religious.[45]

To a great extent it will be a matter between Christ and himself (a superior would intervene only if penance prevented someone from observing the common life or from carrying out his duties) but there is much room here for errors of judgment concerning the how and the how much; it is one of the points on which the advice of a spiritual director may be needed.

The brief examination of conscience referred to above, even if made twice a day, can scarcely be sufficient for those who take spiritual life seriously. In the natural order, anyone who is working to attain some end will keep a regular check on his progress to see whether more effort or a change of method is needed; the same common sense requires it in the spiritual life. Special attention given to some particular point — the "particular examen" of St. Ignatius — has lost none of its value with the passing of the years; what previous generations learned from the old traditional writers is valid in substance, and if their methods are outdated, new methods can be found and adopted without rejecting the substance.

## 6. Retreats

The spiritual life needs periods when ordinary occupations and preoccupations can be set aside and thoughts and energies centered on God. Life should always be directly or indirectly prayerful, but during a retreat the "indirectly" is cut down to a minimum and this brings a sense of freedom.

The annual retreat of eight days, now reducible to six or even five,[46] has long been a universal practice in religious life. The Council recommends it to priests (PO 18,3) and the Church requires it for religious as a preparation for acts of decisive importance: entering the novitiate and making first vows. Most constitutions also prescribe a retreat before final vows.

The form taken by the retreat may vary considerably. In some institutes religious can choose between a preached retreat, a directed retreat or a private retreat. In a directed retreat the giver of it often speaks only once, early in the day, proposing matter for reflection and prayer sufficient for a whole day, which the religious adapt to their own needs; those who need further help or advice can receive it from him personally during the day. It is thus midway between a preached retreat and a private one which is organized and carried out by the individual religious.

The purpose of a retreat is always to deepen and strengthen one's interior life by long periods of prayer; to take time to think things out in the presence of God.[47] Complete silence is found helpful by many, essential by some, but there are forms of retreat in which it may have interruptions.

In a small way, the same is the purpose of the day of recollection very commonly observed each month, though sometimes less frequently and more intensively.

In addition to these, some religious feel drawn to desire other periods of prolonged prayer and reflection for spiritual renewal, and the establishment of houses of prayer to which they can go for this purpose.[48]


We may, then, end this chapter by stressing the title of its first section: religious life is a life of prayer. Every religious is by profession an *orante*.

1. All the documents of Vatican II touch upon prayer in connection with their own particular theme. The first document issued by the Council was the Constitution on the Liturgy; it has been followed by various Instructions and directives from different departments of the Holy See, including an Instruction from the S. Congregation for Worship on 9-5-70. *Evangelica testificatio* deals with the subject of prayer in Arts. 42-49.

A collection of all the texts has been made by T. Urquiri, C.M.F., *Liturgia Conciliar*, Vol. I, 1963-1969 (Madrid: Editorial Coculsa, 1969).

See also Pius XII's encyclical *Mediator Dei* of 11-20-47, AAS 39, (1947), pp. 521-595.

Paul VI's teaching on prayer is collected in a volume, *Si prega oggi?* (Rome: Ancora-Usmi, 1970).

2. We are told in the Acts of the Apostles that they "devoted themselves to prayer, together with the women and Mary the mother of Jesus and with his brethren" (Acts 1:14) and that the first believers "devoted themselves to the apostles' teaching and fellowship, to the breaking of bread and the prayers" (4:42).

3. Cf. the Rule of St. Benedict, Chapter XX, "Of reverence in prayer."

4. ET 42-45.

5. Some make a distinction between *actual* prayer, formal acts recognized as prayer; *virtual* prayer, or actions specifically offered as prayer; and *diffused* prayer, by which the whole life becomes prayerful.

6. The Decree lists as aids to encourage the spiritual life "the table of holy Scripture and the Eucharist, the fruitful reception of the sacraments, especially sacramental penance, daily examination of conscience, spiritual reading, visits to and veneration of the Blessed Sacrament, spiritual retreats and spiritual direction, mental prayer and vocal prayers freely chosen." It speaks of Our Lady as an example of docility to the Holy Spirit and exhorts priests to love and venerate her as mother of the Eternal High Priest, Queen of Apostles and Protectress of their own ministry.

7. This is recognized by the Constitution on the Liturgy, art. 98. Cf. E. Gambari, *For Me To Live Is the Church* (Boston: St. Paul Editions, 1970), p. 231, on the priestly vocation of religious.

8. Cf. Volume I of the present work, ch. XXIX, section 2, on contemplatives, and J.M. Mesa, *Servir es amar* (Madrid: Coculsa, 1959), pp. 189-207, on prayer in the apostolate; a list of articles and books on the subject is given.

9. Cf. PC 8.

10. A minimum would appear to be Mass in common and some collective prayer, morning and evening, which might be the appropriate Hours of the divine office, but there is a widespread movement in religious communities in favor of group prayer or shared prayer at some time of the day. It takes many forms; it may be frequent or less frequent and the number taking part may vary from a small group to a whole community. A typical form of it consists in the reading of a passage from the Bible or some other book, followed by a long period of silent prayer, after which, questions may be asked and insights exchanged. It can be a valuable experience.

11. Allocution of April 22, 1970. In the same discourse the Pope calls the Church "an association for prayer," the family of those who adore the Father "in spirit and in truth."

12. "Liturgie et vie religieuse," in the collection *Donum Dei* (Ottawa, 1964), gives various articles on the subject, which was dealt with at the Plenary Assembly of Canadian Religious in 1963.

A.M. Triacca, S.D.B., in *Per una presenza viva dei Religiosi nella Chiesa e nel mondo*, pp. 333-343, writes on the same theme under the title "Liturgia e vita religiosa" and gives a very useful bibliography.

13. Cf. P. Roberto di S. Teresa del Bambin Gesù, O.C.D., "Preghiera Liturgica e preghiera personale," *La Preghiera Liturgica* (Rome: Teresianum Institute of Spirituality, 1964), pp. 55-102.

14. Cf. G. Fransen, "Prière des religieuses et droit canonique," *La Prière* (Paris: Ed. du Cerf, 1959).

15. Cf. Pius X in the Exhortation *Haerent animo* of Aug. 4, 1908, and *Ratio fundamentalis institutionis sacerdotalis*, 54, recommending it to clerics in training.

For religious, see *Statuta Generalia* on the application of the Constitution *Sedes sapientiae*, art. 37 § 1.

Various proposals have been made to find ways of saying the rosary which are more in keeping with present-day trends but still simple and easy for all.

16. Pius XII praised non-liturgical prayer in the Exhortation *Menti nostrae* of 9-23-50 and in the encyclical *Mediator Dei* (AAS 32, 1950 and AAS 39, 1947).

Cf. also S. Marsili, O.S.B., "Per i Religiosi una liturgia 'propria'?" *Studi Francescani* (1968), pp. 301-312.

17. Paul VI, in the allocution quoted above, made the remark that prayer was on the decline and gave a warning against the tendency to "secularize everything," which is creeping in even among the clergy and religious. The *Instruction on the Liturgy* of 9-5-70 repeats the warning against secularization among the clergy.

18. *Evangelica testificatio* in art. 45 urges fidelity to daily prayer, Other forms of prayer may be weekly, monthly or annual (cf. *Norms* of 1901, arts. 154-159).

19. Preparation for prayer must not be neglected. It is commonly done by the reading of Scripture, commentaries on Scripture and other books which are aids to our spiritual life.

20. "The seeking of God alone proper to the consecrated life gives full scope to the Eucharist to achieve its end in every dimension" (A. Nocent, O.S.B., "Vita sacramentale, liturgia et spirituale di una comunità," *Studi Francescani*, 1968, p. 334).

Cf. also Instruction *Eucharisticum Mysterium* 3,a; 13.

The practice of passing on in one form or another the "pax" salutation of the priest before communion helps to bring home to the faithful the union that the Eucharistic celebration should bring about among them.

21. Communion under the two kinds is permitted to all who participate in the conventual or community Mass (cf. Instr. of the S.C. for Worship, of 6-29-70, which also gives all the other occasions on which Communion under both kinds is permitted, and the Instr. of 9-5-79).

22. Cf. Jn 6:33-40.

23. Normally, the faithful should receive hosts consecrated at the Mass they attend, but the Instruction of 5-25-67 allows Communion apart from Mass for a reasonable cause.

In certain cases lay religious and religious women have been authorized by the Holy See to distribute Holy Communion.

24. The latter part of Paul VI's encyclical *Mysterium fidei* of 9-3-65 (AAS 1965, pp. 753-774) treats of Eucharistic worship and speaks of the fruits it should bear (arts. 31-38), as does the Instruction of 5-25-67 (arts. 49-51).

25. In *Mysterium Fidei* (40) the Pope recalls the bond between the Eucharist and Our Lady.

26. The dogmatic Constitution *Dei Verbum* should be read and meditated on by all, but especially by religious.

27. See Volume I, *Consecration and Service* (Boston: St. Paul Editions, 1973), ch. V, and particularly section 3.

28. The Spirit promised (Jn 14:26; 16:13) and sent by Jesus opens to us the meaning of the scriptures and the light thrown by them on daily events both great and small. In them we see the marvelous condescension of eternal wisdom. The books of the Old Testament show us true divine pedagogy and express sound wisdom about human life; the meaning of the Old Testament was made manifest, however, in the New, where the word of God is set forth and shows all its power (DV 13-17).

29. Although frequently linked together, the commission for interpretation of the Council pointed out that the veneration offered to Holy Scripture is of a different nature from that offered to the Body of the Lord (AAS 1968).

30. It should be at the center of the program of studies, the source of doctrine and the soul of theology (OT 16,1; DV 2,5; *Ratio fundamentalis institutionis sacerdotalis* 78).

31. Before that, Elizabeth had declared that Our Lady was blessed because she had believed the word of God (Lk 1:45).

32. Today it seems surprising to us that so many institutes have waited until now to adopt recitation of the divine office; but those founded in the 18th and 19th centuries followed the customs and ways of praying that belonged to the period.

33. The Rule or the constitutions of the following Orders make it an obligation to say office in choir: the Canonical Orders, monastic and mendicant Orders and Orders of nuns, with a few exceptions, e.g. the Ursulines and the Visitation nuns.

The Clerks Regular do not usually have it, on account of their specific end.

Sometimes, as in Benedictine monasteries, the obligation is so strict that the community is obliged to arrange for office to be said in choir every single day.

A number of institutes both of men and of women have an obligation to say the office in common; some of them have adopted it since the Council.

Dispensations may be granted to individuals by the competent superiors, that is, by major superiors for a just reason.

34. The Instruction *Inter oecumenici* 80 says that a "little office" is drawn up after the pattern of the divine office and can therefore be duly approved if it consists of psalms, readings and hymns and takes into account the hours of the day and the liturgical seasons. The Instruction also refers to the question of translations (83).

35. See Constitution on the Sacred Liturgy, 101.

36. L. Boros, *God Is with Us*, ch. 6.

37. Cf. E. Gambari, *Updating of Religious Formation* (Boston: St. Paul Editions, 1969), pp. 60-62.

38. Cf. A. Vari, "La Penitenza," *Quaderni di Rivista Liturgica*, No. 9 (L.D.C., Leumann, 1967), deals with the whole question of new attitudes to the sacrament of penance, and contains on p. 341ff. a bibliography compiled by Fr. Morganti, O.F.M. *La maison de Dieu*, No. 80 (1967), is entirely given to the same subject. Cf. also F. J. Heggen, "Confession and the Service of Penance" (Univ. of N. D., 1967), taken from Häring, *Shalom*, p. 466.

39. Cf. J. Tilard, "Pénitence et Eucharistie," *La Maison de Dieu*, No. 90.

40. Cf. Volume I, *Consecration and Service* (Boston: St. Paul Editions, 1973), ch. VII. Confession is a means of formation and will be a good one if preceded by the required education. Cf. R. Barbariga, *Educatione e Confessione* (Brescia: La Scuola, 1962), which contains a good bibliography.

41. In the monasteries and houses of formation an extraordinary confessor is also appointed, but the same freedom is left to go to him or not.

42. For houses of religious women subject to a Regular Superior, the latter presents the confessors to the Ordinary, who will grant them approval to hear the confessions of the nuns (Can. 525).

43. It is frequently linked with spiritual direction, which is, however, distinct from confession. The need of a personal guide is often felt as regards our interior life of relationship with God, our inward attitudes and difficulties. Freedom of correspondence on this matter should be allowed, but it is normally now included in a general freedom of personal correspondence.

44. According to the Norms of 1901, it was not permissible for any constitutions to state that no outward penance was practiced in the institute.

45. Religious life in the East has always been markedly penitential, and a spirit of penance in the West could be an ecumenical point of contact.

46. Decree of the S. Congregation for Religious of 6-4-70.

47. A course of talks on renewal or other matters may be connected with it but do not achieve the same purpose and cannot therefore be a substitute.

48. Cf. Volume I, *Consecration and Service* (Boston: St. Paul Editions, 1973), ch. XXXV, section 2.

# Chapter VII
# Prophetic and
# apostolic dimension

## 1. Faith, hope and charity

The prophetic function of religious is to witness to
Christ by a life of faith, hope and charity, and to lead others
to do so; their example and teaching must "spread abroad
a living witness to Christ, especially by means of a life of
faith and charity" (LG 12,1), a life of holiness and true
Christian living. The development of baptismal grace
means development in faith, hope and charity; each of the
counsels is more especially bound up with one or the
other, and the three together give meaning to religious life
in its total belonging to God. Prayer, Christian living, the
apostolate, service, are interconnected in a life of love
centered on Christ; they come from love, they lead to love,
they express love.[1]

Every religious is, then, an apostle. The call to observe
the counsels is a clear and expressive call to bear witness
to the life of Christ in the Church visibly and existentially,
with a clarity and intensity greater than the witness of other
Christians. And all witness is based on faith. Today—and
always—the faith which unites believers to God reaches out
to make believers of all men, so that they may "walk in the
path of living faith, which arouses hope, and works through
charity" (LG 41,1).[2] If the spirit of faith compenetrates
everything, it will be seen in an attitude, a whole mentality,

in spontaneous reactions and casual remarks showing that religious judge current events and other things in the light of faith (AA 4,2-3; PC 2d), but with discernment, so as not to alienate instead of attract.

The call to bear witness is addressed both to the individual and to the community, and OT 14,2, reminds us that in the priest, as in the religious, it is faith which leads to the personal dedication of his whole life. The world needs to see both in the individual and in the community a visible and existential witness to their faith. What people will look for in religious is first of all actions; not so much "what do they say?" as "what do they do? how do they behave?" It is not enough that religious live a life of "continual conversion"; it must be seen by men. And men will usually have fairly definite ideas of what sort of person they expect a religious to be.[3]

A word first about some of the natural virtues: justice, and the desire — leading to action — for justice to be done in the world; sincerity and detestation of hypocrisy; fidelity to a promise given; a kind and welcoming attitude. *Ratio fundamentalis institutionis sacerdotalis* adds willingness to render mutual service, a habit of hard work, readiness to meet and collaborate with people of all social classes. The *Sedes Sapientiae* statutes also speak of sincerity, and of strength of character shown in self-control. All these are extremely important. Confidence and respect for a person in himself is necessary if he is to be accepted as a witness for Christ.[4]

The next step will be to understand that for the religious, these attitudes are the result of the faith, hope and charity which unite him to God; love of God and true love of men are inseparable: one leads to the other. The desire for justice — social, political and international — will be seen in the context of "Thy kingdom come"[5]; moderation in the use of this world's goods, as an expression of the following of Christ in readiness for self-sacrifice; the courage and self-conquest implied in apostolic work, as inspired by the love of Christ. Kind-heartedness rises from being a natural virtue to the fulfillment of the new commandment, to see Christ in all men and love them accordingly.

## 2. Configuration to Christ crucified

*Perfectae caritatis* (25) tells religious that their witness must be seen by all men, but not all will show it in the same way. The characteristic witness of the contemplative will be the life of separation from the world, of prayer and of penance; the configuration to Christ crucified shown forth in their lives is the strongest of protests against the pleasure-seeking attitude seen on all sides, never more than today.

In our time, avoidance of anything penitential is not only a natural human instinct but is supported by theory; penance is labeled Jansenistic and self-denial Manichean, a rejection of the good things of this world as if they were bad in themselves. Christ, however, declared that the new life of the resurrection had to be attained through death and suffering (Lk 24:46-47). Self-denial is no longer simply the road to self-mastery; it is association with Christ on the road to Calvary. Those who know that He said, "Take up your cross daily and come after me" look for some fulfillment of this in His official followers.[6]

They certainly do not expect and would not approve of imitation of the lives of the early anchorites, but they have a right to see religious avoiding over-comfortable surroundings and (as PC 13 says) anything resembling luxury.

Some measure of penance is required of all Christians; all men must shoulder the cross (GS 38) and many are the ways in which religious can set an example. First of all, fidelity in carrying out one's duties even at the cost of sacrifice; again, cheerful acceptance of whatever comes to us without our choosing, however difficult and painful. Both of these, if followed out constantly and in detail, make great demands on human nature without being spectacular; unfailing cheerfulness in the trials of daily life — it is often the unexpected that is hardest to accept — is rare enough to be noticeable, but is not often noticed.

These forms of self-denial are, however, personal. SC 110 says that penance should not only be individual but also external and social. The reference is to fasting, and that indeed seems to be the one form of traditional penance that people of all views are agreed upon. It is true that the Church has reduced the obligation to what may be called a token fast of two days in the year, but most people are willing to do considerably more. The Council document says that it should be adapted to places and circumstances. For many people it is linked with the desire to give more to the poor.

Vigils also have kept and increased their popularity. The contemplative Orders rise in the night to pray, but apostolic workers also sacrifice sleep to join in the voluntary vigils of young people in colleges or of others elsewhere.

*Evangelica testificatio* tells us in Art. 55 that the joy radiating from religious communities will be the best proof that they have chosen well in choosing to belong wholly to God. We may add that there is a special joy born of sacrifice made with a loving heart, and it is a form of witness open to all without exception.

The Pope adds: "May the beloved Mother of the Lord obtain for you that lasting joy which Jesus alone can give." In all their apostolic works, and particularly in all their sacrifices, religious will find unfailing help and encouragement if they say with Our Lady, "My spirit rejoices in God my Savior." In this, as in all else, she leads the way as our example and model.

# 3. Different forms of the apostolate

In their desire to give due weight to the apostolic element in their lives, some institutes have put it in the first place, leaving the question of their consecration somewhat, so to speak, in the shade. It is true that when it is their specific end, apostolic action enters into the very nature of their religious life; their consecration has it directly in view; nonetheless, it is by their consecration that they are religious.

The appearance in the Church of apostolic institutes was like a new understanding and incarnation of the evangelical life, and the Council brought out clearly the apostolic content of all religious consecration; the way is clear for constitutions and methods of formation to show the harmony between prayer and apostolate, consecration and presence in the world. Every religious is an apostle by his whole life and his every act. It is the very depth and closeness of their union with Christ that will enable priests and religious to give His message in language that men will understand.[7]

The pastoral Constitution *Gaudium et spes* has called attention to new fields of action for the Church in the world of today, changed as it is and continually changing. Among religious institutes new forms of life are emerging and new means of achieving their ends; their vitality is proved by their capacity to adapt themselves to the needs of today. In doing this, three main criteria must be kept in mind: their bond with the Church, their specific charism and their docility to the Holy Spirit in renewal. Boundless horizons open out before them.[8] Among others, collaboration with secular institutes enables the message to be given to a secularized world and shown to be profoundly human.[9]

Religious are present in every field of action where salvation history is unfolding in the world; the picture can only be very rapidly sketched here.

The care of souls, in parishes or other organisms, represents the usual work of priests who collaborate with the bishops (and religious priests are called to it more often than formerly); the Council exhorts their superiors to accept parishes, even temporarily, in case of need, and even at the cost of modifying their constitutions if necessary. Considering how much conditions have changed since their foundation, such work may now be in keeping with the spirit of founders who never thought of it.

The bishop has special faculties allowing him to contravene canon law (can. 1423 §2; 1442) by entrusting a parish to a religious institute or erecting a parish in a church or chapel of the same institute, either in perpetuity or for a fixed time (ES I, 32 §1).

The Ordinary can also entrust the parish to one religious in particular, with the consent of the competent superior (ES I, 32,3). In both cases an agreement between the bishop and the superior will be drawn up to specify the conditions. Unless their constitutions positively forbid parish work, permission from the Holy See is not required for the religious.

Clerical institutes were usually founded in view of pastoral ministries, sometimes for particular categories of people or for specialized work; the ministry of religious priests may be contemplative or include professional or manual work. The priest members of the Little Brothers of Jesus present a new type.

A good many Sisters feel called to the direct apostolate, having more immediate contact with people, particularly with adults, and carrying out many of the traditional functions of deacons, especially where there is a dearth of priests, as in Latin America.[10] Catechizing is its most common form, including instruction of converts; others are spiritual help given in retreats or preparation for the sacraments, contacts with families, counseling and direction of youth movements.

Traditionally, teaching and nursing have been the sphere of women religious, appealing, as they do, to woman's motherly instinct; their work began with visiting the poor and the sick, and teaching, but it was checked by the introduction of papal enclosure. New institutes arose to carry it on, at first without the vows of religion and then with simple vows, and it has been completely modernized. Nursing Sisters are as well qualified as any secular. Teaching has been extended from teaching in the institute's own schools to teaching and counseling in state schools, colleges and universities. Conditions are so different that teaching and nursing institutes need to rediscover their own identity and the theological and spiritual basis of their vocation, which gives its richness to their charism.[11]

Care of the sick and the destitute was the earliest form of charity among religious. A modern form of it is social assistance, in which one whose consecration has made her truly the *sister* of all, and at the same time representative of the Church, brings help and assistance in the Church's name. It is a much-needed work that calls for special training.[12]

An apostolate to some extent new is that of social communications or mass media. The pastoral Instruction *Communio et progressio* of March 3, 1971, writes as follows: "Religious institutes should take note of the many important ecclesial responsibilities in the field of social communications and give careful thought to the part they might play in this apostolate, in accordance with their constitutions. Institutes concerned with the apostolate of social communications should collaborate closely among themselves and keep in effective contact with the diocesan, national, regional or continental offices to draw up a common program for this field of work."

Every form of apostolate, direct or indirect, gives opportunities to influence people in favor of Christian attitudes and against all forms of social injustice — local, national and international — but such action must not become merely social, cultural, economic or political.[13] First and foremost it is witness to the Gospel and the teaching of Christ.

# 4. The mission field

Through the centuries, religious have responded faithfully to Our Lord's command to go and teach all nations. When Pope Gregory the Great wanted to convert Anglo-Saxon England, he sent Benedictine monks. In Europe first, then further and further afield, Benedictines, Franciscans, Dominicans, and Jesuits have been followed by institutes founded for missionary work or adding it to their own. Their total availability makes religious particularly apt for such work; one might say there is full correspondence between the religious vocation and the missionary vocation.[14] Many have been drawn to religious life by their desire to work as missionaries; others, already religious, find in themselves the same desire, and it should be taken into account by superiors.

All the different forms of apostolate are to be found in the mission field; some would wish it limited to the direct apostolate, but that is too narrow a view.

The direct apostolate of catechizing certainly has full scope—as indeed it has in de-christianized regions of nominally Christian countries, where the instruction of adults may be more urgent than teaching in schools—but it is not the only form. *Ad gentes* 40,2, asks contemplative institutes to open houses in mission areas,[15] where they bear witness to the inner nature of the Christian calling and may have affinities with innate tendencies in the people of the country.[16]

In other ways also, the direct apostolate may merge into the indirect. Young churches have needs of their own, and the charismatic life can and must be ready to meet them. It has in fact happened that religious in mission areas were ahead of others in methods of renewal.

*Ad gentes* urges that in every country, what is good in customs, tradition and culture should be preserved and assimilated, so that a Christian way of life is formed which is typical of the country and its people.

# 5. Pastoral action

The Decree *Christus Dominus* speaks of religious priests as co-operators of the bishops and says that in a real sense they belong to the clergy of the diocese. A little further on it says that all religious, priests, brothers and sisters, belong to the diocesan family, though the link is stronger for the priests on account of the priestly character which they share with the clergy and with the bishop himself.

Here, then, we have a situation that calls for great qualities on both sides. The bishop is responsible for his diocese and for the apostolate in his diocese; he is the ruler and the center of unity (AG 30,1).[17] The superiors of a religious institute are responsible for the good of the institute, for its fidelity to its charism, for its progress toward holiness. The situation will bristle with difficulties unless there is a real understanding between bishop and superiors—the sort of understanding that comes from true dialogue, in which each party is willing to listen to the other and enter into his point of view.

A particular point that needs delicate handling is that of exemption, by which an institute is removed from the bishop's jurisdiction. CD 35 points out that it refers chiefly to the internal affairs of the institute, but that it might involve the withdrawal from the diocese of a religious of whom the bishop has special need. Then again it is said that the bishop must respect the specific aim of a religious institute.[18]

The need for understanding will begin from the first proposal to found a religious community in the diocese. Frequently it is the bishop who asks for it, but if he does not, where should it be opened and for what immediate purpose? Should it be opened at all?

*Ecclesiae Sanctae* asks religious superiors to show willingness and flexibility in responding to requests from the bishop, especially in cases of emergency and particular need. Religious who work in the diocese may do so in houses belonging to the institute or in houses entrusted to them by the bishop, or in dependence on other bodies public or private. When work is entrusted by the bishop an agreement is drawn up specifying the conditions, even if only one religious is lent, for the individual is lent by the institute or the community.[19] All the religious concerned should feel themselves to be members of the diocese, really involved in the local church and in the parish, if that is where they work.

Planning for the diocese as a whole is obviously required to avoid waste of energy and resources, the doubling of tasks, competition, and posts left unprovided for; willing collaboration rooted in and founded upon charity[20] must be the inward attitude of all, priests, Brothers, Sisters and lay people (CD 35,5).[21] Religious must not make their own arrangements without taking into account the needs and wishes of others.

A very practical means of obtaining this is the setting up of parish and diocesan councils composed of clergy, religious men and women and lay people, who meet to discuss general needs and proposals for action. In addition, meetings should take place between bishops and religious superiors, individually or as a group. National unions of superiors or major superiors examine questions of interest to all. On the regional level the episcopal conferences do the same. In order to bring the two together, *Ecclesiae Sanctae* II, 43, recommends the forming of mixed commissions of bishops and major superiors, to reconcile conflicting interests and ensure collaboration between every kind of religious institute and the hierarchy of the Church.

1. Cf. Volume I, *Consecration and Service* (Boston: St. Paul Editions, 1973), ch. XIV, "Striving for the perfection of charity."

2. The inward urge of charity is to give itself in a dialogue with the world, transmitting the message of Christ which is truth and life. The whole of Part III of *Ecclesiam Suam* treats of this dialogue.

3. The Rule of St. Benedict, chapter IV, gives a list of actions to be done or avoided by religious under the heading "The tools of good works."

4. The Council emphasized the value and necessity of the natural virtues as a basis for personal relationships of faith, hope and charity.

5. We have already considered the part played by religious institutes in spreading the kingdom of God (Volume I, *Consecration and Service*, Boston: St. Paul Editions, 1973; chapters XVIII, XIX, XXX, XXXII). The statement that every religious is an apostle holds true for all institutes in different ways.

6. Cf. the Instruction *Poenitemini* of 2-17-66 (10); PC 12,2; 25; ES II, 22.

7. Cf. *Renovationis causam* 5; 13,II; 23,I; 25,I, and the present writer's comment; *Updating of Religious Formation* (Boston: St. Paul Editions, 1969), pp. 55, 57, 77, 78, 97. See also *The Religious Adult in Christ* (Boston: St. Paul Editions, 1971), chapter IV on apostolic formation. Vatican II has given the necessary directives on this subject for priests *(Optatam totius)*, for missionaries (AG 25-26) and for the laity (AA 28-32).

8. Council texts which suggest new fields of action for religious are those on the Mission Activity of the Church *(Ad gentes)*, the Apostolate of the Laity *(Apostolicam actuositatem)*, the Ministry and Life of Priests *(Presbyterorum ordinis)*, Education *(Gravissimum educationis)*, Ecumenism *(Unitatis redintegratio)*, the Media of Social Communication *(Inter mirifica)*.

Encyclicals such as *Ecclesiam Suam, Pacem in terris, Populorum progressio* and the Apostolic Letter of May 14, 1971, on the 80th anniversary of *Rerum novarum*. contain directives for the action of religious institutes in the social field and especially among developing nations and classes.

The Holy See has set up various secretariats and councils, including the Secretariat for Christian Unity, the Council of the Laity, the Pontifical Commission for Justice and Peace, the Secretariat for Non-Christians and for Non-believers.

9. The Church which raises man to the dignity of a child of God, at the same time makes him more human with the humanity taken by the Wo·d of God in the Incarnation.

10. In Mexico, for instance, a Sister who visits villages to catechize the people is deputed by the priest to do everything for them that a priest would do except say Mass and hear confessions. She baptizes, witnesses or validates marriages and preaches in the church.

The second general Conference of the Bishops of Latin America at Medellin in 1968, discussed the theme *Religious life and participation in development* and summed up very well the part religious should play in those regions today.

11. Though teaching in school is not a form of direct apostolate, it opens the door to it in many ways. The effect that teaching Sisters have had on Catholic life in the United States, for instance, is incalculable.

The declaration on Christian education *Gravissimum educationis*, after a statement on the rights and duties of the Church and the principles concerning Christian education, recalls the importance and the purpose of the Catholic school and concludes by an expression of gratitude to "the priests, religious men and women and lay people" who carry on this work and an exhortation to persevere in it.

12. Cf. the present writer's article, "Lo stile della presenza della Religiosa nell'attività sociale," *Religiose nell'Assistenza Sociale* (1965).

13. New methods of social or professional action must be approved by the competent authorities and based on adequate training and a deep interior life.

14. Careful study of the Decree *Ad gentes* on missionary activity is more incumbent on religious than on others. It should form a part of the program of formation.

15. Cf. *La preghiera e il lavoro apostolico nelle missioni* (Rome: Gregorian University, 1954): four conferences on contemplatives in mission countries.

A very interesting experiment is being made by some English Benedictine Fathers in India, living in the style of the country.

16. Cf. Volume I, *Consecration and Service* (Boston: St. Paul Editions, 1970), ch. XVII, and *For Me To Live Is the Church* (Boston: St. Paul Editions, 1970), pp. 145-200. M. Maziers, "La place des religieux et religieuses dans une diocèse, *Vocation* (Jan. 1970).

17. In CD 35,4, and in ES I, 23-26, it is specified that religious are under the authority of the bishop for all that concerns public worship, the care of souls, education, catechetics and apostolic works.

18. For undertaking work not included in the specific end of an institute, three conditions are required: persons in urgent spiritual need, a request from the bishop and the consent of superiors.

19. Such is the situation of religious who work in the offices of the Holy See.

20. Cf. Pius XII, Allocution of February 17, 1958.

21. Sisters and lay religious will always have more frequent occasions to work with the laity, both in their houses and outside. To do so in a spirit of fraternity is an apostolate in itself. It may sometimes be desirable for the religious to leave certain tasks to lay people and thus free themselves for more urgent work of their own.

# Chapter VIII
# The life-style of religious

## 1. Outward form and framework

If there are any who have not yet read Paul VI's *Evangelica testificatio,* they will be well repaid for making good the omission; it gives a complete and satisfying summary of the meaning of religious life.[1]

In arts. 33-34 it points out that in spite of the extremely varied forms of religious life today, there are certain fundamental requirements for living in that close union with God which is the end and aim of all of them. Outwardly, it requires a certain style of life distinguishing it from the life of seculars.

Outward surroundings must be favorable to spiritual growth, and their importance must not be underestimated. It should be possible to "pass from external activities to a life of recollection with more prolonged moments of prayer." The atmosphere should be one of cordiality, team-spirit and friendliness, in which "all strive to understand what each one has at heart" (39).

The history of religious life shows it as an ordered existence lived according to certain rules and regulations; it is sometimes called a life of regular observance. In this framework the life of the religious is lived day by day; it guides the community and its members in their relations with persons and things. Without touching the substance of the evangelical counsels, it regulates the manner of observing them according to the character of the institute and its specific end.

Monasticism is marked out by its detailed manner of life in common, much of which was passed on to the mendicant or conventual Orders; little by little many points, including the very important one of cloister, became part of Church law[2] and so found their way into the constitutions of later institutes for which they were not well suited. We have seen how St. Vincent de Paul evaded the difficulty by declaring that the Daughters of Charity were not religious.[3]

*Evangelica testificatio* (30) admits that it is not easy today to find a life-style that combines discipline with religious freedom in a way that satisfies everybody. It must not crush spontaneity and a sense of responsibility; it must not substitute the letter for the spirit, and yet it is of great value, not only as a safeguard against instability and caprice but for building up a community into an integrated whole, made up of persons whose self-possession aids the development of strong personalities.[4] Any group of people joined in the pursuit of a common aim draws up regulations for itself. For religious, however, observance must aid, not stifle, the spirit; more efficacious than rules will be formation to a sense of responsibility and of fidelity to a given pledge or promise. Rules and regulations today have a different character from those formerly in use; they will not only take into account, as PC 3 tells us, the demands of culture and social and economic conditions, but differences of mentality from one region to another. An institute working in a number of different countries will not expect uniformity of observance everywhere; there may be differences not only between institutes but between provinces of the same institute.[5] Nor will there be any attempt to regulate every detail of daily life. Customs concerning meals and recreation may even vary from house to house (cf. ES 2,26).

In general, we may say that the life-style of an institute should give its members the support that they need, individually and collectively, and also be a witness to the world of the nature of religious life itself.

## 2.  Residence and cloister

The traditional and normal unit of religious life is the local community, and a community needs a house to live in.[6] In monastic and semi-monastic life it has always been taken for granted that going out of the house was an exceptional thing, done only for a particular reason and with permission, and for the shortest possible time. In monasteries of contemplatives no special need has been felt to modify that attitude; their separation from the world is of a kind that calls for the silence and solitude only to be found within their own buildings and grounds.

What has changed is the idea that *all* religious life demands this kind of separation. To see how revolutionary this change has been we need only look at the life lived by the Little Brothers and Little Sisters of Jesus, who live in small groups among the poorer social classes; their "house" may be a caravan or a houseboat, to which they return as to a spiritual center after their working hours, and in which they welcome all visitors. Admittedly, their vocation is exceptional and at the farthest possible extreme from the monastic ideal; but it is one that has a great appeal nowadays.

Meanwhile, Church law has recognized by rescripts, Instructions and Decrees[7] that all apostolic institutes need a certain freedom to go out and also to be absent for long periods from the houses where they live in community.[8]

Between the two extremes are a great number of apostolic institutes whose members feel a need for contact with the neighborhood in which they work, both by going out and by admitting others into their houses. Some have tried the experiment of a completely open house; but this has been seen to have disadvantages. Religious need some place in which they can find quiet and silence, at least at certain hours. They also need periods of solitude, as we remarked when speaking of prayer. Each institute, taking into account its specific aim, will lay down in its constitutions and establish in its customs the degree and manner of openness required to attain that end, in docility to the Spirit.

To return now to the contemplative Orders. Cloister, for them, has lost none of its meaning; it is "a sign, a protection and the characteristic form of their separation from the world" *(Ecclesiae Sanctae* II, 30). In former days high walls and locked doors were a necessary physical protection, as were walls for towns and sentinels at their gates. That time has passed, and the high walls are now symbolic. The use of mass media is permitted, with special rules for its use.[9]

Papal cloister is still in force for Orders of both men and women.[10] For men, it has always meant simply the exclusion of women from any part of the building or grounds included in the cloister, except the wives of heads of state; for women it means not only the exclusion of men and all other persons — except in case of necessity (e.g. priests, doctors, workmen) and with due precautions — but also the rule that nuns may not go out except for certain specified reasons. Such reasons now include attendance at sessions or meetings considered necessary for the cloistered life, for instance, meetings connected with federations of nuns (cf. *Venite seorsum* 12). The severe canonical penalties for breaking the rules of cloister have been abolished, but its observance is a grave obligation.[11]

All other religious, whether men or women, in pontifical institutes or diocesan, must have some rules excluding persons of the other sex from certain parts of the house. The question is regulated by the constitutions, which may go almost as far as papal cloister, as do the Passionists, or allow great freedom both for going out and for admitting outsiders. Some would object to the use of this term, saying that no one is an outsider for a religious community; nonetheless, as remarked above, a community needs some places and times when recollection can be undisturbed. Christ used to withdraw from the crowds to pray.

## 3. Communication with others, in the community and outside it

There is perhaps no sphere in which religious today have stronger feelings and claim more liberty than in the matter of communication with others, both within the community and outside it. Unless it is left entirely to the judgment of those concerned, it is said, there is undue lack of respect for the person, undue limitation of responsibility. All kinds of communication are concerned, including correspondence.

It must be admitted that real problems may arise here. The religious state has its own demands; it has been freely embraced and its demands cannot simply be ignored. It is a question of interpreting any existing customs or rules in all straightforwardness. If they do not fulfill the purpose for which they were made they can be set aside. To take an example, many institutes have moved with the times by giving great freedom of personal correspondence.[12] The use of the telephone will be a matter for the custom of institutes or houses according to their specific needs.

It must be borne in mind that former limitations or communication were based chiefly on the need for detachment. It is another case of shifted emphasis. It is true that religious "leave all things" to follow Christ, but some human values will be a greater help by using them than by giving them up. A particular instance of this is communication with one's family, which is now included among the forms of indirect—and sometimes direct—apostolate. Visits home have been gradually extended from occasions such as the serious illness of a parent to a fairly general custom of visits from time to time with no special motive except that they do good to all concerned, including neighbors and friends. For many years the stricter enclosure of women prevented it—as it still does for contemplatives, who make this sacrifice among many others—but if undertaken in the right spirit it is seen to be a real apostolate.[13]

To speak of communications is to speak of mass media, universally at the disposal of apostolic institutes. Newspapers, periodicals, radio, and television—all must be made use of with the same sense of responsibility. There are good courses on the use of the mass media, and at least some religious ought to attend them; superiors will have a general eye on their use; but the practical daily decisions will in the end be made by individuals in the light of their personal responsibility. The essential thing therefore is to give them every help in forming and strengthening their general attitude of being at God's disposal because they belong totally to Him; they cannot then close their eyes

to the fact that this often means giving up their own preferences; nor will they wish to close their eyes, but rather
to see what His preferences are, in order to follow them.
It is for superiors to give general directives; they would
intervene if serious abuses arose, as they would in any
sphere of religious life.

Another point that the word "communication" brings
to mind is that of silence. A word has been said of it as a
necessary preparation for prayer and that is its main importance; in silence man finds God, finds himself and pre-
pares to meet God in his brothers.[14]

Silence must also be considered from the angle of
community life. Charity will discern occasions when to
speak would be good but to refrain from speaking would
be better; and it will respect the times and places allotted
to those who wish to work undisturbed. People coming
in from the noise and bustle outside should be able to
find a peace and quiet that contrasts with it.[15]

# 4. Religious habit

The religious habit has always been considered the
sign of those who have embraced the state of profession
of the evangelical counsels in a public way. From the time
of Cassian it was so understood. The habit also signified
a call to an inward conversion corresponding to the change
of outer garb.[16] In the case of consecrated virgins the distinctive sign, right from the earliest times, was the veil.
Later the habit came to distinguish a particular institute.

As a sign of call and of community the habit has an
ascetical and spiritual function. This is why it has been
the object of legislation, both in canon law and in the
rules of particular institutes. Thus canon 596 prescribes
that religious should wear their habits both inside and
outside their houses unless superiors see grave reasons
to make an exception. It is true that there is no canon
which obliges religious institutes to adopt a habit in the
first place, so that canon 596 does not apply to the institutes, like the Daughters of the Heart of Mary, which were

approved without a provision in their constitutions for distinctive garb. These institutes constituted exceptional cases, however, with the exception being dictated by the kind of apostolate undertaken by the community, and the particular circumstances under which the religious worked.

The general practice of the Holy See has been to require the prescription of a religious habit, even when the founders had not had this idea or had even decided against it. The absence of a general canon requiring new institutes to adopt a habit is really to be ascribed to the fact that the habit was so common that there was no need to make a law about it. Vatican II likewise did not prescribe the religious habit explicitly; in *Perfectae caritatis*, however, it called for the adaptation of the habit according to certain criteria. These were essentially the criteria already given by the Holy Father in 1950, when the religious were asked to look to the poverty and practicality of their garb. The Council stressed sign value, simplicity, modesty, poverty, becomingness, and suitability to the needs of different times, places, and ministries. To the extent that the existing habits did not meet these requirements, the institutes were asked to change them.

In the course of such change there has been a tendency to stress active presence in the world and to attenuate or eliminate the distinctiveness of the sign formerly attached to the religious garb. As there has been less sensitivity to the ascetical and spiritual function of the religious dress, there has been a rather widespread movement of recent years to do away with religious garb. In some institutes the adaptation of the religious habit has been carried so far as to lose its religious character altogether, with the adoption of dress completely secular except for some small emblem or pin.

Admittedly it is not easy to fix the exact moment in an ongoing process of adaptation at which a religious habit becomes a uniform, or a uniform becomes simply ordinary lay garb. In order to evaluate a change it is rather necessary to look at the motives behind it. The religious habit in itself is not of the greatest importance; what is important are the reasons for which it is worn and the reality of which it is an expression. In thinking of the habit we can adduce considerations of poverty, of saving time, of safeguarding modesty and simplicity, and of mortification. But much more important than all these is the theological, spiritual, eschatological and ecclesial reality of which the religious life is a sign and to which the habit bears witness.

Obviously the habit cannot well be a sign in an environment unsympathetic to such a sign or to the reality for which it stands. This consideration of the environment is stressed by those who wish to give up the habit. They claim that in certain circles they will not be accepted as religious, and that therefore their apostolate will be less fruitful. Others question whether religious really ought to be separated from people in the world, and maintain that a habit makes dialogue more difficult. This is the reason, of course, why secular institute members do not wear distinctive dress, and there is perhaps an influence on religious from the example of secular institute life. But when these reasons about not being distinguishable from lay persons are given by religious, we may perhaps wonder if there is not some influence from an atmosphere of secularization, or even some unconscious secularism. The Pope and the organs of the Holy See have at several stages called the attention of religious to this point. Pope Paul has stressed that they should not go from one extreme to another, and has warned against a certain identification with the world in a bad sense.[17]

We ought, however, to consider seriously the reasons given in certain cases for eliminating distinctive signs. These reasons perhaps occur more frequently in our time. For instance, the institutes which have professional activities may find that changed circumstances justify a style of life and therefore a habit which reduces the outward distinction of religious.[18] Especially when the apostolate is at stake there can be valid reasons for such a change. Pope Paul, though insisting on the ordinary need of a habit for religious men and women, did widen the possibility of laying it aside in environments or activities which required that. Nevertheless, the garb, even the secular garb, to be adopted by religious in such circumstances, should, said the Pope, express, or at least not contradict, the consecration they have made, and hence it should be different from clearly secular forms of dress.[19]

When such changes are made, moreover, it should be done according to the directions of legitimate authority. This means that when the General Chapter of an institute of pontifical right judges that the habit should not be worn, we hold that the intervention of the Holy See is necessary.[20] This approval is required because the religious habit, for the reasons already set forth, is not only a part of the distinctive shape of a certain institute, approved as such by the Church, but is also, in a global way, a feature of religious life in general. As to cases in which superiors can judge, either for individuals or groups, that the reasons justifying an exception to canon 596 are present—these are probably more numerous today. It should also be observed that when circumstances in certain kinds of activity or certain regions warrant changes in the garb, these changes need not be introduced in an absolutely uniform way.[21] Finally, we may say that when the Constitutions take up the question of habit, they should limit themselves to fundamental points—leaving all the rest to supplementary directories.

## 5. Work and other activities

The life-style of religious includes their way of earning their living and the forms of relaxation they make use of.

*Christus Dominus* 35,4, tells us that they are subject to the local Ordinary in what pertains to the decorum proper to the clerical state and *Ecclesiae Sanctae* mentions as examples public use of the mass media, presence at public entertainments, membership of associations disapproved of by the Church and the wearing of secular dress.

Forms of relaxation call for no lengthy treatment. Some women religious may congratulate themselves on being free to take long country walks instead of being confined to the house and garden. Attendance at public entertainments will be regulated by the constitutions and by local custom, taking into consideration the nature of the institute. To lay down any general rule would be difficult, but public opinion anywhere would surely agree that a priest should not be seen at a gaming-table.

Work is a much wider subject. Church law enters into considerable detail concerning the ways in which priests and religious may suitably earn a living; it will usually vary a good deal according to country and region, but the local bishop, who has the general duty of supervision, will know how to judge of this. It seems fairly obvious that they ought not to take upon themselves administrative or other work involving financial responsibilities, give their names as guarantees for loans, etc., and they are directly forbidden to engage in commerce. Domestic industries are permitted even when seculars share the work, and the sale of objects thus made is not counted as engaging in commerce. A living may be earned by keeping hostels or homes, and, needless to say, by keeping schools or hospitals, but religious are warned against the real danger of causing scandal by the prices they charge if they seem to be catering only for the very rich. Manual work done at home has always been a way of helping to support contemplative monasteries, and is now recommended more than ever, since public opinion looks askance at begging or living on alms. Begging is still tolerated, but strictly regulated (cf. can. 621-624; ES II, 27). "Drives" for fund-raising require the bishop's permission.

Work in itself, whether manual, intellectual or artistic, forms part of a human being's normal activity; the picture of creation given in the book of Genesis represents God as telling man to cultivate the earth, that is, to share in the work of creation by developing all the resources hidden in the material world and to be discovered gradually, as well as developing his own faculties and talents and placing them at the disposal of God and his fellow men so that "earthly progress may contribute to the growth of Christ's kingdom" (GS 33-39).

If the world and man were rightly ordered, work would be a pleasure and not a penance, for it can give profound satisfaction; as things are, however, people have to be reminded that idleness and lack of effort can be seriously wrong. In this matter as in so many others, our fellow men ought to be able to look to religious to understand and enter into their own difficulties and help them to be true to their best ideals. Religious should be a sign, a stimulus and an example.

1. Apostolic Exhortation of His Holiness Pope Paul VI *On the renewal of the religious life according to the teaching of the Second Vatican Council* (Vatican Polyglot Press, 1971). The articles particularly concerning this chapter are 30-35.

2. A number of these were put together in the Norms of 1901, but all canons relating to non-essential points in religious life can be changed or can disappear. For instance, since the Council the traditional regulation of the novitiate has been changed.

3. In some texts "religious life" refers to the outward framework within which it is lived.

4. Cf. E. Gambari, *Renewal in Religious Life* (Boston: St. Paul Editions, 1967), Part I, ch. IV.

5. The unity of the institute must, however, be safeguarded.

6. The religious house is the legal domicile of each religious.

7. Cf. *Cum admotae, Religionum laicalium* and *Renovationis causam,* all of which have been referred to in the present work.

By the two first-mentioned, superiors general are authorized to give permission for absence of a year, and more in case of illness or for apostolic work. For further explanations see E. Gambari, *Facoltà speciali dei Superiori generali,* pp. 84-91.

*Renovationis causam* permits absence to test a vocation, and although it refers to religious under temporary vows it furnishes a criterion for other cases.

8. Absence from the house is not the same as exclaustration; the difference is explained below in ch. XVI, section 3.

9. See the Instruction *Venite seorsum,* Norms 10-11.

10. Dispensation from papal cloister can only be granted by the Holy See or by those who hold special faculties. Minor papal enclosure, now suppressed, was instituted by the Statutes of *Sponsa Christi* for contemplative monasteries of which some members were engaged in apostolic work. They must now either give up the work or find some other solution.

11. On June 4, 1970, the superiors general of the Canons Regular, the Mendicant Orders and the Clerks Regular were authorized to mitigate the rules of cloister in their houses and adopt those which apply to institutes of simple vows (AAS 70, 1970). The document does not mention consultation of their respective councils or chapters, but in practice it would take place; cloister would be regulated according to their needs and to their constitutions.

The suppression of canonical penalties concerning cloister for nuns applies also, no doubt, to the men's Orders.

12. Intervention when judged necessary by the superior remains within his rights. Church law permits freedom of correspondence with the Holy See, Nuncios and Apostolic Delegates, the local bishop, superiors of the institute and (for nuns) superiors of the men's Order in charge of them; correspondence on spiritual direction has always been considered as free from inspection.

13. A visit home is recommended for postulants and novices before they decide definitely to request admission.

14. Silence which is a mere absence of noise and of words has no spiritual value. "The search for intimacy with God involves the truly vital need of a silence embracing the whole being" (ET 46).

15. At Montecassino on October 24, 1964, Paul VI spoke of the need to recover one's personal life, which is threatened by the feverish excitment of modern conditions. "Man is in need of silence with its own interior language, in need of order, in need of prayer and peace, in need of his true self" (AAS 56, 1964).

16. Cassian, *Institutiones coenobiticae*, IV, 5. On the significance of the religious habit see J. G. Guy, S.J., "Le vetement religieux hier et aujourd'hui" *Vie Consacrée*, A. 39 (1967), pp. 81-93. N. Barwig, *Changing Habits*.

17. Address to General Superiors, July 3, 1967. The Pope spoke of the meaning of the religious habit, and in discussing the kind of religious garb worn, put his hearers on guard against worldliness.

18. The changes demanded by actual circumstances in the framework of community life are reflected in the habit. Cf. J. Beyer, *De vita per consilia evangelica consecrata*, pp. 213-214. A.M. Perrault, O.P., however, warns against closing oneself to anything but emotional arguments on this issue. He points to the value of the habit as a sign and stresses some important sociological and psychological considerations. See *Il rinnovamento della vita religiosa* (Vallechi), pp. 439-440.

19. ET 22.

20. Cf. *Ecclesiae Sanctae*, II, 6 and canon 495. See also Gambari, *Il rinnovamento della vita religiosa*, p. 181.

21. History favors the religious habit as a distinctive sign, but history does not always favor uniformity here — just as in the regulations for the dress of priests, which have many points in common with those for religious. St. Benedict in his Rule, chapter 55, provided for a certain variety by reason of climate and the places where the monks lived.

# Chapter IX
# Religious meet and unite in the Church

## 1. Religious meet in the Church

Many of us can remember a time when the fact of being religious was scarcely felt as a real uniting factor among religious as such, that is, among all religious. It was much less strong than the sense of unity among priests. And yet, just as the common ordination and mission of all who are in communion with the bishops and the Holy See unite them in one and the same priesthood and ministry (cf. LG 28; CD 28; PO 7-8), so too, all religious constitute within the Church a special body made up of the totality of religious institutes.[1] They share with one another the profession of the evangelical counsels; their dependence in virtue of the vow of obedience upon the Pope as their highest authority, binding all of them to the Church in a special way (LG 44,2; 45); and their availability for the good of the Church and the service of their fellow men. Their spirituality and their apostolate are mutually complementary, and together they form one whole.[2]

Aided as they are by modern means of communication and the general mentality which seeks union rather than isolation, the institutes and their individual members should show a spirit of openness and a desire for communication; dialogue and exchange of experiences will lead to greater friendliness and readiness to help one another. There is no question of imitating one another or losing personality; it is a matter of joining forces, especially in certain fields such as the encouragement of vocations, the area of formation,[3] the apostolate and aggiornamento. The gravity of the problems is out of all proportion to individual efforts, and calls for study, planning and action engaging all. Happily, religious today are more conscious of what unites them, have more *esprit de corps* and less tendency to isolation. The spirituality of the Mystical Body gives them a deeper sense of union with all the other members of the Church, clergy and laity.

# 2. Conferences or unions among religious

The need for religious to meet one another has given rise to meetings and congresses, of which the most important was the *General Congress of the States of Perfection* in Rome from November 29 to December 8, 1950, which ended with the discourse of Pius XII, *Annus sacer*, the starting-point of the movement for renewal in religious life.

Congresses in other regions led to the setting up of permanent organizations of major superiors called Conferences, Committees or Unions, and these were followed by the International Unions of Superiors General, one for men and the other for women.

In addition to, and sometimes before, these unions vertical in character, horizontal unions were formed in various countries by religious engaged in similar activities, nursing, education, social assistance, direct apostolate or the training of their own members.[4]

The Pontifical Year-book for 1972 shows a great network of federations and conferences of religious at national, regional and international levels, covering the whole world, and in addition to those erected by the Holy See there are privately formed associations of those engaged in similar work, who find collaboration helpful.[5]

The conferences founded by the Holy See are considered as juridical moral persons with capacity for action within their respective spheres of competence, toward the religious institutes who are their members as also toward the hierarchy and ecclesiastical and civil organizations.[6] Their structure, functions and field of action are laid down in their statutes, adapted sometimes to the region, but usually providing for officials with defined duties as well as the collaboration of all the members.

Membership of such organizations is optional, for institutes enjoy autonomy, but if they are to take effective action and speak in the name of all the religious of the region in what concerns their common interests, it is clearly desirable that all should join them; it might even be a moral obligation.[7] Their decisions are not binding even on their own members unless the statutes say otherwise, but here again, circumstances might make it a moral obligation for all to accept them.[8]

*Perfectae caritatis* expresses the Council's interest in conferences or councils of major superiors and speaks of co-ordination and co-operation with episcopal conferences in the exercise of the apostolate.[9] Religious cannot be members of an episcopal conference,[10] though sometimes invited to a meeting as auditors; mixed commissions of bishops and major superiors are recommended on the national level by *Ecclesiae Sanctae* 43; but it is highly desirable that the major superiors should have an opportunity of making their voice heard at the episcopal conference and be called to collaborate on various questions in study, planning and execution. ES 42 suggests a link between the Union of Superiors General (men) and the S. Congregation for Religious and Secular Institutes,[11] and there is actually a council of sixteen members as liaison between the S. Congregation and both Unions of Superiors General.

The Union of men's Superiors General elects ten of its members to take part in the Synod of Bishops.[12] Collaboration takes place with all kinds of ecclesiastical organizations at different levels and is particularly useful at the diocesan level, to foster brotherly union, to plan and carry out pastoral work. Conferences and unions can speak with an effective and representative voice.

# 3. Regrouping of institutes

## Fusion

Vatican II, desirous that religious institutes should give their full value in the Church of today (PC 1,4), warns against founding communities which are needless or lack sufficient resources (PC 19) and says that existing communities or monasteries possessing no reasonable hope of further development should be forbidden to receive novices[13] (PC 21); if possible, they should be combined with other more flourishing communities whose scope and spirit is similar, and thus not lose their right to live the religious life.

This is a union of extinction. It sometimes takes place not because a community has no hope of survival but because it wishes to rejoin the family from which it broke off in the past.[14]

In the post-conciliar period the Holy See approved several unions of institutes which united on an equal level to form a new institute; they gave up their autonomy by merging it in a new juridical moral person and elected a new superior general; if necessary, they divided it into provinces on a geographical basis. The spirit or charism which they shared was not weakened but strengthened by their action.[15]

This kind of union comes about between institutes so closely allied as to be considered parts of the same family, with a common origin, spirit, constitutions and activities,[16] but it can also be formed by institutes having no common origin but a marked similarity in their aim, their purpose and their constitutions, so that the advantages of union are apparent.[17]

*Ecclesiae Sanctae* II, 39-40, says that for forming any union there must be proper preparation — spiritual, psychological and juridical; that the character of each institute must be taken into account as well as the freedom of each member. Under Leo XIII there began a movement in this direction exemplified by the Roman Union of Ursulines, the Company of Mary of St. Jeanne de Lestonnac, later on the Union of Sisters of Mercy in the United States and a number of others. Among the men's Orders also, such as the Trappists and the Franciscan Friars Minor, a movement toward greater unity appeared at this time.

## Federations[18]

When institutes unite but keep their autonomy they form what is called a federation. One type of this is a monastic Congregation. For men, these were made obligatory by the Council of Trent. For nuns, they were strongly recommended by Pius XII in *Sponsa Christi,* and Vatican II emphatically repeats that those who belong to the same religious family should form federations (PC 22). Many monasteries of nuns have followed the recommendation and greatly gained by it for adaptation and renewal. The religious at the head of a federation can intervene in certain matters as far as its statutes allow, but if the autonomy of the monasteries were diminished it would no longer be a federation but a union.[19]

If several monastic congregations or federations unite, they form a confederation. In 1893 the Benedictine monks did so, and in 1959, the Canons Regular of St. Augustine.

## Associations

An association is formed by a group of institutes, for mutual help and permanent collaboration in certain spheres: the apostolate, for instance, or formation, but without constituting a new corporate body with organs of direction; it is usually made up of representatives of the institutes concerned and regulated by an agreement or convention. The link between them is some common interest either in their origin, their purpose, or some work undertaken jointly.[20]

The documents quoted show that the Holy See desires and encourages union and collaboration of all kinds; it is unfavorable to any separatist movement within communities. Occasionally and for good and grave reasons it has regretfully given approbation to the division of an institute, stipulating that relations must be maintained; future union or federation is thus left as a possibility.

# 4. Links between men's and women's institutes

Relations between men's and women's institutes have varied a good deal over the centuries. Church law at present makes a clear distinction between monasteries of nuns and women's congregations.

## Monasteries of nuns

These may be dependent upon a Regular superior and exempt from the jurisdiction of the bishop; others may not. For each Order the dependence is regulated by the pontifical documents, the Rule, the constitutions and age-old practice. For some Orders it is considered normal, as for the Discalced Carmelite Fathers and nuns; for others each case is decided as it arises[21]; in some places, as in Spain, the Holy See has for special reasons made all the monasteries subject to the local Ordinary.

Dependence can be of different types. There are monasteries of Benedictine nuns who follow the Rule of St. Benedict and consider themselves as incorporated into the Order, a monastic Congregation or a men's monastery; spiritually and juridically they form part of a whole and are subject to its chapters and superiors. Such are the Trappists.

The nuns belonging to the Mendicant Orders form their Second Order and as such are linked with the First Order. *Ecclesiae Sanctae* I, 9, for this reason says that their aggiornamento is to be guided by the highest authority in the Order.

At the present time and in accordance with the spirit and directive of Vatican II the tendency is to give greater autonomy to the nuns and emphasize the spiritual help which the men's Orders can give.[22] The formation of federations among the nuns is in keeping with this movement.

## Women's congregations[23]

There are three ways in which these congregations may be linked with men's Orders: there may be a spiritual aggregation or union by which the women share in the merits and prayers of the Order, or a bond entrusting the Order with care and direction of the Sisters, or a bond of real authority. The connection may arise from belonging in some way to the same religious family, or having the same founder and by his express wish, or from work undertaken in common; it ensures the permanence of certain benefits, spiritual, pastoral and governmental.

Except for the aggregation of tertiaries living in community, still provided for in can. 492 § 1, the Holy See has for some time disapproved of having a priest at the head of a women's congregation, and this was stated in the Norms of 1901. The Instruction *Cum Sanctissimus* applies the same rule to secular institutes. Several requests were refused, both because such links limited the authority of the bishops and because experience has shown them to be unnecessary. Benedict XV said "Let the women be governed by women."

A few exceptions have been admitted. The Daughters of Charity of St. Vincent de Paul are directed by the Lazarists; the Daughters of Mary, Help of Christians *(Salesian Sisters)*, by the Salesians; the Daughters of Wisdom by the Montfort Fathers.[24] In other cases the religious are spiritually directed by a men's Order, as the Franciscan Missionaries of Mary by the Friars Minor.

1. It has been called the *Ordo religiosorum* corresponding with the *Ordo sacerdotalis* of priests. The unity and variety of institutes have their center in the Church. Cf. Volume I of *Consecration and Service* (Boston: St. Paul Editions, 1973), ch. XXII.

2. G. Nardin, "Il movimento d'unione tra gli Stati di perfezione, *Commentarium pro Religiosis* (Rome, 1961), pp. 105-108, quotes texts of Pius XII.

3. Cf. E. Gambari, *The Religious Adult in Christ* (Boston: St. Paul Editions, 1971), Part II, ch. VI.

4. The principal organization of religious concerned in the training of candidates is the *Sister Formation Conference* (SFC) in the United States.

5. Nardin, *op. cit.*, p. 399. *Las Organizaciónes de los Religiosos para la renovación de la vida religiosa* (Madrid: Confer, 1958), p. 96.

Soeur M. Madeleine, *Les Unions des Religieuses dans l'Eglise de France*, Centre National des Vocations (Paris, 1961).

During the year 1972 there were 130 conferences in 76 different countries.

On October 16-19, 1972, a very successful meeting of representatives, men religious and Sisters, was held in Rome to discuss the state of religious life in different parts of the world.

6. Unions of this kind have sometimes acquired civil personality enabling them to act in defense of the interests of their members; some of them behave in some ways like trade unions, drawing up forms of agreement, etc.

7. If the communities are asked to adhere to the appropriate conferences, this supposes that the conferences will faithfully follow the directives of the Holy See, by whose authority they themselves were established.

8. There is a certain analogy with the episcopal conferences, but it must not be pressed too far.

9. It was providential that CD 36-38 and PC 23 brought out the importance of both. *Perfectae caritatis* says that the conferences or councils have much to contribute in many fields: in helping individual religious institutes to a fuller achievement of their ends, in fostering a more effective co-operation for the good of the Church, in a more even deployment of preachers of the Gospel and also in handling business of common interest to religious and arranging for co-ordination and co-operation with the episcopal conferences.

10. Cf. Reply of the commission for interpretation of the Council, 10-31-70, in *Communicationes* II, pp. 165-166.

11. The Apostolic Constitution *Regiminis Ecclesiae Universae*, 73 § 5, asks that after founding conferences and unions the S. Congregation for Religious should make use of them in the way that seems most opportune.

12. Cf. the *Regolamento del Sinodo*, art. 5 § 1,1.

13. Sometimes the house is simply closed.

14. For historical or political reasons a group left the parent stock to form an independent unit.

15. There was sometimes an experimental period before the definitive union.

16. Circumstances in the past often led to the breaking up of an institute when it spread into other dioceses or countries; the Sisters of St. Joseph, for instance, and the Sisters of Mercy set up a separate government in each country or diocese.

17. This happens most easily when institutes belong to the same Third Order — Franciscan, Dominican, Augustinian — or were founded for the same purpose — teaching, nursing, parish work — and inspired by the same spirituality.

18. Cf. E. Gambari, "De Monasteriorum Foederationibus," *Acts of the General Congress of the States of Perfection* (Rome, 1950), Vol. IV, pp. 205-250.

19. Cf. E. Gambari, *loc. cit.*, pp. 206-212.

20. For example, the opening of a joint house of studies.

21. Some Orders, such as the Dominicans, have shown unwillingness to undertake the guidance of nuns of their own Order.

22. Cf. J. Leclercq, "Moines et Moniales," *Lumen Vitae* (Brussels, 1971).

23. Cf. G. Van den Broeck, "La dépendance des Communautés de Religieuses à l'égard d'un institut de religieux," *Revue de Droit Canonique*, 1968. E. Wagner, O.F.M., "Formae aggregationis, unionis, subiectionis inter diversas religiones, Societates et Instituta saecularia," *Acts of the General Congress of the States of Perfection* (1950), Vol. II. In the same volume is a paper read by P. Guido Cocchi, C.M., on the same subject.

24. Even in these cases dependence is limited to what is strictly necessary and really desired by the Sisters, who must retain a certain autonomy.

# Chapter X
# In union with the hierarchy

## 1. The link with the hierarchy

The special bond which links religious with the Church links them also with the hierarchy, whose duty it is to give them care and guidance (LG 44,2; 45,1).

From the beginnings of religious life, its development has brought it more and more effectively into the life, action and structures of the Church, especially through the clerical institutes and the apostolate; as soon as it became a particular state of life, social, juridical and public, it called for regulation by the hierarchy with whom it is associated in its mission and in a part of its authority.

The attitude of the religious, who have special duties toward the Church,[1] will be one of respectful and filial submission to those placed in authority in the universal Church or in local churches; there is no cleavage between the mystical Church and the Church seen as an institution; the *sensus Ecclesiae* will remind the religious that because they act in her name more than the other faithful, they must show docility, readiness, generosity and constancy with regard to her teaching, directives and norms.[2] The charism or prophetic character does not give exemption from obedience in life or work carried on in the name of the Church (PC 8, 2).

## 2.  Religious and the Sovereign Pontiff

In virtue of their vow of obedience, religious are subject to the Pope as their highest authority; this is not merely a juridical norm but follows upon the theological and spiritual consequences of the primacy. It is exemplified when exemption from the jurisdiction of the local bishop places an institute under the direct authority of the Pope, and also every time the Holy See erects an institute or raises a diocesan institute to pontifical status.

History shows what the Sovereign Pontiffs have done for religious,[3] and the part religious have played in the defense of the pontifical primacy and in carrying out apostolic work at the wish of the Pope.[4] Their total availability makes them valuable instruments of evangelization, and they in their turn find in it the source, increase and defense of their universality. Its logical consequence is the availability of religious to all bishops in communion with the Holy See, who make use of them to fulfill their responsibilities toward the universal Church and toward the local churches most in need.

When dealing with religious and their institutes, the Pope acts through a Department of the Roman Curia[5] entitled the Sacred Congregation for Religious and Secular Institutes.[6] It is divided into two sections: one for all that concerns religious institutes, their erection, their guidance, their suppression, the defense and pursuit of their particular end, their government and discipline, property, privileges, the formation of their members and their life according to the special character of the institute; constitutions and dispensations from canon law; the other section of the Department does the same for secular institutes.[7]

It also falls to this Department to promote the renewal, adaptation and development of religious life, and to establish unions or conferences of major superiors.[8]

In certain determined fields religious depend on other Departments, e.g., for the Eucharistic fast on the S.C. for the Sacraments, for scientific or academic training on the S.C. for Catholic Education, for action in missionary countries on the S.C. for Evangelization.[9] It would seem logical, however, that for what concerns their religious life all missionaries should depend on the S. Congregation for Religious and Secular Institutes.

The S.C. for Religious concerns itself with the needs of particular institutes as occasion requires, but on broad lines with all institutes. To keep its information up-to-date it used to receive a five-yearly report on the conditions in every institute; this is not now asked for, but the reports of all general chapters must be sent in.

Nuncios and apostolic delegates often have special faculties for acting on behalf of the Holy See to grant permissions or dispensations to religious institutes in their territory.

The role of the Cardinal Protector was, as his title implied, to protect institutes — particularly of women — from undue interference and to give help and support when needed; but the function is being phased out as no longer required.

# 3. Relations with the bishop and the diocese

A good deal has been said on this subject under the heading *Pastoral action* in a preceding chapter.

The bishops are the guides of all the People of God, leading them into rich pastures (LG 45,1); and among these are the religious (LG 44,4). They are a special, chosen portion of the bishop's flock, members of the diocesan family; and it is for him to see that the diocese benefits by their presence as fully as possible, by drawing them into his general pastoral plan and taking account of each institute's particular character. A very important part of the bishop's duty toward them is the encouragement of religious vocations, by himself and by his clergy and by any help he can give to the institute's own vocational work.[10]

In the Council documents relating to these and similar questions, it is clear that their aim is to introduce a new spirit into the relations between bishops and religious, a spirit of mutual understanding and charity leading to willing collaboration, less insistence on juridical rights and greater emphasis on union and unity.

Juridical dependence has been diminished by the widened faculties granted to superiors general.[11] The attitude of the religious must be a co-operative one of availability and flexibility.

In many dioceses a Vicar for religious has been appointed in addition to the vicar general; he has the title of episcopal vicar,[12] and is in charge of pastoral action insofar as it concerns religious. His duties call for prudence, sound doctrine, tact and respect for institutes and persons; it is no easy office to fill, especially at the present time. Obviously he cannot go beyond what the Bishop has power to do, and there may be a considerable danger of his interfering in the initiatives of religious women, either by putting a brake on them or by pushing them too much. Religious men are subject to him as they are to the Bishop, unless the latter has made exceptions.

## The clergy

Various Council texts recall the closeness of the bond uniting all priests in virtue of their common sacred ordination (cf. LG 28,3; 41,3; PO 7,1, 8; 14,3; SC 57).

The Council emphasized the link with the diocese of those priests who belong to it—and for this reason liked to call them diocesan rather than secular—but emphasized still more the universal dimension of the priesthood of Christ, and asked all priests to realize it by their availability for work wherever it was most urgently needed.

Pius XII, in the allocution *Annus sacer* (12-8-50), said that no priority exists between the secular and regular clergy; neither can claim a prerogative of divine right; the authority extends to both and both are subject to the Pope; in their submission to the Pope all priests meet.[13]

Every religious priest should be and should feel fully active in the diocese; all who share in the one priesthood are co-workers with the Bishop, each according to his own vocation.[14]

The document of the Synod of Bishops in 1971, on *The Ministerial Priesthood*, asks for closer relations between the diocesan priests and the religious priests in genuine brotherhood and special mutual aid, including spiritual aid (cf. II Part II, 2).

## Councils and other organizations

United pastoral action means that religious must have contacts and dialogue with clergy councils, pastoral councils and other diocesan organizations. In fact, it is considered that some religious priests should be on the clergy council and both men and women religious on the pastoral council (cf. CD 27, ES I, 15-16 and the Circular Letter of the S. C. for the Clergy of 4-11-70). In this way they are fully in the life of the diocese, "sharing and implementing its undertakings and aims" (cf. PC 2c), and their collaboration will be a source of renewal and enrichment for the diocese and for themselves. Directives given by the competent diocesan authority will be followed by them for the sake of unity in ecclesial life and discipline, without prejudice to the discipline of their own institute.

## The parish priest

Religious are not dependent upon the parish priest except insofar as they do parish work.

As a general principle, whoever is exempt from the jurisdiction of the bishop is also exempt from the authority of the parish priest; in a clerical institute the superior takes his place for the administration of the sacraments and for funerals, and can also dispense from the obligation of fasting and abstinence. In all such matters lay religious and women are dependent on the parish priest, unless, as often happens, their chaplain takes his place (cf. can. 464 § 2).

## Councils or senates of religious men or women

In some dioceses consultative councils or senates of religious men and women have been established to carry out functions similar to those of the councils or commissions of major superiors, that is, to promote co-ordination, provide information and give assistance to the bishop and his representatives by means of dialogue, study and planning; they are distinct from other diocesan councils and from the conferences or committees dealt with in Chapter IX, which are broader in scope. They are concerned only with their own diocese, in which they can render valuable service by fostering union among the religious and discussing problems which concern the bishop and themselves. All institutes should be represented in them, and religious who work on different levels, not only superiors. Some experimentation will probably be needed as regards their composition.[15]


# 4. Religious and priests[16]

The deeper the union with the Church, the more vital are the links between its members.[17] Theologically, spiritually, liturgically and juridically, priests and religious find their meeting-place in the Church. They share in Christ's call to holiness, to celibacy, obedience and poverty, and in the means of responding to it.[18] They are officially charged with the worship of God, so that their whole life is a liturgy; they are at the service of the Church and of their fellow men; they have the interests and the good of the Church at heart, and their oneness in brotherhood will help them to work for the unity of the human race. Priests and religious men and women can be said, each in his own way, to speak in the name of the Church.

Nor must it be supposed that contemplative religious are excluded from this relationship; in the words of *Venite seorsum,* they are "at the heart of the Church." The Council declares that the first duty of religious toward the Church is to offer prayer, penance and the example of their lives (CD 33,1).

The links that unite them spiritually in the Church lead naturally to union in the life and work of priests and religious, which will gain in every way and be of great value for the faithful as an example of collaboration in Christ.

Many are the ways in which they can be, and feel themselves to be co-workers for the same end, thus lessening the sense of isolation that comes to those who work alone. The words of *Lumen gentium* 13, are very apt here: "Through the common sharing of gifts and through the common effort to attain fullness in unity, the whole and each of the parts receive increase." The services which communities of women render to priests, who in their turn bring them guidance, light and strength, unite all in their common effort.

Priests are at the disposal of religious men and women, as also of their brother priests, to give them help in their spiritual life; it is a delicate task and a great responsibility, but also a source of hope and joy; they owe more to those who have given more to the Church, but they can hope for more fruit from the seed that they sow.

In the ministry of the word by preaching, catechetics and teaching, women's communities expect much from priests; and the further women progress in their studies, the greater care is needed in preparing the homilies and instructions to be given to them. In particular, every priest should from the time of his training learn about religious life. The decree *Optatam totius* 19, says that students must "learn to help religious men and women that they may persevere in the grace of their vocations and make progress according to the spirit of their institutes." This implies not a superficial knowledge of the meaning of vows, but something of their theological basis and its implications, especially at the present day.[19]

A very important corollary to this duty is the encouragement of religious vocations—and, naturally, of priestly vocations also; the Council documents point out that this requires pastoral action on a large scale, prayer, catechesis and preaching; in a word, all that goes to the making of a fervent parish community, and not least is the example of the priests themselves (OT 2; PO 11; CD 15,3).

The attitude of religious toward priests should be, in proportion, the same as their attitude toward the bishop, that is, esteem, respect and due obedience, but above all the support of their prayer, the interest shown in their undertakings, their collaboration wherever it is needed. A genuine and universal desire for union will go far in making the Church present to the world of today; young people in particular will recognize it, appreciate it and, by the grace of God, respond to it.

1. Cf. E. Gambari, *For Me To Live Is the Church* (Boston: St. Paul Editions, 1970), Part II, ch. I; ch. V, 5-6; Part IV, ch. II.

2. What Vatican II says of the duties and bonds which link priests to the hierarchy (cf. LG 28; CD 28; PO 7-8) applies to a certain extent to religious men and women, though not always in exactly the same way.

3. Cf. E. Gambari, *op. cit.*, Part I, ch. II.

4. J. Ratzinger, *Das neue Volk-Gottes, Entwürfe für Ekklesiologie,* (Düsseldorf: Patmos-Verlag, 1969), on the Mendicants and the papal primacy.

5. The function of this Department is the same as that of all the Departments of the Roman Curia, as set forth by Paul VI, in *Regimini Ecclesiae universae* of August 15, 1967 (AAS 59, 1967).

6. The new title of the Department makes separate mention of secular institutes to avoid any confusion with religious institutes. The Department deals also with Societies of common life, Third Orders and Associations which intend to become Institutes of perfection.

7. Cf. *Regimini Ecclesiae universae* 71-74.

8. It was from the S. C. for Religious that the movement for aggiornamento was actually launched.

9. Cf. *Regimini Ecclesiae universae* 73 §2; 88. It would seem logical that even religious institutes founded for, and active in missions, should be subject, inasmuch as they are religious, to the specific department.

10. *Ecclesiae Sanctae* III, 6, speaks of special encouragement of vocations for missionary work.

11. The situation of non-exempt religious with regard to the Ordinary is not the same for all, clerical and lay. The powers of superiors general have been widened by the Decree *Religionum laicalium* (cf. E. Gambari, *Facoltà speciali dei Superiori Generali*, pp. 71-81) and by the rescript *Cum admotae.*

In post-conciliar documents the major superiors of clerical institutes are considered as Ordinaries (cf. M. P. *Ministeria quaedam*, 8-15-72, art. IX and *Ad Pascendum* Ib).

The M.P. *De episcoporum muneribus* of 6-25-66, excludes laws concerning religious from the bishop's power to dispense from the universal laws of the Church.

12. Cf. E. Gambari, *Figura del sacerdote incaricato dell'assistenza alle Suore*, Acts of the first Assembly of priest-assistants to women religious in Italy, USMI, Rome, 1968. On pp. 30-33, it treats of the episcopal vicar, whose function is not the same as that of a priest-assistant to organizations of women religious at different levels.

13. See also Card. A. M. Larraona, "Hierarchia utriusque cleri," *Commentarium pro Religiosis* (1963), pp. 29-71; 167-190.

14. Ordination for a particular diocese strengthens the bond with it and with its bishop and gives a special juridical and pastoral title to be a member of its clergy, but this should not outweigh the theological bond of unity among all who share in the priesthood.

15. Although only consultative in character, they can put forward proposals for common action such as meetings, retreats, study days, etc., with the approval of those responsible.

16. Cf. E. Gambari, "The priest's collaboration with professed religious," *Seminarium* (1970), pp. 255-267. The Council documents, especially PO, emphasize the links between priests and religious.

17. The depth of Our Lady's union with Christ was the source of her relation of motherhood to the faithful, all of whom are her children.

18. Religious life brings out and utilizes to the full the priestly element in baptismal consecration. Cf. E. Gambari, *For Me To Live Is the Church* (Boston: St. Paul Editions, 1970), Part III, ch. 3.

19. This is even more necessary in the periodic formation of religious. Religious life should be studied in its theological, spiritual, apostolic, historical and canonical aspects. Cf. ES II, 6 § 2.

# Chapter XI
# Principles underlying
# the structures of government

## 1. Community of service

Structures, and particularly authority, have become for many a sign of contradiction and a stumbling-block.

The new way of looking at the human person and his dignity and the consequent sense of freedom, of democracy, of co-responsibility and collegiality have created an atmosphere which is to a large extent new. It is in this atmosphere that religious vocations are born, and into it the Church and religious institutes must enter; in it they must carry on their work.

The Council has shown us authority in a new light based on the Gospel, setting forth its theological, spiritual and pastoral basis and emphasizing its function of service; we thereby have the criteria for bringing its exercise up-to-date. *Perfectae caritatis* tells us that the manner of governing religious institutes is to be examined, and this includes not only the manner but the actual structures of government, so that all may be adapted to the modern physical and psychological circumstances of the members, and to the demands of culture, and social and economic conditions (PC 3).

Paul VI, in his allocution of 11-4-64, remarking on the increased importance attached to personality, individual freedom and the moral primacy of conscience, spoke of the difficulties already arising with regard to religious authority.[1] In his discourse of 1-12-67, he warned the whole Church of the need and the duty to meet the new tendencies and welcome the ferment that is acting among the People of God insofar as it is an expression of God's will in the signs of the times. The renewal of structures actually taking place in the Church shows the institutes the way they should go.[2]

The fellowship existing between those who share the same charism gives rise to the need for structures and authority, but at the same time it gives life and shape to those same structures. *Koinonia* shows itself today in the call for personal contribution and mutual service on the part of all the members, whether it be the service of authority or of obedience, which are complementary; each in his place is there for the good of the Church and of the human race.[3] *Lumen gentium* says well and clearly: "All share a true equality with regard to the dignity and the activity common to all the faithful for the building up of the Body of Christ" (LG 32,3).

Community of service is the source of rights and duties rooted in love (Gal 5:13). In due proportion, we may repeat for religious what Paul VI said to the second Synod of Bishops in his discourse of October 11, 1969: collegiality is first of all communion in love and in the duty of service.

Like any other group of people joined in the pursuit of a common cause, the religious community has established for itself links of interdependence and norms of behavior. To one person, or to more than one, may be entrusted the task of stimulating and guiding, and, on occasion, of making decisions; in certain cases it may fall to the whole community. There is, however, no clear-cut line between this task and the general duty binding on the group and on each of its members. It is shared by those who decide and those who give active and responsible obedience; their paths converge and meet in the pursuit of the common aim. Notwithstanding the active participation of all in the common good, and, indeed, to make it more efficient in religious institutes, authority with precise rights and duties is necessary (ET 25).

The Council has reawakened the sense of co-responsibility in the members of the Church and the members of institutes, drawing them closer together, and this discovery has given a new richness to the common life in religious institutes. Paul VI, speaking in *Ecclesiam Suam* of our relations with non-Catholics, says, "We readily accept the principle of stressing what we have in common rather than what divides us." Men all over the world today are linked together by reciprocal needs; they find more and more that they are dependent on one another; like them, religious are learning to experience the demands and the benefits of service given and received.

# 2.  Structures in religious life

Just as we speak of the mystery of the Church with reference to its inner spiritual reality, we can, by analogy, speak of the mystery of religious life.[4] In the Church, the mystery, or inner reality is expressed and embodied in the outward and social reality of the People of God (LG ch. II)[5]; in religious life, the mystery is expressed by the institute itself and every one of its parts in its canonical form, involving rights and duties toward God and toward the group and the juridical means of enforcing them.

These juridical structures in religious life must always exist, precisely because they are at the service of the charismatic reality, safeguarding and promoting its vitality and efficacy in the measure found to be necessary. If at any time a particular structure becomes a hindrance to the community charism or to the life of communion in charity, it would not only lack a reason for being but would be counter-productive, and should therefore be replaced.

A religious institute, like the Church, may be likened to an organic living body of which all the parts are necessary. St. Paul speaks of "the whole body, nourished and knit together through its joints and ligaments" (Col 2:19).

Structures are the shape given to the various relations, functions, tasks and positions involving rights and duties, which support and guide the activities of the group and determine the conduct of those who join it for a common purpose.

In the Church, there is a head, who, as the Vicar of Christ, presides over the whole ecclesial body; the bishops, in charge of local churches and united by collegiality; parishes and other Church organisms dealt with in the Code of canon law, from the Pope down to the rector of a church.

In religious life there is the institute itself, the parts into which it is divided, provinces and houses, the various organs and offices of government, the rules concerning formation, the apostolate, community life, etc.

Common sense shows that these structures must have stability and that decisions cannot be left solely to the inspiration of the moment or of individuals. Structures will only be appreciated and respected, however, if they have demonstrable value in themselves and are justified by their necessity and usefulness here and now. They must correspond with the religious purpose of the group, and with the present needs of the Church as made known in the promptings of the Spirit.

The will of the legislator is not enough to give them full value and efficacy. To be understood, they must clearly express the positive values that carry weight today, such as brotherhood, solidarity, and participation. They must be well adapted to the end in view, flexible and dynamic in spirit,[6] encouraging initiative or at least not hindering it. Above all, they must not be looked upon as substitutes for personal conviction and a sense of responsibility which guide spontaneity and creativity, within the framework which has been set up.

The principles for the renewal and evaluation of structures may be synthesized as follows: respect for persons; diversity of functions; liberty joined to responsibility; the contribution of all to the common good; unity in plurality. Each of these can be expressed in a rich variety of ways.

## 3. Basic principles

### Respect for the person

The recognition of the dignity of man and the basic equality of all for the building up of the Body of Christ

(LG 32,3) does not spring from the general mentality of our time; it has its source in the Gospel, which tells us that we are all brothers under the one head, Christ (Mt. 23:8). *Gaudium et spes* repeats it (26).[7]

The person is at the center of the structures and of all religious life. Community life does not mean the loss of personality in a nameless crowd; it is a person-to-person relationship among those who share the same charism and have been called to a new personal relationship with Christ. Structures should therefore be shaped so as to encourage the development of each member's own personality.

The dignity of a person is closely bound up with his liberty and responsibility. Without liberty, responsibility cannot exist; anyone who has been given a task is not expected to produce the result automatically, like a computer, no scope being left for initiative on his part. This kind of automatic obedience is not what is required. A task given should be accepted by the religious with a full sense of responsibility for carrying it out to the best of his ability, and giving the thought and effort necessary for the purpose; only thus will he reach maturity. The aim of a superior should be to guide the community and every member of it to maturity.[8] Structures exist for guidance, not as a substitute for effort. Like the rails on which a train runs, or the banks of a river, they give speed and strength by guiding and directing.

Authority is not the sole principle of action; the Holy Spirit can assist us in other ways. We are not exempted from listening attentively to Him and keeping our eyes on Him; nor are we excused from using our initiative and making our personal contribution. Authority itself expects this from us.

Respect for the person starts from the time of formation, which must take into account the individual's intellectual capacity and personal talent (PC 18,2); the gifts of nature and grace must be developed so that each religious can serve the Lord with his whole self and his whole strength.

The next point is that as far as possible each one should be given the occupations and tasks by which he can best contribute to the common good, and this distribution is made on the basis of equality. If each is to have his rightful place in the diversity of duties, there will be no question of privileges or exemptions, even less of a right of domineering, but simply of placing each religious where he can best serve the common good, recognizing always that the common good can and does require sacrifice. If this is done each will give, each will receive, and all will recognize and respect the distribution of duties required by the common life.

Service, which was one of the central ideas of the Council, is service of God and our fellow men. The service of government is for the benefit of those who are governed; structures are organized for the good of persons taken individually and collectively, and in the hierarchy of values, persons have the priority; the person's true welfare may not be sacrificed to the structure. But the common good is not something extrinsic to the individual; it is made up of the personal goods and the individual labors of those who pursue a common end, the specific end of the institute with its charism. In the planning of formation and the distribution of offices and assignments, the needs of the institute must therefore be kept in view.

This brings us to a delicate problem which can sometimes present real difficulties. How is the good of the institute to be combined with the good of the individual when they seem to conflict? It is especially difficult when the individual religious seems to have a personal vocation within the general charism of the institute. Now, it is true that the good of the person must not be sacrificed to the structure, but it is his real good that is in question, and his real good does not exclude sacrifice. Those who receive will expect sometimes to give, and a sacrifice made for the common good can be the most valuable of personal contributions. Clearly, an authoritarian attitude which looks only at efficiency and takes sacrifice for granted is wrong. To avoid errors of judgment, prayer, an objective approach and a frank discussion with the person concerned are the essential means; it may be advisable to consult the community; in the end, the competent authority must decide.

## Participation or sharing

The principle of personal responsibility widens out from individual actions to the collective action of the community and its shared responsibility; structures must allow for both.

A share in decision-making can fall under the head of co-responsibility, comparticipation, democracy or collegiality, according to the angle from which it is looked at and its degree of efficacy in action. The aim in view is, to quote Cardinal Suenens, "a systematic convergence of effort, a mutual collaboration in an atmosphere of confidence." [9]

The sharing in a common life makes it a duty to work for the good of the whole institute and each of its members, feeling an obligation to do all that one can for them. All that concerns the institute and the Church will be a matter for concern to every religious, who will take the burden, as it were, upon his shoulders and be prepared for self-sacrifice when the good of the community calls for it.

Co-responsibility is, as the word itself shows, sharing a common responsibility, each in his own place and his own way, so that through the diversity of the members the kingdom of God may be built up. To feel it as not only a right but a duty will prevent passive acceptance of a situation that calls for action. As St. Paul felt himself under obligation to all (Rom 1:14), each member of the institute will feel responsible for the good of all (cf. ET 39) [10]; it is the concrete fulfillment of the doctrine of the Mystical Body, and it will lead naturally to comparticipation.

Structures should provide for the religious to work together not only in carrying out decisions but in the preliminary thinking out, planning and discussion, and this implies information, consultation and dialogue. The way in which Vatican II appealed to all religious to take part in the work of renewal shows the meaning of comparticipation. [11] Superiors were asked to invite the collaboration of all; ES 18 remarks that chapters and councils should express the involvement and the concern of all members of the community for the good of the whole (PC 14,4) and goes on to say that this will be the case especially if the members have a real and effective part in the choice of chapter and council officials. [12]

The tendency today is to have as many people as possible, and in the most efficient way, taking part in deliberations and the carrying out of decisions.

This applies at all levels — general, provincial or inter-mediary, and local, and wherever a group of people work together, as in the area of formation.[13]

Democracy, when it is spoken of in connection with religious structures, must be properly understood. The word has sometimes been forcefully rejected because it was taken to mean a political system in which questions are decided by a majority vote, or the political theory that authority has its source in the body of the people. In a religious community democratic structures are those by which every member has a share in decision-making, either directly or indirectly. On the occasions when a whole community discusses and decides together, every religious can express his personal opinion and has a direct share in the result, whatever it may be. When decisions are made by an elected chapter, his share is indirect but real; he gives his opinion as to who should take part in the chapter. The democratic spirit is one in which everyone has a right to speak and to be listened to.

Collegiality is the strongest form of collaboration.[14] A college is a group with certain collective powers and responsibilities. In a juridical sense it is a group whose members have equal power. The best example of this is the general chapter, at which each person is free to speak and when a decision is made all votes have equal weight. The present-day tendency is to widen the field of action of general and provincial chapters and increase — or re-store — the importance of the local chapter, which formerly took an effective part in community decision-making. A council also in certain clearly defined cases can act as a collegiate body in which all votes have equal weight. Collegiality in a broad sense covers comparticipation by consultation, discussion and dialogue as preliminaries to action. The means used for consultation is left to the choice of the institute; but ES, speaking of special chapters, says it must be "free and ample."

## Distribution of functions

The principle of sharing does not apply only to the sharing of the individual religious in the action of the group; it applies also to the spreading out of the actual decision-making among different groups, to the extent that experience shows it to be profitable.

The two principles that chiefly come into play here are subsidiarity and decentralization. The motives underlying them are similar and almost — but not quite — identical. Both have their root in respect for the liberty and responsibility of the person. Subsidiarity in a general sense concerns all structures and organizations[15]; it consists in giving those responsible in any particular sphere the faculties and powers required for the normal fulfillment of their tasks and thus avoiding too frequent and needless recourse to higher authorities.[16] It applies to a superior, to a group in charge of some work, to an individual with a task to fulfill. It does not mean isolation or the rejection of any other authority. A member of a community has rules and directives to follow and must keep in touch with his superior, refer to him when necessary and accept intervention on his part; but apart from this, he should be given power to fulfill the responsibilities which normally belong to his office.

The combination of dependence and independence which go to make up subsidiarity cannot be a matter for meticulous rules; it will work satisfactorily if applied in the right spirit. There must be trust on both sides and a genuine desire to collaborate for the end in view.

Decentralization has this in common with subsidiarity: it passes on to subordinate authorities action that might have been taken at a higher level but is better dealt with by those on the spot; in many cases the subordinate would be actually hampered in his task by lack of sufficient power to act.

We have said that structures should be adapted to the end in view. Centralization has certain advantages, and the apostolic institutes of the 19th century were all founded with centralized structures; but the general movement toward decentralization in our day shows that it, too, answers a felt need. Provided it does not go too far, the general work of the institute will gain in speed and practical efficiency by decentralization. It will also be better adapted to local conditions. Diversity of cultures calls for diversity of action, and those on the spot are in the best position to see what is needed; they should be able to make certain decisions according to circumstances.

The rights thus passed on to others carry with them corresponding duties and responsibilities, particularly that of maintaining unity in diversity. A practical and regular system of links and contacts between center and periphery is essential, for without it, diversity might slip into disintegration; it may be organized in whatever way is most convenient and efficient, but it must be faithfully maintained. Fidelity to these contacts will be the mark of fidelity to the common aims of the institute and its common effort. The highest authority is ultimately responsible for the institute as a whole, and must be in a position to ensure not only unity of spirit but a certain measure of general outward discipline.[17]

Diversity may concern regions, provinces, houses or individuals, and at every level the higher authority must combine the different elements into a whole. All work together for a common end and their action is complementary and convergent; this is true of a community with its superior, who is not outside it but a member of it acting from within, where the bond of union is Christ. In the end, true unity in diversity of structures and activities is the result of the pervading influence and presence of Christ Himself.

1. In his allocution, the Pope referred to a certain spread of a Protestant and modernist attitude which denies the need of an intermediate authority between man and God.

2. He spoke of a purified view of the hierarchical structure of the Church and the community aspect of it (10-9-68). The acts of the chapters bear witness to the importance of this.

3. The Church and every local community is bound together in a *koinonia* or brotherhood because every person in the Church is bound to Christ in the most intimate fellowship. He is the source of authority because as Head of the Church all graces and gifts are distributed by Him. (cf. Fr. Barnabas Ahern, C.P., at the meeting of Superiors General of women's institutes at Rome, November, 1970, pp. 74-75.)

4. The mystery of religious life is treated of in Volume I, *Consecration and Service* (Boston: St. Paul Editions, 1973).

5. The structure of the Church is set out in this chapter of *Lumen gentium* and is reflected in the structure of the religious community: its members possess the dignity and liberty of the children of God with

the indwelling of the Holy Spirit, the new commandment to love one another as Christ has loved us, and the end and aim of establishing the kingdom of God until creation itself is set free from its bondage and obtains the glorious liberty of the children of God (Rom 8:21).

6. "The possibility for change and diversity should be permanently incorporated into the structure." Canon F. Houtart, *The Eleventh Hour,* (Herder, 1968).

7. The recognition of the dignity of the human person will encourage the sense of co-responsibility in institutes and the consciousness of acting from a sense of duty and not through any external coercion.

8. The training to act with liberty and responsibility should begin from novitiate days. *Renovationis causam* says that candidates should be taught "to work at the ordering of their own life" (31, II 3).

The whole of the Instruction emphasizes liberty and responsibility. See *Updating of Religious Formation* with comments by E. Gambari (Boston: St. Paul Editions, 1969).

9. L. J. Card. Suenens, *Co-responsibility in the Church* (Herder & Herder, 1968). *The Jurist* (1971), 1, gives a series of articles by different authors on this subject.

10. There is also a co-responsibility with regard to the Church and the whole world.

11. C. Riva, *La partecipazione nella Chiesa* (Rome: Ave, 1970), p. 130.

12. By analogy, the same principle would seem to apply also to a certain participation in the choice of the persons who are to be superiors, in whatever manner might be judged suitable.

13. Nowhere in the Church is the democratic character better expressed than in religious institutes. The present tendency is toward collegiality; the highest authority connected with the Departments of the Holy See is the Plenary Assembly of the Cardinals and Bishops; in the S. Congregation for Religious and Secular Institutes there are also superiors general who are members of it.

In each Department the Congress is the collegial organ (cf. *Regimini Ecclesiae universae*).

14. The juridical character of the institute as a collegiate moral person, which applies also to the separate houses, is based on a spiritual and moral collegiality. Cf. G. Lesage, O.M.I., "La collégialité dans le gouvernement ordinaire des religieux," *Acta Conventus internationalis canonistarum, 1968* (Vatican Polyglot Press, 1970), arts. 456-472.

In the explanatory note to Chapter III of *Lumen gentium,* it is said that "college" referring to the group of bishops all together is not to be understood in a strictly juridical sense but as a stable group whose structure and authority are to be deduced from revelation; it can also be called an Order or body. Equality between the head and the members does not exist.

15. Subsidiarity was first mentioned in Church documents in connection with the rights of citizens as against undue interference by the state in the economic field. Cf. Pius XI, *Quadragesimo anno* and various texts of Pius XII and John XXIII.

It was afterwards applied in other spheres. The Council mentions it with regard to education (GE 3, 6) and international co-operation (GS 86).

Cf. also G. Lesage, *Le principe de subsidiarité et l'état religieux*, *Studia canonica* (1968), Vol. 2, and various articles in the *Acta Conventus* mentioned in note 14.

16. Pius XII applied this principle to the life of the Church "without prejudice to its hierarchical structure" in his allocution of 2-20-46.

It is applied by the Holy See in *Cum admotae, Religionum laicalium* and especially in *Renovationis causam*.

The above documents could also be given as examples of decentralization, which includes the reform of the Roman Curia.

17. What was said at the Synod of Bishops in 1969, concerning relations between the Pope as head of the universal Church and the bishops, applies also to religious institutes.

As in the Church, brotherhood and authority are complementary to each other. Cf. Paul VI, 1-27-65.

# Chapter XII
# Authority in religious life

## 1. What is religious authority?

Vatican II had much to say on the subject of authority, and this is not surprising; the Council sees it as a central field for renewal. All agree that authority calls for renewal and adaptation; objection is not usually raised to the existence of authority as such, but to the manner in which it is exercised.

There is so much questioning today with regard to authority and obedience that we need a clear line of thought; we need first of all to go back to the Gospel. That Christ conferred authority on the apostles and especially on Peter is beyond question, and yet Paul VI thought it necessary to quote the well-known texts when he spoke of authority and obedience.[1] But Christ did not only confer authority. He said "I am among you as one that serves." And the Council has given a new aspect to authority by defining it as service.

For hundreds of years the Pope has had the title "Servant of the servants of God." And yet it comes to us as a new aspect. The Council achieved this by bringing out the theological, spiritual and pastoral content of authority and showing it as a function of service. *Perfectae caritatis* 14, which sketches out the duties of a superior, uses this word, and Paul VI, in the allocution just referred to, developed this concept at some length.

It is true that authority implies dependence. If directions are given, someone must carry them out. If all the emphasis is placed on the juridical aspect, however, the religious superiorship comes to look too much like civil authority, a realm in which the separation of rulers and subjects can look like division and even opposition. Such an identification in religious life can easily lead to a defensive attitude among the religious.

To understand religious authority properly we must look at the sphere in which it is exercised. Like the Church, the religious community is mystical and spiritual and at the same time social and juridical, human and divine[2]; authority concerns both aspects, but it has its roots and draws its strength from the divine, not the human element. *Lumen gentium* says of the Church that Christ as its Head gives gifts to its members, the gifts of the Spirit, and authority is one of these. There is only one source of authority, God our Creator. By reason of their creaturehood, all men are subject to Him and not to one another. The dignity of man is such that he is subject to other men only insofar as God has given a measure of authority to them, and this He does in various spheres. When that takes place, dependence on them unites us to God. The highest authority is that which Christ conferred on the Church through the apostles. The Church in its turn delegates authority and, in particular, the religious authority which is the subject of our present discussion.

## 2. Authority as service

In what sense is authority service? In the ordinary sense of the word; it serves a purpose; it is offered to persons to supply a need, to assist them in some way. Paul VI, in the allocution above-mentioned, pointed out that the role of authority is to co-ordinate the means best adapted to attain the end for which a society exists.

The Church exists to carry out God's salvific will for mankind; religious life exists within the Church—and therefore the rights and duties of superiors exist—to attain union with God by the practice of the counsels. If we apply this principle to the different functions of religious superiors, we shall see how all fits into place. Religious authority is derived from the Church which guides men through faith to holiness; and the superior carries on the work of the Church, united to those for whom he is responsible and co-responsible. Authority in the Church and especially in religious life means communion with God and union with fellow men. The superior is linked vertically to God and horizontally with his brothers in religion. He is a unifying and a vivifying force uniting individuals to God and to one another. He acts from within the community, not from outside. The institute, the province and the house are each a group of persons united in the love of Christ and bound together by the same charism and the same authority.[3] It may be said of them as of the Church that they are united in the unity of the Father, the Son and the Holy Spirit.

The first purpose and aim of authority in religion is, then, to lead the religious to holiness through the practice of the counsels; those who are called to follow Christ in this way, striving for the perfection of charity, desire the constant union with the will of God which they find in the religious state and cannot find elsewhere.[4]

But the very mention of the religious state reminds us that the counsels can be better practiced in a community; and a community, like the Church within which it exists, needs a head. At the head of the Mystical Body is Christ, represented in the Church by the Pope; at the head of the community is a superior. Authority is a particular mode of the Lord's presence and actions in a community; and the superior fulfills a theological need more than a juridical one, though that exists also, as we shall see. He animates and unifies a group gathered together by the love of Christ.

In apostolic institutes there is a third reason for the presence of authority. The apostolate is carried out by the mandate of the Church and in her name. An apostle does not act in his own name; he is sent. Obedience has in itself an apostolic and redemptive dimension since it was the path that Christ trod.

For the above reasons the Church considers authority to be essential to the existence of a religious institute.[5]

Here, then, we have the three principal ways in which authority serves the religious by enabling them to do what would otherwise be out of their power.

## 3. The service of the superior

Let us see how this takes place in a typical community today. But let us first see how a religious community comes into existence.

At the origin of an institute there is a person or a group in possession of a charism which attracts others, willing to be guided by the founder and to live in a manner agreed upon. If the founders are several, one personality usually stands out as the leader and his authority is accepted. The charism as such is not a source of authority but of a manner of life. At this stage the group is a private association directed by one who is at its head by the will of its members.

After a time the association wishes to become a religious institute and applies to the Pope or the bishop to establish it as such and approve the rules it has drawn up for itself. When this has in fact taken place, the institute becomes an ecclesial body and its authority becomes ecclesial authority, that is, exercised in the name of the Church and with the authority of the Church; its constitutions have the binding force of Church law; the Pope becomes its highest superior.[6]

The existence of the institute has two sources: the action of the founder, moved by the Holy Spirit, and the action of the hierarchy; its authority likewise comes from the will of the hierarchy, and from the will of the members inasmuch as they have been given a certain power of self-government which has been raised and elevated to an ecclesial character.[7]

The service of the superior is due to God, to the Church and to his brethren. He serves God by seeking His will in docility and loyalty to the Holy Spirit, using all the means at his disposal, in order to transmit it to his brethren. He serves the Church by obedience to its norms and directives, which remind him that his position is one of dependence and does not admit of an authoritarian attitude. Finally but very really, he serves those under his care.

The "rights and duties of superiors" is a phrase commonly used, but the duties of a superior far outweigh his rights, or rather, whatever rights he may have are given to him only to enable him to carry out his duties. The Pope is the Servant of the servants of God by the charity which sums up the life of one who lives for others.[8] A religious superior is different from one at the head of a family, a school, an army or any other group, even groups within the Church; he acts in the service of a charism.

## Social and juridical aspect

The Church has a threefold power: teaching, ministry and government or jurisdiction.

Exempt institutes share in the power of jurisdiction; others have what is called governing power (can. 501§1). *Cum admotae* gives the superiors general of pontifical clerical institutes the power of jurisdiction within their own institutes, with the faculty to subdelegate to other major superiors with the consent of their council.[9]

Governing power includes all the powers necessary for dealing with organisms, persons and property in view of the institute's end and aim. In law they are known as *normative* (to make rules), *executive* (to have them carried out), *judicial* (to decide disputed questions), *coercive* (to impose penalties) and *administrative* (to administer property). A religious superior has all the powers necessary to carry out his duties with regard to groups, persons and property. His ordinary power is contained in the office itself; he can have a vicar to act either in his absence or (like the vicar general of a diocese) without his absence; and he can delegate authority except in matters for which delegation is forbidden.

Not all superiors have these powers in the same measure, nor do they exercise them in the same manner. In the religious state there is no strict division of powers, though they are allocated according to the functions and rank of superiors. Normative power belongs chiefly to the general chapter; the task of a local superior is mainly executive. All this is set out in the constitutions of each institute, and in them, as well as in the general law of the Church, each superior will find the terms of his authority.

The general principle is given in can. 501: "Superiors and chapters, conformable to the constitutions and to the universal law, have governing power over their subjects, and in every exempt clerical institute they have ecclesiastical jurisdiction both in *foro interno* and in *foro externo.*" Can. 502 applies the principle to superiors general and other superiors: "The superior general has authority over all the provinces and houses and members of the institute, but he must exercise it as prescribed by the constitutions; the other superiors have authority within the limits of their charge."

Various degrees of authority are set out in the constitutions. Higher superiors deal with more general questions upon which the unity of the institute depends; those on the spot should be able to deal with concrete situations; they are not simply representatives of the higher superiors but receive their authority from canon law and the constitutions.[10] Higher superiors can act as guides and in certain cases intervene (e.g. at a canonical visitation) but they cannot take away or limit the authority of the local superior unless in exceptional cases and according to the norms of the law. Relations between superiors at different levels are of the greatest importance. As members of the same institute, they should work together in a sense of communion and mutual service.

The efficacy of authority does not depend on frequency of intervention—rather the contrary—or on the rigor and force of its action, but on the union with the will of God to which it leads. Like the rocket which puts the spaceship in orbit, it gives the right direction and then leaves the ship to pursue its course.

## Spiritual and pastoral

There is no dividing line between the juridical and the pastoral, which overlap and merge into one another.

Like the bishops in the Church, superiors should act by counsel, persuasion and example, but also by making rules when necessary, judging and regulating what concerns the life and action of the group. They have a right to give orders with binding force. The vow gives obedience a sacred and religious character but does not create or increase authority. Religious profession indicates voluntary acceptance of established authority for the sake of the kingdom.

A superior receives his mission from the Church and speaks in the name of the Church, but he is also the representative of the community and the Church usually leaves him free to act as such. He acts within the community and *with* the community, animating, moderating, pointing out mistakes, co-ordinating the actions of persons and groups and concerned also with each individual member, guiding, supporting, encouraging and helping all to live in communion with the will of God. The rights and duties of superiors are necessary means to attain the end—union with God; by his decisions he mediates the will of God to the religious.

## 4. Discussion and dialogue

The superior must work with the community to seek the will of God and plan its fulfillment in particular cases, taking an objective view of the situation and weighing the possibilities; later on will come an evaluation of what has actually been accomplished.

Dialogue does not take the place of authority but it helps it to work efficaciously and recognizes the co-responsibility of the community and the individual (ET 25).

Techniques for dialogue in a group have been worked out, but more important than any technique is the inward attitude, especially willingness to listen; something has been said of this in Chapter V above; all must be convinced that *all* have something to contribute (1 Cor 12:7-11). In general, the art of dialogue still needs much study, practice and good will; but provided the good will is there, as it usually will be, discussion in common is extremely valuable.[11] It enlightens the superior (who has to make the final decision) and shows him the lines along which the community thinks and the variety of tendencies; it enlightens those who will have to carry out the decision, and will do so with a greater sense of obligation after hearing the reasons for it. A consensus may be reached and ratified.

It should be remembered in passing that a superior cannot always give all his reasons, and all will admit this in principle. The fact is that for dialogue as for all mutual relations there must be trust on both sides. Everyone expects trust, needs trust and should deserve trust.

Furthermore, consultation of the community or council will only concern questions of a certain importance; it would be a waste of time and energy to use it for trivial matters. Nor can the whole responsibilty for community life be left to collegial discussion. Checks can be devised as a safeguard against arbitrary action, but a superior needs a certain freedom, especially for decisions concerning individuals, which will usually be dealt with in consultation with the person concerned.

When dialogue is between a superior and one person, the need for each to listen willingly is even greater than in a group. The need for mutual trust is greater also.[12] Tact and respect for the person opens the way to the ideal of authority as service; the superior should help the individual to unify his own life and his work. For no one does a superior make all the decisions; for each he should give the general lines within which the religious must make use of his own resources of nature and grace in docility to the Spirit.

Charity seeks the real good of each religious and collaborates with the Spirit in helping him to grow to full stature (Eph 4:13). He must therefore do his best to search out God's designs for this particular person; it is a matter of co-operation and of obtaining the willing consent of the one concerned. Between superior and individual there must be "unity of mind and heart." Only free and responsible action on the part of the religious enables the superior to act in spheres which involve certain personal rights. A particular point is the freedom to consult a priest when desired. Obviously the superior cannot intervene in matters of conscience.

The twofold function of a superior, administrative but above all spiritual and pastoral, will be more easily accepted by his community if it is framed in conduct which reflects the way in which God treats His children. The superior should be a replica of Jesus, the Good Shepherd, living and acting among his brothers. Personal holiness does not create authority, but it contributes greatly to its efficacy.

What *Renovationis causam* (32) says of the novice master among his novices is true of any religious superior. He must "try to build up a climate of confidence, docility and openness so as to guide their generosity toward a complete gift of themselves to the Lord in faith."

# 5. Superiors and Our Lady

Our Lady has been proclaimed Mother of the Church, and therefore Mother of the shepherds and Mother of their flocks.

In Paul VI's allocution to the Second Synod of Bishops, gathered in St. Mary Major on October 25, 1969, he recalled the relations between Our Lady and the Church and went on to speak of the special relation that exists between Mary and those members of the Church who carry out certain functions, particularly the service of pastoral guidance. "Mary," he said, "is our Mistress. She teaches us, who have the office of teaching the People of God, by doctrine and example"; and he gave details of what those in authority can learn from her.

Many years ago Pius XII presented Our Lady as an example to the superiors general of women's institutes, especially as a mother, and there are theological reasons for this as well as reasons of devotion.

Mary does not enter into the hierarchical order of the Church, but she does hold a position that raises her above every creature, makes her Queen of Apostles, and puts her at the center of the group that awaited the coming of the Holy Spirit in the Upper Room.

As a response to her "superiority" she declared herself the servant of the Lord, and hastened to express this in action by placing herself at the service of her cousin Elizabeth. Superiors who take her as their model will serve God, the Church and their brothers, and they will serve them well.

1. Allocution of 1-28-71. Mt 28:18-19; 18:18; 16:19; Lk 10:16; Jn 20:23; Cf. L. Laberthonnière, *La notion chrétiemme de l'autorité* (Paris, 1955).

2. The priority of the Church as *mystery* is shown in *Lumen gentium,* which treats of it in Ch. I, before dealing with the hierarchical constitution in Ch. III. Authority is treated in sociology simply as a social phenomenon, but we see it with other eyes.

The juridical content of authority is not fixed and permanent; it depends on concrete circumstances and can change with them.

3. A modern writer has said that the special role of authority is at the service of the charism which gathers the community together.

4. "He who has my commandments and keeps them, he it is who loves me" (Jn 14:21).

*Congregavit nos in unum Christi amor.*

5. The manner in which authority is allocated, organized and exercised is examined a little further on. It depends on many circumstances and on the character of the various institutes.

6. Cf. E. Gambari, *For Me To Live Is the Church* (Boston: St. Paul Editions, 1970), Part II, ch. V. In 1958, Pius XII told a group of superiors general (men) that he looked upon them as his associates in a special way and delegated to them a part of his sovereign jurisdiction.

7. The members cannot be considered a source of authority in the sense of having the power to give, withdraw or limit the powers of superiors without reference to the Church. Their authority, such as it is, comes from a certain power of self-government given to the institute by the Church.

The question is connected with the right of association within the Church (cf. Volume I, *Consecration and Service,* Boston: St. Paul Editions, 1973, ch. XXV, section 3).

8. Paul VI said (2-25-65), "There is no authority in the Church which is not a service."

In the Franciscan family the highest superior is called the Minister General, and St. Vincent de Paul gave to the one at the head of the Daughters of Charity the title of Sister Servant.

9. There is something priestly in the exercise of all authority. The task of the one in charge of a community of priests has a character of its own. Cf. E. Gambari, *Facoltà speciali dei Superiori Generali,* pp. 71-81.

10. By can. 209, the Church supplies for the lack of jurisdiction in cases of common error, when the person who acts is thought to possess powers which he has not in fact received.

11. Cf. A. M. Perrault, O.P., *Formazione e Dialogo alla luce del Concilio,* Centro Studi U.S.M.I., (Rome, 1967).

12. Distrust of authority may come from over-confidence in self, and that very fact will make it difficult to overcome.

# Chapter XIII
# The institute and its parts

## 1. The institute as an organism

The general elements of the religious state, the specific elements of a particular form of religious life, and the group of persons gathered together to live according to the same gift or charism with the sanction of the Church and by duly approved rules, make up a religious institute, Order or Congregation.

An institute is mainly thought of in terms of the people belonging to it, and therefore has a personal even more than an institutional character; although an organism, it constitutes a moral person and juridically it is a collegiate moral person. It possesses a life that is spiritual and interior as well as social and juridical, and a vital force inspiring its members with love of God and the brethren.[1] All the parts that go to make it up are similar organisms and groups of persons.

## Autonomous local communities

A religious institute or Order may take the form of a single community which fulfills its aims without being linked to other communities in a wider organism. Such are monasteries of nuns and each community of any Order composed of autonomous houses. The juridical term is a house *sui juris*, that is, self-governing, even if it forms part of a wider organization, provided it has a notable degree of self-government.[2] It is decentralized, its local independence being much greater than its dependence on any outside authority.

There may be spiritual and even juridical links between houses of the same Order, as happens with monasteries of Congregations or Orders of monks, or with monasteries of Federations of nuns. These links however, do not aggregate these groups into a higher organization, as this is not required by their nature and purpose. Further details on this question are given in Chapter IX.

## Centralized organization

More frequently the Order or Congregation is so structured that the institute forms a wide community divided into lesser groups strictly united among themselves and all sharing in the same charism; it is an organic whole of which every subdivision is a vital part.

It may be divided simply into houses, but when sufficiently numerous, houses may be gathered together to form provinces; the institute will thus in its own way reflect the hierarchical organization of the Church, divided into dioceses and subdivided into parishes.

At the head of each subdivision there is an authority subordinate to a higher authority, not merely in name but in fact, each having clearly marked functions, taking into account the principle of subsidiarity.

The purpose and aim of centralization, including, as it does, a central authority possessing real power, is not merely administrative efficiency, though efficiency should result from it; it is the safeguarding of a spiritual and apostolic unity linking the communities together as parts of a whole and expressing the ideal of the founder and of the Church which approved it. Provinces and houses should work together to carry out their vocation and mission for the general good of the Church; for this purpose their charism was granted, and their charism is one. It must not be lost sight of in a desire to update structures, for it is quite compatible with updating.

## Present-day tendencies

There is today a strong tendency toward decentralization, which gives greater powers to provinces and to local communities. Much is to be said for freedom to adapt rules and customs to different countries and regions, but in the revision of their constitutions some institutes have gone so far that it is not easy to see in what their centralization consists. The claim is made that spiritual unity is more important than administrative, and of course it is so; but if decentralization goes too far, an institute might lose its substantial unity and become simply a federation of groups or houses.

In the opposite direction there is a tendency to join forces for a common end, emphasizing points that unite rather than points that differentiate and divide. Society as a whole is feeling its way toward a stronger community spirit, and the fragmentation of religious communities could stand for the very opposite of updating religious life. The unity of religious institutes in the past has constituted a paradigm of efficient organization of forces in the service of the Church and remains a providential means of serving both Church and society.

# 2. The religious house and the local community

The religious house, as a group of persons united in brotherhood by spiritual, apostolic and juridical bonds, shows the common life actually being lived in its normal environment. Greater importance is attached to it than formerly. It offers its members most of the services which religious expect from the institute, and in it they carry out most of the obligations resulting from profession. Their lives are largely conditioned by the local community, for it is in everyday life that holiness is acquired and the apostolate put into practice. The principles of subsidiarity, co-responsibility and comparticipation find their best fulfillment in the local community.

It is therefore one of the most important fields for updating; no other can take its place or produce such good results (cf. ET 39-41). New forms of community are being sought, better adapted to modern psychology. Interpersonal relationships today require a new style and have created new needs which must be answered.

We remarked above that a religious institute is thought of mainly in terms of the people belonging to it. What has been said of religious life and of institutes is true in miniature of a local community; the fact that it is called a house has led to thinking and speaking of it as a place where religious live; but a community is not a place. It is a group of people[3] living "a shared life for the better service of Christ" (ET 39) in surroundings which help them to carry out their ideals. If those ideals are apostolic, then, though the new forms must in their own way be faithful to the common life, the structures will not be such as would be established exclusively for the contemplative life.

Ordinarily, a religious community is a group with a fixed residence, an organized way of life with a superior at the head, and a permanent function to carry out; it must also have due authorization for its establishment, but this need not, for validity, be given in writing. If one of these features is lacking, it does not constitute a religious house.

In special circumstances, however, especially in mission countries, a group of religious within a specified territory may be considered a community even if they live alone or in twos and threes, provided they have a superior at the head of them all.[4]

A religious house in its juridical aspect has certain rights and duties toward the Church and the institute which are set out in Church law and the constitutions.

It is assumed that it possesses a certain stability and autonomy in a sphere of action responding to its specific aim, such as the apostolate or formation. A minimum of three religious is required, but normally there should be a sufficient number to lead a real community life, and a common purpose or interest that brings them together, not only materially but also spiritually.[5] This is perfectly compatible with a diversity of occupations which is not only necessary but desirable.

A *regular* house is one belonging to an Order. A *formed* house must have at least six religious; in a clerical institute, at least four must be priests; a house *sui juris* is autonomous[6]; a *branch* house is one that does not exist independently but forms part of a larger community, as, for instance, a holiday house or one in charge of a school or hospital; at the head of it is not a superior but a delegate.

Various terms are used in constitutions: e.g., monastery, priory or convent for a religious house; residence, hospice or mission for a subordinate one. Sometimes there is simply a group of religious trying out a particular work or way of life in view of a foundation; these include what are known as *experimental communities* in search of new forms and structures.[7]

The opening and closing of religious houses is a matter which concerns the Church and the diocese and is therefore dealt with in canon law.[8] Until recently the permission of the Holy See was required for the opening or closing of an exempt house, as well as the written consent of the local Ordinary; this is still the case for monasteries *sui juris* of contemplative nuns, but by a Decree of the S. Congregation for Religious and Secular Institutes, dated June 4, 1970, for all other houses the consent of the local Ordinary is sufficient. To open a house in the territories under the S. Congregation for Evangelization, the consent of that Department must be obtained.[9]

A branch establishment such as a school or hospital may be opened with the permission of the Ordinary (can. 497 §3); no permission is required for enlarging an existing house or taking on new work, unless stated otherwise in the authorization to open the house. That authorization, unless it states otherwise, implies permission to carry on the institute's usual work; for a clerical institute it includes the right to have a church or public chapel and to carry on the priestly ministry.

A diocesan congregation wishing to open a house for the first time in another diocese must have the consent of both bishops, the Ordinary of the place where the motherhouse is situated, and the Ordinary of the place where it is desired to make a foundation (can. 495 § 1); the canon adds, however, that permission should not be refused without a grave reason, and thus emphasizes the fact that even a diocesan congregation is by its nature universal and destined to extend beyond its own diocese.

The closing of a religious house always strikes people as a piece of sad news, whereas the opening is joyous. It may be that the reasons for closing it are really sad and regrettable for the Church, such as the lack of vocations. There may also be other good reasons, but before deciding to close a house or some particular work, superiors should bear in mind the duty to aid and support local churches; the consent of the Ordinary is required by law, except for the exempt communities. Bishops, for their part, should show sympathetic understanding of the needs and difficulties of the institute and remember their co-responsibility for the good of the Church as a whole. Straight-forward and friendly discussion should lead to agreement.[10] A house belonging to a diocesan institute can be closed by the Ordinary after discussing it with the superior general, but if it is the only house and closing it means suppressing the institute, the permission of the Holy See is required.[11]

To change the use of a house to something not provided for in its foundation requires the same authorization as the opening of a new house, unless it is a matter of organization within the institute, such as transferring the juniorate to the novitiate house. Changing one form of apostolic activity for another is a question for agreement with the local bishop.

Other conditions and formalities concerning the opening, closing or changing the use of houses are laid down in the constitutions. Hitherto it has usually been a matter for the central government, which either decides, on the recommendation of the provincial government, or simply confirms a decision taken by the latter.

A religious house in an apostolic institute is frequently the place where the apostolate is carried on; the school, the clinic, the refuge is identified with the convent, because the work enters substantially into the religious life and forms part of it. This is why the opening of a house implies permission to carry on its work.

Proposals are made nowadays for complete separation between the religious life and the work, not only by a separate dwelling-place but juridically and financially, responsibility being handed over to others, to whom the religious lend their services under contract. Preoccupation with money matters, in this view, is considered unsuitable for religious.

Such a system may be suitable in particular places or circumstances, but not universally; the fusion of community and work may be required for the efficacy of some kinds of apostolate.

Another proposal is limited to having a separate dwelling-place. This may be partly in view of ensuring a quiet place to which religious can go after working-hours, but basically both proposals stem from a desire for more radical poverty. *Perfectae caritatis* lays it down that religious institutes have a right to possess "all that is necessary for their daily life and work," but some would like to reduce the notion of "necessary" to a minimum.

## 3. Small communities

The desire for a more intense experience of the benefits of community life is at the heart of a strong movement toward the setting up of houses composed of a rather small number of religious and toward the organization of larger communities into little sub-groups.

It is maintained that real fraternity is possible only when the group is small enough to favor truly personal relations among all the members, as well as mutual spiritual and apostolic support. Each member will find in the group an aid to the integration and development of his own personality.

In a large community it is rather easy to remain isolated. Individuals, whether through their own fault or that of others, really never become vital parts of the group. In order to avoid this kind of individualism, it is being proposed that communities should be organized not just with a view to the apostolic work to be done, as in industry, but that the number and choice of the members should take into account the needs of single persons and of the group itself. It is further suggested that large communities can give the impression that they are primarily administrative organizations, and can be associated with the idea of material comfort and worldly power.

Still another reason given for avoiding large houses is that their buildings, their daily order, and even the locations in which they are found, bring about a separation from their human environments, and from the way of living of the common people. This can be avoided, it is said, by establishing family-size groups which will be open to others and which are thus more able to express the mystery of the Church in both its personal and communitarian dimensions.

The arguments given do have their cogency and they explain the phenomenon of small communities, called fraternities, which characterizes some recently founded institutes like the Little Brothers and Little Sisters of Jesus. The reasons cited are also at the base of many attempts to find a new expression of monastic life. Very many communities are facing the problem right now of how to convert large communities into small communities, or how to organize the existing houses into small sub-groups.

This, of course, is a question of renewal which has to be studied in each institute. The study, however, and the solutions adopted, should take into account the needs of religious life itself, the characteristic form of the single institute, the good of the apostolate, and the requirements of the general legislation laid down for religious.

In evaluating the whole movement toward small communities, many questions and difficulties arise from the fact that some of these experiments have been linked to other doubtful innovations. Some of these are: an absence of real authority in the group, a lack of any order in the daily life, an economic set-up which prescinds from the vow of poverty, an undesirable way of making up the group. Cardinal Antoniutti has observed that when small communities represent reactions of independence and secularization which are not in harmony with poverty and obedience, they cannot be approved.[12]

This does not mean that religious life cannot be lived in a framework and style different from that to which we have been accustomed. But religious life must remain. There must be some minimum, at least, of the dependence, the poverty, the common exercises, and the separation from non-religious which should characterize a religious institute. In the matter of government, it is necessary that there be some authority which is not merely collegial. Even if he does not live constantly with the little group, there should be a personal superior. Furthermore the provincial or general superior should be concerned with the make-up and working of the group. More or less spontaneous groupings are not enough; a mere likeness in ideas is not sufficient to guarantee the stability of even a small house. Much, of course, will depend on the charism of the institute and on the goal envisioned by the group.

In all of this, moreover, it seems only fair to say that we ought not to exaggerate the difficulties of true communitarian life in large houses, provided that all have good will and use the means that are at hand to realize a family spirit and mutual aid and friendship. In a world as pluriform as ours, differences in age, culture, taste, and profession can be very positive factors, and experience has shown that groups characterized by such heterogeneity can be even more stable.

This balanced attitude toward both kinds of groupings is well illustrated by Pope Paul, who pointed out in 1969, that he had known of regular admirable small communities in Milan, which were "living lamps" for the people of the city.[13] In the same talk he voiced some apprehension about other small communities whose discipline, or lack of it, seemed to constitute an impoverishment of religious life. In his recent Exhortation he returned to this theme, recognizing the reasons which justify the creation of smaller communities, but noting that such groupings, far from presenting an easier form of life, are actually more demanding. At the same time he asserted that large communities are particularly suitable for many religious.

# 4. The province

The province is an intermediary structure between the central government and the local community; it becomes necessary when communities are too numerous and widespread for a central government to deal with them individually. The movement toward decentralization, the principle of subsidiarity, and the need for flexibility in action were reasons basic to the division of the institutes into provinces.[14]

Although an organic part of the institute, the province has a personality of its own, spiritual and apostolic; it is by no means simply a juridical subdivision. This is particularly evident when it represents a particular language or culture. Its basis is usually territorial, but may be partly personal, consisting of religious occupied in some specific work; and it may possess a house or houses outside its own territory, as, for example, a financial center for a mission or a newly opened house in a territory for which no province yet exists.[15]

The personality of the province is made up by the individual houses contained in it, each with its own individuality; and the provinces together make up the institute. Juridically, each has a certain autonomy, and a superior acts in his or her own name, though in dependence on the central government.

It is normal for a province to be mainly self-sufficing as regards persons, works, government and finance. On particular points the constitutions will give more detail; experience has shown that it is advisable to leave a certain liberty and flexibility for dealing with the concrete circumstances which led to the formation of a province.

There is a rich variety in the organization of provinces in the religious Orders and Congregations, and this allows for their effective adaptation to the concrete needs of each institute.

Division into provinces may become necessary as time goes on; it will then be a question for the general chapter to examine, taking into consideration all local needs and circumstances. The present-day tendency to decentralization will be against waiting too long, but the problem must be studied objectively. Houses or regions not yet in a condition to form a province may be provided for in some other way. It is always possible that direct dependence on the central government will best fulfill the purpose of certain houses (e.g., houses of formation which serve the whole institute), but there should be a serious reason for it.[16] In general, the Holy See prefers that any division into provinces should apply to the whole institute. The first time it occurs, it must be approved by the Holy See, but subsequent changes can be made by the proper authority of the institute, including the formation of new provinces and the subdivision or suppression of existing ones.[17] If, however, it were desired to suppress all division of the institute into provinces, the permission of the Holy See would be required.

In some institutes provinces with common interests and problems and speaking a common tongue are united to form groups within the same region; there are obvious advantages in this. At times these groups of provinces play a special part in the structure of the institute and the representation of the different regions at the general chapter or the organization of the central government, or both.

Membership of the province is a matter regulated by the constitutions, as also the rights it confers. Normally, a religious belongs to the province in which he makes profession. In many women's institutes the superior general designates the province after the first profession or when the time comes to embark upon apostolic work. In some centralized institutes, temporary or permanent transfer from one province to another can be authorized or imposed by the central government; when the institute is less centralized, the link with the province is stronger. When a province is divided or a new one erected, the religious may be allowed to choose which they will belong to, or it may be assumed that they are divided according to nationality or according to the house in which they are working.

## 5. Organisms similar to provinces

Various terms are used to describe divisions of an institute alongside its provinces or when it is not divided into provinces; such are: vice-province, quasi-province, provincial vicariate, commissariat or district.

Those at the head of these groups are considered to be major superiors and they possess ordinary powers exercised either in their own names or in the name of the one whom they represent as vicar.[18] The groups themselves may be dependent on the central government, in which case they have practically the same function as a province, or they may depend on a province and have a superior who represents the provincial.

The motive for setting up such organisms is frequently a matter of national or cultural prestige, which calls for the more responsible authority on the spot and less dependence on superiors living at a distance and in different surroundings.

A group of houses or communities may have a superior who in practice acts as a major superior but with delegated power only, that is, such power as the major superior chooses to give him; such a group is called a regional delegation. Some institutes, on the other hand, give ordinary power to the superior even though only as vicar, and the organism is then similar to a province, with representation at the general chapter.[19]

These groups of various kinds are not provided for by canon law, but the fact that they exist indicates that they fulfill a need. Sometimes the constitutions do not even mention them, and institutes have set them up on lines that meet their purpose. By analogy it may be said that since can. 488 speaks of superiors equivalent in their powers to provincials, it implicitly allows for groups similar to provinces.

## 6. Relations between the houses and provinces of an institute

A religious institute is a vital whole, theological and spiritual, and each of its parts has this same character; together they form a living organism expressing the ideal of their founder.[20]

The juridical and administrative forms which are a practical necessity are at the service of spiritual unity and communion of life. Elsewhere we have quoted the remark: "The special role of authority is at the service of the charism which gathers the community together," and the sharing of the charism leads the local community to broaden its horizons and take into its life the life of the province and of the whole institute. Nor will the sharing be spiritual only; *Perfectae caritatis* reminds us that temporal goods should be generously shared with houses or provinces in need.

Decentralization will not harm unity if the bond of a common spiritual patrimony is given its true value. Better knowledge of the founder and his first inspiration, the spirituality, vocation and mission of his religious family, spread among the provinces and houses and strengthened by meetings and personal contacts, will bring about union and unity in mind, heart and work.

1. The Capuchins, in their constitutions of 1969, define their Order as an organism which unites the friars in the imitation of Christ, so that in the diversity of tasks and services they contribute to the building up of the Church in charity.

2. The law does not lay down any minimum of self-government necessary for the use of the term *sui juris*.

3. This is taken into account in the changes introduced for the novitiate by *Renovationis causam* and for the seminary by *Ratio fundamentalis institutionis sacerdotalis*.

4. The same system has been provided for elsewhere, especially for sisters working in different schools. Emphasizing the personal aspect of a community as a group of religious allows for much greater mobility. Even those working in isolation can enjoy some of the benefits of community life.

5. Community life means living and working together, and the number of persons should make reasonable allowance for this; its primary purpose is not ascetical self-denial and sacrifice, but the living of a fuller life.

6. Houses *sui juris* are to be found in certain women's institutes with simple vows, such as the Sisters of Mercy and Sisters of the Presentation. Many of them have joined to form a religious Congregation with a superior general.

7. The term *experimental communities* is used for various types such as a group without a superior; a group formed by co-opting its members; a group living in a house or flat among seculars, or admitting secular members or members of other religious institutes. Some go so far as to eliminate all structures and form what cannot even be called a religious community.

8. The former stipulation that a house might not be opened without a guaranteed means of financial support is no longer to the purpose in our day. Some people would even prefer a religious family to rely on the same means of support as a family in the world.

9. That is, a house in the canonical sense, not a branch house.

10. It would seem reasonable that agreement after consultation and discussion should be required for the closing of diocesan houses also. It hardly seems equitable that a bishop can persist in refusing to close a house when the institute has urgent reasons for doing so. If no agreement can be reached, recourse might be had to the Holy See.

11. The canons concerning erection and suppression of houses and provinces are 492-496; can. 1162 § 4 concerns churches and public oratories.

12. Letter, November 24, 1969.

13. Message to Superiors General, Rome, November 22, 1969.

14. Provinces in the strict sense do not exist in the monastic Orders; their Congregations do not fulfill the same function.

15. If possible, it is better to avoid having more than one province occupying the same territory.

16. Members of such houses sometimes send a representative to the general chapter. In some institutes they retain active and passive voice in their respective provinces.

17. Cf. Decree of June 4, 1970, referred to above. The S. Congregation has always considered three houses as the minimum number for constituting a province; the minimum number of religious varies according to the constitutions.

18. A superior with ordinary powers usually has the right to represent the institute with the ecclesiastical or civil authorities and to be a member of the Assembly of major superiors.

19. A vice-province or quasi-province is practically equivalent to a province, but sends fewer delegates to the general chapter.

20. The theological, charismatic and spiritual content of the common life is examined in Chapter V.

# Chapter XIV
# Organs of government and collaboration

## 1. Functions and responsibilities

The service of government is a carefully organized whole. Like the human body it has its members and parts, and their combined action is fused and welded together for the benefit of all. Each has its place and each its distinct function.

The structures that go to make up the institute follow the same pattern; each is a body, and since a body needs a head with its specific function, there is someone — either a person or a group — at the head of each part.

For the whole institute the highest authority is the general chapter, and when no chapter is in session, the superior general, aided by a council; in a province and in a community there is a superior similarly aided. In addition there will be persons and groups to carry out various tasks — e.g., commissions, secretariats, consultative bodies, those who engage in research, dialogue, communication and execution — but these do not exercise authority; neither do the religious who directly or indirectly share in decision-making by means of votes, consultation, proposals and dialogue. The part they play is active and important, but not the same as the task of those in charge.

## 2. Chapters [1]

### Nature and functions

The chapter is an authoritative body, collegial in nature, that is, a group whose members have equal power; it may be general, provincial or local; the assembly of the local community is called a chapter when it meets for elections or has the power to make decisions. [2]

A *chapter of elections* is what its name implies; a *chapter of affairs* deals with other matters concerning the institute; it is *ordinary* when held at the time and for the purpose provided for, as, for example, a vacancy in the office of superior general, for which the chapter must elect a successor; it is *extraordinary* in any other case. [3]

The frequency is determined by the period for which the offices are held, which are filled by chapter elections; intermediate chapters are often provided for also, and the tendency is to greater frequency. [4] A certain latitude is usually allowed, so that a chapter may meet from three to six months earlier or later than the date foreseen, with, if necessary, a consequent shortening or lengthening of periods in office.

The chapter's special task is to provide for the general good of the institute or province, encourage and increase its spiritual and apostolic vitality, and work in the spirit of its charism to ensure unity and constant renewal in structures and members.

The importance attached today to collegiality and co-responsibility means that greater importance is given to chapters; the provincial chapter plays a more effective part in the life of the province and often elects the members of the provincial government.

Chapters, according to can. 501 § 1, possess dominative power, and in clerical institutes the power of jurisdiction also; they are, in fact, superiors.

The general chapter is the highest authority in the institute and acts according to the constitutions; it makes rules, decides matters of prime importance and elects the principal members of the central government. [5]

Chapters of elections and chapters of affairs have the same powers; a chapter of affairs, once it is assembled, can transform itself into a chapter of elections if, through resignation or for any other reason, an office falls vacant which it is the chapter's duty to fill.

Questions concerning the constitutions or other general codes of rules in the institute are reserved to the general chapter, as also any problems considered important for the life and unity of the institute itself.

It is sometimes said that the general chapter is the highest *extraordinary* authority, because neither the general nor the provincial chapter is stable or permanent but meets only at certain times and for as long as is necessary.[6]

The work of renewal has given chapters a better knowledge of their duties and powers, particularly as an expression of the interest of all religious in the good of the institute. Within the limits laid down by the constitutions, chapters have authority over superiors, who are bound to carry out their decisions.

While the general or provincial chapter is in session, the work of the institute is carried on as usual, but from the time of its convocation no changes or transfers of personnel may be made which might affect its composition.

Decisions made by a chapter remain in force until the following chapter, unless it is otherwise stated.

## Composition

The chapter should be a full and complete expression of the community; the general chapter is supposed to represent the whole institute and the provincial chapter, the whole province, not only juridically but objectively expressing its thoughts and its wishes. The choice of its members is therefore a matter in which all the religious should effectively take part (cf. PC 14,4; ES II, 18). If an institute were small enough, all its members might take part in the chapter itself, which would then resemble the local chapter of a monastery *sui juris* formed by the assembly of all its members.

It follows that the election of delegates to the general chapter should take place on the widest possible basis; all the religious who have made perpetual vows should have active voice.[7]

The general chapter, however, has a right to lay down conditions for active and passive voice; the reasons for limitation should be well founded. Some institutes give it only to religious professed for a certain number of years; others refuse it to those who have applied for secularization or exclaustration, or who have obtained leave of absence for personal reasons.

Implicitly, the Council wishes the number of capitulars chosen by the religious to be sufficient to make their weight felt in decisions; there should be a certain proportion between the number of *ex officio* members and of those elected. In some institutes the elected members must be more numerous than those who attend by right. It should be remembered, however, that even those who attend by right are there partly by a general wish, since the religious now have a more active share in the choice of officials at different levels.

The tendency today is to limit the number of *ex officio* members, especially if attendance is looked upon as a privilege or reward for past services, as for example, those who have been superior general; but it would be imprudent to exclude, on principle, the category of members who attend by right of occupying certain posts; their experience can be of value to the assembly.

It is most important that the chapter should not appear to be divided into two blocks with conflicting interests: representatives of those in authority and representatives of "the others." There must be no *them* and *us*, but a body entirely concerned with the real good of the whole institute.

The choice of delegates is therefore a great responsibility; it is an effective participation in the elections and other acts of the chapter. A delegate, however, does not go simply to speak in the name of those who elected him; he must bear their wishes in mind, but, like every capitular, he must seek the good of the institute according to his own convictions.

A most important principle to bear in mind is that representation has a qualitative as well as a quantitative aspect.[8] As far as possible, the choice of well-qualified persons should be ensured, as well as the true interests of the institute and of the province, of different categories of persons and occupations and different geographical regions. Various systems exist, providing opportunity for the expression of different points of view without being dominated by one extreme or the other.

The systems most commonly used are the following:
— election by houses and groups of houses on a numerical basis of members;
— division into groups by age or length of profession, to ensure reciprocal knowledge and representation of those viewpoints;
— groups according to occupations, so that all kinds of work and apostolate have a place in the chapter;
— a single list of all those who have passive voice, from which each one chooses the number of delegates required;
— a fusion of two systems, single list and groups; after the election of delegates by groups, the remaining delegates are elected from the single list;
— election by two stages: each religious first sends in a list of those considered to be suitable as delegates; from among those named, the actual election is made.

Election of the delegation is followed by election of substitutes for those who are unable to attend the chapter. Institutes have great freedom to regulate the composition and manner of selecting the members of their chapters, and the constitutions may give a general chapter the right to fix the conditions for future chapters.

The following points are commonly observed.

If the institute is divided into provinces, the general chapter consists of the members of the central government,[9] together with superiors and delegates of the provinces; there are usually two delegates from a province and one from any similar organism, but there may be more than two from larger provinces, without strictly proportional representation; the latter might give undue power to a single very large province.[10]

The constitutions may allow the chapter to add persons of special competence in some sphere, but very few; it can always invite other religious to speak as experts or to be present as observers. Some institutes allow all who wish it to attend as observers.

Provincial chapters, or the general chapter of an institute not divided into provinces, are organized in the same way. When delegates to a provincial chapter are elected in the communities, the number of them may vary with the size of the community.

## Procedure

*In general*

In can. 101 § 1, we find the rule concerning the acts of collegiate moral entities: a decision requires an absolute majority; if two scrutinies do not give an absolute majority, in the third, a relative majority suffices.

The absolute majority consists of more than half the votes; it is commonly said that it requires half the votes plus one, but in fact if the total is an uneven number, it can be less; for instance, out of a total of 19, 10 would constitute an absolute majority.

If the votes are evenly divided the president has a casting vote; in the case of elections, if the president does not wish to use his right, the senior of those with an equal number of votes — that is, senior by ordination, religious profession or age — is deemed to be elected.

By jurisprudence and the practice of the Holy See, constitutions do not give the president a casting vote in the case of elections; it is laid down that when votes are equally divided, seniority by ordination, profession or age is the deciding factor. Constitutions may, however, adopt other criteria.

*Elections*

The canons concerning elections (162-178) should be observed by religious unless — as is usually the case — their constitutions give rules for them.

The main points of canon law are as follows: for the chapter to take action its members must assemble; those who are absent have no right to vote; if, however, they are in the house, the tellers will go to collect their votes.[11]

Some institutes allow voting by proxy if the proxy is a member of the chapter.

Constitutions usually require the presence of two-thirds of the capitulars. No one may vote for himself. In order to be valid, votes must be free, secret, certain and unconditional (can. 169).

A president and two tellers supervise the voting after swearing to fidelity and secrecy. The votes are then counted; if the number is correct[12] the voting papers are opened, the results announced and the papers burned; the secretary writes a complete report of the proceedings.

The person who receives the majority of votes as required by can. 101 § 1 is considered to be elected unless the constitutions say otherwise. As soon as the election is accepted he acquires all the rights belonging to his office.

# Preparation

For efficacious work, a chapter needs careful preparation in the form of questionnaires, inquiries and research; pre-capitular study commissions awaken the interest of all members of the institute and obtain positive contributions.

Preparation for the chapter includes its convocation and all the action that precedes it in provinces and houses. The convocation of a general chapter falls to the superior general or the person taking his place. Choice of the meeting-place usually requires the consent of the council.

The efficacy of the work done depends to a great extent on the rules of procedure; the chapter should be free to draw up its own plan of work, and decide, for instance, at what point the elections should be held. Some institutes have introduced the practice of allowing it to choose its own president, thus emphasizing the equality of all; others have a council of presidency, or a group of moderators who preside at the meetings; greater freedom is felt when it is not the superior who presides. On these different points many institutes have profited by the experience gained in their special general chapters.

# 3. Superiors

The term *superior* is used for the religious at the head of one of the organisms we have just described; in a strictly juridical sense he must be a single person endowed with authority, and the organism must be an entity complete in itself; a novice master is not a superior; nor is a councillor at any level; nor is a delegate or a vicar, except when he is acting as substitute for the superior.

The powers and duties of superiors are laid down in Church law and in constitutions (can. 488,8; 501-516); three levels are distinguished: general, provincial and local; major superiors are the superior general (sometimes called the moderator), the provincial or anyone holding an equivalent office, and the superior (man or woman) of a monastery or house *sui juris*.

The titles given to superiors are varied: abbot, minister, guardian, president, animator, co-ordinator, *responsible* or *responsabile* in French and Italian. Nowadays the actual word *superior* is disliked by many, including many superiors themselves, because it implies inferiority in other religious. It is not easy to find an English term that gives general satisfaction, and, in fact, it is not the term that is important but the function. Avoidance of the word means, for some people, that they would like to suppress the function.

The function of a personal superior exercising real authority is required by Church law and by the nature of a religious community. It may be variously defined in different institutes; it must allow for the recently introduced practice of consultation and other principles laid down by Vatican II, which are intended to guard against the two extremes of authoritarianism and the mere carrying out of decisions made by a chapter or a council; but its personal nature cannot be suppressed. The guidance of the community and the guidance of individuals, the making of final decisions for everything after community dialogue, the spiritual influence in the service of the charism—all this cannot be entrusted entirely to a group of persons; the function of a superior can only be adapted to its purpose by the action of a single person, whether man or woman. All that has been said in the preceding chapters of this book on the institute and its organization fits in with this statement, which was reaffirmed by the Decree of 2-2-72.

# Designation

Superiors may be designated by election or appointment, or a combination of the two through consultation, presentation or confirmation; various methods of giving the. religious a voice in the appointment can be used.

The superior general is always elected by a general chapter[13] and the election requires no confirmation or intervention by other authorities.[14] In the Orders, and more and more frequently in institutes with simple vows, the provincial superior is elected by the provincial chapter. The central government usually intervenes either by confirmation after the election or by approving a list of names to choose from.

Even if it is often no more than a symbolic act, it seems desirable that in centralized Orders or Congregations the superior general should intervene in the election of a provincial, either by previous approbation or by subsequent confirmation. The intervention of the general government expresses the unity of the institute. There is at present no law making it obligatory. When the central government appoints the provincial, the province intervenes either by the presentation of names or by previous consultation. Presentation in the strict sense obliges those who make the appointment to choose from the names sent in; consultation has no binding force, but should be taken into consideration.

In centralized institutes the local superior is usually appointed by the provincial government with or without confirmation by the central government; he may also be appointed by the central government, with presentation or at least consultation of the provincial government. In institutes not divided into provinces, local superiors are usually appointed by the superior general with the consent of his council. In some institutes, especially for reappointment of the superior actually in office, the community itself is consulted.

In monasteries and houses *sui juris*, superiors are elected.[15] In some Orders local superiors are elected by the provincial chapter. Election by a local community is a rare exception.

In centralized institutes, where general needs have to be considered, the election of local superiors by individual houses does not seem a good method. A general consultation asking for the names of any religious who appear suitable for the office of superior may be profitable, and it is sometimes done.

*Postulation* is the name given to the election of a person not considered eligible by canon law, as, for example, not being of the required age; there are special norms distinguishing it from an ordinary election (cf. can. 169-182) and it has no force until it is confirmed by a higher authority.

Postulation requires two-thirds of the votes. If, after two scrutinies, this is not obtained, the practice of the Holy See is that the postulation cannot proceed and everything starts afresh. The reason for this is that in a third scrutiny, if the postulated person drops out, the relative majority might go to some other religious with comparatively few votes and not represent the real wish of the chapter.

The most frequent case of postulation is the re-election of a superior general whose legitimate term of office has expired. Can. 507 § 3 says it is extraordinary and may only be used if the constitutions provide for it or do not forbid it. In general, the holding of an office for too long a time is disapproved.

The provincial is sometimes elected not by the chapter but by all the members of the province, in the same manner as the election of delegates to chapters.

## Requirements

Certain conditions are laid down by Church law for holding the office of superior, including a minimum age.[16] As an experiment, the Decree of the S.C. for Religious, of 6-4-70, lowered the requisite age for a superior general to 35 years and for other major superiors to 30; it suspended the condition of legitimacy except in certain cases, and even for these, dispensations are easily granted.

Constitutions can fix their own conditions and requirements for the office of superior, but far more important than juridical requirements are the spiritual and moral qualities enabling a superior to carry out his task today, which is more pastoral than authoritative. In particular he needs a capacity for dialogue and collaboration, which imply some knowledge of psychology, and he must know how to take on his own responsibilities.

## Term of office

The superior's term of office is fixed by the constitutions, and the present tendency is to discourage prolongation and provide for more frequent change. Superiors are now very rarely elected or appointed for life.[17] Six years is a usual period for a superior general, with possibility of a second term; beyond that, in women's institutes postulation is required and must be justified by serious reasons; repeated re-election would end by being in office in perpetuity. Provincials, on the other hand, after a six-year or three-year term, are sometimes repeatedly re-elected.

Perpetuity is provided for by the constitutions of certain Orders and Congregations, most frequently for abbots, abbesses or other superiors of monasteries; also for some superiors general, including the Jesuits and the Premonstratensions; others have recently given it up.[18]

Local superiors may not be appointed for more than three years (can. 505) with the possibility of a second term but not for a third in the same house. The rescript *Cum admotae* and the decree *Religionum laicalium* authorize superiors general to allow a third term after consulting the local bishop.

In former times it was common for local superiors to remain in office for long periods and even for life. The reaction of many women's institutes today is to be more rigid than canon law and to forbid repeated reappointments of the same person even in different houses, without at least an interval out of office. It is true that being in office for too long can produce a disposition to look on the power to command as a personal right, and it can bring about some loss of sensitiveness to the needs of others and to community thinking. On the other hand it does seem more prudent not to adopt absolute norms here, but to foresee some exceptions, while also taking care that there be some rotation — which is the best means of preventing eventual abases and of making all feel that they share in providing for the common good.

A superior's office terminates at the end of the period for which it was conferred, but the normal practice is that he remains in office until a successor takes over his duties; there is no period of vacancy. The office may also terminate by resignation, transfer or deposition. Resignation does not take effect until it is accepted by the one who made the appointment or by a higher authority. The resignation of a superior general can only be accepted by the Holy See or by a general chapter.[19] Transfer by appointment to another office incompatible with the first implies the cessation of the first; the good of the institute may justify it. Deposition requires serious and valid reasons. Can. 560, which says that a novice master may not be removed from his charge without a just and grave cause, may be applied to superiors; respect for the person and the stability provided for in the constitutions alike forbid deposition without proportionate reasons.[20]

# Formation

The formation of superiors presents an urgent, important and difficult problem; it might well be said very urgent, very important and very difficult.

Institutes have great need of good superiors; the fate of communities and their members depends on them to a large extent, and at this time their task is particularly difficult and calls for uncommon gifts of guidance. Renewal in religious life demands renewal in those responsible; its adaptation depends on adaptation in superiors. They must study and assimilate the doctrine and spirit of Vatican II; updating of constitutions and other texts will serve no purpose unless it is put into effect; and yet any precise directions or suggestions for the preparation of superiors cannot easily be found. The best way of preparing for responsibility remains the time-honored one of giving it by degrees, and (more than formerly) encouraging a spirit of initiative.

Superiors actually in office need special help. They need—and do not always have—a space of time reserved for reading and reflection. Community meetings and dialogue with the religious will be helpful to them. Contacts with other superiors and discussion with major superiors serve a very useful purpose. Courses and retreats for groups of superiors or of others in responsible positions, with opportunities for exchange of ideas, can be extremely helpful; even in the juniorate, distant preparation can be given in the shape of a certain modest exercise of responsibility and explanation of what it implies. To all religious superiors may be applied what is said on these points in *Perfectae caritatis* 18,4 and in *Ratio fundamentalis institutionis sacerdotalis* 30,2.

### Duties

The main duty of a superior is to be in touch with his own religious, a local superior in the community and a provincial habitually in his province; the superior general should keep in contact with the provinces, the houses and the religious.

Regular visiting of the houses by major superiors has lost none of its value, though it has become much simpler and more familiar than the former canonical visitation and the word *canonical* has tacitly been dropped.

Contact with the hierarchy is part of a superior's duty, especially with the Holy See through its Decrees and Acts (can. 503 § 1).

## 4. Councils and councilors

As far back as the time of St. Benedict, the value and necessity of a council in the living of religious life was seen and understood.[21] A council is an aid, a guarantee and a brake on the action of superiors, and signifies com-participation and co-responsibility in the functions of guidance.

In the government of the Church the College of Cardinals acts as a council for the Pope, and the Chapter or a group of ecclesiastics for the bishop. Vatican II and post-conciliar documents have extended the principle by setting up the Synod of Bishops,[22] clergy and pastoral councils, and other groups for the study of problems by representatives of those interested. The function of councils in the Church today often goes beyond what their name implies.

The general law of the Church says that religious superiors, general, provincial and local—at least in formal houses—must have councilors; the nature and functions of such councils and councilors are shown in constitutions and in the practice of the Holy See; they vary from one institute to another in their duties as governing bodies, collaborators or simply consultative and advisory bodies, but a religious institute has its own way of governing, especially by the principles of collegiality and participation, and its councils differ from other ecclesiastical councils. The council might act collegially more often, but the superior must have a sphere of action in which he can use his authority for the good of the institute; if he has no power to act alone, he cannot be considered a superior.

The general council is usually composed of the superior general as president and a fixed number of councilors; the president is a member of the council and votes like the others.[23] In some institutes the general chapter can increase or diminish the number of general councilors, and in some, the central government or the provincial chapter can decide on the number of provincial councilors. The full council including the president should be an uneven number, to avoid the inconvenience of equally divided votes.

A full council is the term used when all the members are present; it is usually required for the making of appointments to offices or other important matters.

More frequently than in the past, an *extraordinary* general or provincial council has been introduced to treat of particularly important questions; it meets more rarely than the permanent ordinary council to which, for this purpose, other members are added, some *ex officio*, who hold important posts, and others chosen for the purpose; all come from different parts of the institute or the province, so as to collect a variety of opinions. Its powers of deliberative voting should be limited, but as a consultative body and a source of information it is very valuable.

Some institutes have introduced, instead of an enlarged council, a deliberative body more like a chapter in permanent session; in fact, as a council can act collegially, it will not always be easy to say whether this new body is a council or a reduced form of chapter. Other institutes are experimenting with different councils or deliberative and consultative groups to deal with different categories of affairs: one for the destination of persons, one for the acceptance and guidance of apostolic work, and so on.

The local council in small houses and sometimes in larger ones consists of all the members of the community and is the same thing as the local chapter. This does not appear to be contrary to canon law, which does not fix the number of councilors, and it seems a good thing to interest the whole community in the affairs of the house. It is another question whether all the purposes of a council can be fulfilled by one of this kind; there are matters which of their nature are confidential and should be known only to a few; many institutes therefore provide for a small council with two or four members to deal with certain important questions, in addition to the council formed by the whole community.

## How councils act

A council shares in the government of an institute in various ways: as a collegial body, by deliberative vote,[24] or by consultative vote, giving its opinion when it is asked.

The general principle is that the authority of the superior is only limited by the council on the occasions and in the measure clearly set out by the law; presumption is in favor of the superior.[25] Strictly according to law, therefore, if it is said that the superior must consult his council or act with his council, he need only ask its opinion and is not obliged to have its consent. However, the text must be interpreted objectively and in the whole context.

The different cases in which councils at the different levels must intervene, and in what manner, are set out in canon law and in the constitutions, supplementary rules and acts of the chapter. The constitutions usually contain a list of the matters for which the council acts collegially or with deliberative or consultative vote. The council itself cannot impose a limit on the superior's authority unless this is specifically provided for in the constitutions.

The tendency today is for the council to act collegially in the more important affairs of the institute or the province, as, for example, when the general council acts as a substitute for the general chapter in appointing a general councilor to fill a vacancy.[26]

A deliberative vote has binding force (can. 105) and a superior cannot validly act against it. Some institutes make no difference between a deliberative and a collegial vote.

If the vote is only consultative the superior can act against it, but should not do so without strong reasons. In our day particularly, this is strongly felt, and a superior would feel that the wish of the council, especially if unanimous, carries a certain moral obligation not to oppose it.

Whatever kind of vote is in question, if a superior is obliged to lay a matter before the council and omits to do so, the subsequent act is invalid.

The procedure for councils is practically the same as for chapters. Frequency of meeting is indicated in the constitutions and is usually greater for the general council than for others. Meetings must be announced in advance and copies of the agenda sent around. All members must be summoned to the meetings; the omission of even one might result in annulment of the acts.[27] Many institutes require the presence of at least two-thirds of the councilors. For important matters a full meeting is necessary, and a substitute must be supplied for any unavoidable absence.[28] Some constitutions may provide for action by the council without an actual meeting, the councilors being individually consulted, but the ordinary rule is that consultation requires the group to meet.

As stated above, the superior who presides at council meetings is considered to have the same rights and duties as other members. The objection that he should not vote on matters proposed by himself has no value, but it would be well for the constitutions to mention explicitly that the president votes exactly like all the others.

The problems to be discussed at council meetings are usually proposed by the superior, and this seems normal as it is he who has called the meeting, but the councilors also can put forward suggestions and it is often done.[29] Discussion should take the form of true dialogue, straightforward and objective, in an exchange of views which throws light on the matters to be decided.

When discussion is finished the vote should be taken on a formula giving two clear alternatives to choose between; a vague formula leads to confused and indecisive voting. A secret vote is sometimes obligatory and may always be requested by anyone who desires it; money matters are voted on secretly, as also the dismissal of a religious under temporary commitment (can. 647).

After the meeting the secretary draws up the minutes.

## Councilors

All councilors, though they have no authority outside council meetings, have an important duty to help superiors in every way. In nearly all institutes there is a desire to give greater scope to the general councilors, within the council and outside it, emphasizing their co-responsibility for the institute; some would like each one to specialize in a particular field such as formation, the apostolate, missions, etc. As a group, they should be marked by unity in collaboration and by the vital energy without which nothing is achieved. Individually, they should have a personality that can bring something positive to the collective effort.

It is looked upon as extremely important that the councilors should ensure contact between the center and the periphery, and that it should be fairly frequent.

General councilors are elected by the general chapter. Provincial and local councilors in various ways, sometimes two being appointed by a higher authority and two elected by the provincial or local chapter or by the whole province or community.

As a rule, the members of the council remain in office as long as the superior, and when the latter is changed, the council is renewed. Councilors can usually be indefinitely reappointed.[30]

General councilors are obliged by the constitutions to live with the superior general, though a small number may live elsewhere provided they can be present at council meetings. They must be available to carry out their duties and free from other obligations which would be a hindrance to this; a general councilor cannot, for instance, be a provincial; theoretically the offices are not incompatible, but in practice distance would be a problem, and it would be difficult to find time to give adequate attention to both.[31]

In some institutes the general chapter designates one of the general councilors to act as vicar in the absence of the superior general; in others, the constitutions provide for the choice of a vicar at the time when the superior's absence makes it necessary; very often it is the rule that this function falls to the first councilor or, in his absence, to the second and others in order of precedence. In some ancient Orders it is the superior himself who appoints a vicar in case of his absence or illness or approaching death, but it is normally the constitutions that give all necessary rules in the matter, saying when a vicar is required, what powers he has and how he is to exercise them.

During a period of vacancy of the office the vicar has all the powers of the superior to carry out his functions; whoever acts for a superior absent or unable to act has the superior's powers for normal cases, unless the latter has reserved any matters for himself in accordance with the constitutions.

## 5. Other groups with special functions

Union and communion as a basic spiritual idea cannot exist simply in theory; if it exists at all, it must find concrete expression in the form of actual meetings and contacts, some permanent, some temporary.

Meetings and assemblies at every level, general, provincial and local, serve a valuable purpose by providing opportunity for the exchange of views representing different aspects of questions and problems; even when not destined to lead to immediate action or even immediate decision, they pave the way for it. If a consensus is reached on any subject, that fact in itself is very helpful to those in authority. Contact with superiors and religious of other institutes broadens the horizon and gives new ideas, leading sometimes to valuable common action.

## The community assembly

The development of true community life is an essential factor in renewal and adaptation, and it can be brought about to a great extent by meetings of the whole community rightly understood, well-organized and prepared.

Such meetings can take over the functions—in a different form—of the former chapter of faults; they can take the shape of what is now called revision of life; to achieve their purpose, they need religious trained in the art of dialogue, but the meetings themselves give training, provided people have the patience and perseverance to get over the inevitable early difficulties.

The younger religious in particular feel the need of community life in which help is offered and given in the interpersonal relationships of a group—help in the spiritual life, in carrying out the apostolate, in learning how to tackle difficulties.

In old times the monastery chapter aimed at something of this kind,[32] and present-day community meetings can take on the functions of chapter, council, discussion group and dialogue, with an exchange of positive and constructive criticism which helps individuals and community to reach maturity.

## Commissions

In an age of specialization religious institutes cannot do without specialists at both general and provincial levels;

superiors cannot know everything, and they appoint individuals or groups to study particular matters concerning the institute and its work; it is their business to keep their information up-to-date so that it is available when needed.

These commissions, of which some are permanent and others temporary, serve as links between the government and the different houses with their activities.

Their conclusions and reports are not binding on superiors in any juridical sense, but if well drawn up they carry great weight on account of the specialized knowledge of their members. The moral authority given by competence and prestige has great influence in our time.

# 6.  Organs of communication

## Secretaries and procurators

The unity of an institute and a province rests on a system of communication and rapid, objective information, which should be handled by secretariats and various organs of information.

Not only must records be kept and acts drawn up, but the higher levels of government must be constantly in touch with houses and individuals, giving and receiving information, asking and answering questions. The part played by the secretariat of the central government is of an importance not easily exaggerated. The same may be said of the secretariat attached to a general chapter, and, in proportion, to other secretariats.

The general and provincial secretaries are usually appointed by their respective councils. In some institutes, there are secretariats and secretaries for particular fields of activity: formation and studies, missions, the apostolate in general.

Can. 517 § 1, prescribes the appointment of a procurator general in pontifical institutes of men, for relations with the Holy See. A similar official has been found useful in women's institutes also.

The superior general, man or woman, can always deal directly with the various offices of the Holy See, especially the Congregation for Religious, but it is a good thing for one person to have such matters in hand.

The procurator for business with the Holy See used to be elected by the general chapter; now he is often appointed by the general council and is usually a member of the general chapter.

# 7. Church law concerning the organs of government

In the revision of structures and organs of government,[33] which is the sphere in which a need for far-reaching changes has been most felt, institutes sometimes ask which of them are prescribed by the Church and how they should function. The answer is to be found in the Code of canon law and other papal documents of a universal character. If there is no law or canon making a particular organ obligatory and defining its use, the institute is free to use it or not.

Canon law speaks of chapters and personal superiors (can. 501) for the whole institute (can. 502), the provinces (can. 488,8; 502; 504) and individual houses (can. 502, 505). According to general law, moreover, the personal superior is part of the very structure of an institute, a province or a house.

Chapters are not considered essential at all levels; and, as a matter of fact, although the provincial chapter normally has its place in a province, some institutes have had provinces without them. In a centralized institute the general chapter is the highest authority; but the local chapter, to which so much importance is attached in autonomous houses, is not obligatory.

Can. 516 says that there must be councilors and bursars, and can. 617 prescribes a general procurator for pontifical institutes of men.

No other structures of government are dealt with in canon law. The very nature of chapters and councils requires secretaries to draw up their acts.

Chapters and superiors have governing power which must be exercised "in conformity with the Constitutions" (can. 501 and 502), and other canons concerning the rights and duties of superiors likewise refer back to the constitutions (can. 505, 507, 511, 516). All such references will in the future take account of the new form that constitutions may take after the revision required by the Council.

A minimum of authority, rights and duties, is essential for the office of superior, but it is not easy to define. The experiments now being made may prove helpful here.

# 8. Updating in practice

In virtue of the liberty which they enjoy, institutes have often restructured existing organs of government and introduced new ones, providing for the participation of all, linking up chapters and superiors with others throughout the institute for decision-making, consultation, research and opportunities of discussion, proposals and dialogue.

The institute thus appears as a body built up and joined together by organs for decision, mediation, consultation, research, planning, execution, communication and information, which engage a larger number of persons and indeed all the religious. In this way we do not have the impression of a community divided into two groups or strata: a small one active and responsible and a larger one whose duties are passive, the carrying out of orders.

The movement that results from better understanding of authority and obedience is a movement that brings people together in *koinonia*, the union of all the members.

The institutes, while keeping the principle of authority intact, have used a variety of methods for the distribution and linking up of functions and duties.

We have passed to a more collegial form of government; the power of decision-making has also been extended to peripheral organs; the system by which everything was meticulously regulated by authority has given way to greater freedom of decision and liberty of movement for the individual.

The liberty allowed for by Church law, however, finds limits in the purpose of the structures and of authority; their efficiency and adaptation to them ends. Structures have sometimes been created which delay and complicate the exercise of authority, or do not provide those in authority with the faculties necessary for carrying out their duties. Experimentation will be judged by its fruits, and where mistakes have been made, remedies will be found and applied.

1. See *Il Capitolo Speciale*, (Rome: U.S.M.I.), p. 291. Marinus a Neukirchen, O.F.M. Cap., *De Capitulo generali in Primo Ordine Seraphico* (Rome, 1952), p. 543. G. Lewis, *Chapters in Religious Institutes* (Catholic University, Washington, D.C., 1943), p. 158.

2. The local chapter is the earliest in the history of chapters; it has great importance in monasteries *sui juris*.

Even without the title of chapter, the community assembly can have collegial powers for certain questions and elections, in which case its decision is binding on the superior also. Ordinarily its task is one of discussion, dialogue and consultation (PC 14,3).

3. In some institutes any chapter held outside the normal frequency is called extraordinary.

4. Some institutes have provided for a general and provincial chapter every three years.

5. What is said here of the general chapter applies to the provincial chapter in its own sphere. Normative and legislative power is, however, often reserved to the general chapter.

6. This is the common practice of the Holy See and of institutes, though two sessions were allowed for the special general chapter (ES 3).

It is not forbidden for any general chapter to suspend its work for a limited time, especially to enable the commissions to prepare material for the sessions.

7. For clerics it is often required that they have finished the normal course of studies.

8. Ancient law used to distinguish between a numerical majority, *pars maior*, and a majority of wisdom, *pars sanior;* but how to ensure that the wiser persons are elected is a problem not easily solved.

9. They remain members of the chapter until its termination, even if not re-elected.

10. Institutes with few provinces have more than two from each one.

11. The constitutions may allow those absent to vote, and say how it is to be done. Proper arrangements must be made to safeguard authenticity and secrecy, but to allow it is in the spirit of collegiality.

12. There may be abstentions, in which case the number of voting papers would be less than the number of capitulars.

13. The Holy See is unfavorable to an election by universal suffrage except in small institutes; consultation of all the religious is allowed.

14. In diocesan women's institutes the bishop who presides at the election has the right to confirm it; in pontifical institutes the bishop of the place where it is held presides at the election and announces the result. In the present day it would seem a good thing to have the same procedure for women as for men.

15. Can. 506 § 2 says who is to preside at the election of the superior of a monastery of nuns.

16. Some institutes fix a maximum age beyond which a person cannot be appointed superior. It seems preferable to leave those who appoint or elect to judge of the suitability of the person.

17. Up to the present there has been no limit of time for ecclesiastical offices outside religious life. *Ecclesiae Sanctae* I, 11 invites bishops to resign at the age of 75. The Apostolic Constitution *Regimini Ecclesiae universae* of 1968, says that the Prefects and Secretaries of the Roman Congregations (General Norms, ch. I § 5) are appointed for a period of five years.

18. Election for life has been abolished by the Oblates of Mary Immaculate, the Redemptorists and the Religious of the Sacred Heart.

19. While the chapter is in session the superior can offer his resignation.

20. A sufficient cause would be that serious harm was being done to the community, but it would be preferable to advise the superior to resign.

21. P. Hofmeister, *Der Ordensrat* (Bonn: Ludwig Rôrsheid Verlag, 1937), p. 117; *Consiglio,* General Assemblies 1960-1961 (Rome: U.S.M.I.), pp. 109-161.

22. The Synod was instituted by the Motu Proprio *Apostolica sollicitudo* of October 15, 1965.

23. If the constitutions say that the superior presides at council meetings but is not a member and has not a vote, they must be observed.

24. The word *decisive* is not correct, since the final decision lies with the superior; he cannot act against a deliberative vote, but he can refrain from action. The constitutions should make it quite clear what the different kinds of vote imply.

25. The constitutions may establish that presumption is in favor of the council.

26. *Ecclesiae Sanctae* II, 7 gave the general council the powers of the special general chapter for the period between two sessions of that chapter, according to the decisions of the chapter itself.

27. If a councilor is known to be against some proposal there might be a temptation to hold a meeting in his absence, if that is foreseen, but such an action would prove that relations within the council are not what they should be.

28. In some institutes provision is made for the appointment of a substitute.

29. There is a difference between moving a resolution on which the council is obliged to vote, and merely making suggestions or drawing attention to particular points. The latter falls within the duties of all councilors (cf. Norms of 1901, art. 279).

30. Some institutes prescribe that the whole council should not be changed at the same time but one or two left to ensure continuity.

31. A bursar can be a councilor, but he has no vote in the approval of his accounts.

32. Under a new form, the value of certain monastic traditions has been discovered.

33. The Pope himself is giving us examples of change in this sphere. The special general chapters have started experiments of the greatest diversity.

# Chapter XV
# The possession and administration of property[1]

## 1. The possession of property

Some institutes have limited the right of their provinces, and still more of their houses, to the possession of property,[2] with a view to co-ordinating the efforts of the whole institute and its members to carry out the mission entrusted to it. In missionary institutes the provinces have little independence; they exist simply for the foreign missions.

More frequent is the case of men's or women's institutes not divided into provinces, in which all landed property belongs to the institute itself; or of institutes whose provinces are the owners of all land and houses within their territory.

The administration of the property is thereby simplified and a fair distribution made easier, houses with a surplus giving up some of it to help those in need and bringing about a greater equality among them. The general fund is used by the institute or the province for its common ends.

Other institutes have introduced a system of *subordinate possession,* by which both provinces and houses can own property and are responsible for their own debts and obligations; but the ultimate ownership lies with the higher authority — institute or province — which can dispose of the property in its own right.[3]

## Acquisitions and debts

The constitutions and other codes of the institute should decide what acquired property is to be added to the patrimony of the institute, province or houses (cf. can. 580 § 2 and 583) and how the contributions of the houses to the province, and the provinces to the institute, are to be fixed.[4]

If a house is closed its property passes to the higher authority, province or institute; if a province becomes extinct, the right of disposing of its property belongs to the general chapter, or, outside the time of the chapter, to the superior general with his council (can. 494 § 2).

Can. 536 states the rules concerning indebtedness:

1. If a corporate entity (whether an institute, a province or a house) contracts debts and obligations even with the permission of superiors, it is personally responsible for them.

2. When a regular, with the permission of superiors, contracts debts and obligations, the corporate entity whose superior has given the permission bears the responsibility; if it is a religious with simple vows, he himself is responsible, unless he acted, with the superior's permission, on behalf of the institute.

3. If a religious contracts debts without any permission from superiors he himself is responsible, not the institute, the province or the house.

4. In every case, it is a rule that an action can always be brought against him for whom the contract has been a source of profit.

The present tendency is to hold the institute or the house responsible, even when the superior does not give explicit permission but by his silence implies approval of what the religious is doing.[5]

# 2. Administration

Poverty calls for wise and prudent administration, which consists in all the action required for the preservation and development of property, putting it to the best use and ensuring that it serves the ends for which it is destined (cf. can. 352).

Administration can be divided into ordinary and extraordinary. Ordinary administration is concerned with the habitual and day-to-day acts done for the above purpose. It is extraordinary when the acts are exceptional, either of their nature or by their infrequency, as, for example, buying or selling which involves the patrimony. Some people consider extraordinary anything which goes beyond the bursar's normal activity and therefore requires permission from the superior.

Can. 532 § 1 says that property must be administered in accordance with the constitutions[6] and with canon law.[7] Details are laid down in the constitutions and by general chapters, but the main concern of all religious administrators must be the Gospel ideal; they should not aim chiefly at safeguarding and increasing their possessions; but look higher, at the good that can be done, the purpose for which the property is intended, the witness to be borne to poverty and love of the poor. Pastoral considerations and the knowledge that religious property forms part of the patrimony of the Church and should benefit the poor will save them from any temptation to wish for wealth or the power that it brings. In particular, religious must show great concern for social justice, the payment and treatment of workmen and all those employed, including exact payment of the insurance required for social security.

On the principle of co-responsibility, there is a desire for communities to be given more information as to expenditure and the disposal of property.

## Bursars and superiors[8]

Can. 532 § 2 names superiors and those appointed by the constitutions as the administrators of property; superiors can validly incur expenses and carry out the ordinary acts of administration, but the constitutions usually attribute this work to the bursar.

Can. 516 § 2 prescribes the appointment of a general bursar for the whole institute, a provincial bursar for the province and a local bursar for the house; the local superior may if necessary be the bursar, but not the general or the provincial.

The corporate entity is responsible for the acts of its lawful representatives (cf. can. 536 and 1527).

It is stated by canon law (can. 516 § 2; 502) that all bursars carry out their duties under the direction of their respective superiors, and direction implies vigilance, accountability and some guidance; the bursar cannot act as a superior in his particular sphere. It does not, however, give the superior the right to take the bursar's duties upon himself and simply give him orders to carry out; his rights and duties are defined in the law of the institute, which determines the frequency and modality of the vigilance and accountability to be exercised.[9] The superior guides and directs, but the bursar carries the responsibility for organizing the administration and seeing that all is done in an orderly way. He is called to council meetings when financial matters are to be discussed.

The general and provincial bursars should follow up those of lower rank.[10]


In acts of extraordinary administration superiors have a direct part to play; their authorization, and at times that of their respective councils, is required for buying, selling, borrowing, lending, extraordinary expenditure, etc. The constitutions and the general chapter fix the sums that may be disposed of by superiors at different levels and say whether the deliberative or consultative vote of the council is required; in practice, the constitutions refer the question to the chapter, for it is not a thing that can be fixed permanently.

The Roman Pontiff being, according to canon law, the supreme administrator of Church property and therefore of the property of religious, (can. 1518; 499 § 1), the permission of the Holy See must be asked for the alienation of property or the contraction of debts above a certain value (cf. can. 524 § 1). Specific sums are mentioned in the Code, but the continual and rapid depreciation of currencies tends to make the fixing of any amounts meaningless within a short time; the episcopal conferences are authorized to increase them in their own countries when necessary, and religious may apply to themselves the totals fixed for Church property.[11]

For nuns and for diocesan women's institutes it is the bishop who authorizes alienation and borrowing, approves the investment of dowries and can, if he wishes, inspect the accounts of all the houses; in other institutes he approves the use of funds given to the parish or to the house for expenditure on divine worship or on works of charity (cf. can. 535 and 533).

## Duties of administrators

The first duty of an administrator is fidelity; the property he administers belongs to others, and he can neither act as if he were the owner nor neglect what must be done to use it profitably.

The Code in can. 1522 and 1523 says that administrators of Church property must make correct inventories, keep accounts of receipts and expenditure and the documents relating to them, and be careful to observe both canonical and civil law.

Administrators or bursars may not make presents or give alms except conformably to the constitutions and with the superior's permission. A sum that is set aside for almsgiving is usually fixed each year by the community, ensuring that charity is not limited to what is too easily spared.

Besides his professional duties the bursar has duties of relationship in community; the superior must see that his work does not clash with the duties of others, and the bursar himself must realize that his personal attitude — kindness, consideration, true charity — is of great importance for creating in the community an atmosphere of peace and joy.

1. Only the more important points are mentioned in this chapter. For further details any good treatise of canon law can be consulted.

2. Cf. Chapter III above, on collective poverty.

3. Subordinate property takes effect within the institute, not outside it.

4. The contributions are often fixed on the basis of income, or of the number of persons. The fund thus built up enables the province or the institute to help other provinces and houses.

5. Permission in itself does not imply any guarantee or responsibility; when the Holy See authorizes a loan, it does not take responsibility for it.

6. The constitutions and the general chapters determine the duties of each administrator, the method, conditions and modality of certain

acts, the financial competency of the different organisms, the acts to be considered ordinary or extraordinary, and the general system of administration in view of a certain uniformity.

7. Cf. can. 534 for alienation.

8. Some institutes have appointed a commission at the different levels which includes the superior and the bursar.

9. Ordinarily the accounts must be approved by the council at the level concerned, which, at certain fixed times, inspects the financial statement, the registers and the cash-box. The report to be presented to the general or provincial chapter has also to be prepared and approved.

10. Not infrequently the bursar is the legal representative of the institute or the house for dealing with civil authorities.

11. Cf. M. P. *Pastorale munus*, art. 38. and E. Gambari, *Facoltà speciali dei Superiori Generali*, pp. 53-63.

In 1970, the sums fixed were £100,000 for Scotland, £50,000 for England and Ireland, $300,000 for Canada. The episcopal conference in the United States has not yet fixed any limit.

# Chapter XVI
# Separation from the institute[1]

Separation from the institute can take place in different ways; either by transfer to another institute, or by returning to secular life at the expiration of temporary commitment, or by secularization, or again by expulsion or dismissal from the institute itself.

The giving up of religious life must appear as something abnormal or exceptional for one whose consecration to God is looked upon as lifelong, to be expressed in the final "it is finished" (Jn 19:30).

## 1. Transfer to another institute

There is *transfer* when a religious leaves his own institute and is incorporated into another without interruption of his vows or of his belonging to the religious state. The vows made in the institute which he leaves are absorbed and taken up into his profession in the institute or monastery which he joins.

Juridically, and by the practice of the Holy See, the procedure of transfer applies to members of Societies of common life or of secular institutes with regard to religious institutes and vice versa, and also among themselves.

The conditions for a transfer are as follows.

## Permission

No religious can pass to another institute or independent monastery without authorization from the Holy See (can. 632); *Pastorale munus,* art. 38, permits the authorization to be given by the local Ordinary for diocesan institutes, or by the Apostolic Delegate (arts. 22-35 of the faculties granted to the Nuncios).

Acceptance is required on the part of the competent superiors of the institute it is desired to enter. It is normal that the superiors of the institute the religious is leaving have the possibility of expressing their opinion; usually their consent is asked; can. 544 § 5 requires them to give a written testimony.[2]

## Novitiate followed by profession

The one transferred must complete the full novitiate, during which he is bound by his vows and must, in virtue of the vow of obedience, obey the superiors of the institute he is entering and the novice master; during the novitiate the rights and particular obligations he had in the institute he is leaving are suspended (can. 633 § 1).

When the novitiate is ended the superior has the right to prolong the period of probation for a further year (can. 634); this seems entirely reasonable, especially if it is a change-over to contemplative life.[3]

At the end of the probation, if the novice is not admitted he must return to his own institute unless his vows have meanwhile expired; if he is admitted he makes profession in the new institute; if he had already made perpetual vows, he will make perpetual profession immediately (can. 633, 2-3). This profession absorbs the previous one and the rights and obligations attached to it no longer exist (can. 635). If his previous vows were solemn they cease to be so, unless the Holy See ordains otherwise (can. 636).

One who passes from a monastery *sui juris* to another of the same Order—for instance, a discalced Carmelite to another monastery of discalced Carmelites — neither makes a novitiate nor repeats his profession (can. 633 § 3); but it is obvious that there should be a suitable time of probation before the definite transfer.

Any property he has acquired as a religious remains with the first monastery (can. 580 § 2 and 582) but the dowry and personal property (if any) follow the person (can. 635,2).

### Motives

Transfer to another institute is usually motivated by a desire for a form of life more in keeping with a person's particular vocation, as, for example, the contemplative life or a missionary life; it can also be due to dissatisfaction or a lack of comprehension in his own community, or to the sort of transformation of the institute that makes a person say, "This is not the Order I entered."

The principle of fidelity to one's institute as expressing God's plan for us is undoubtedly good, but the experience even of some saints shows that transfer to another institute sometimes also enters into His plan.

Nevertheless, it is all too easy to deceive oneself and consider a call from God something which really is only the product of whim, instability or mere desire for change.

# 2. Leaving the institute at the expiration of vows

### Voluntarily

Canon 637 tells us that those who have made profession of temporary vows may, when the term of the vows has expired,[4] freely leave the institute. They are not bound by any obligation assumed with the act of profession. Some use the term "juridical freedom" for this, leaving it to be understood that fidelity to one's vocation may be a moral obligation, especially when vows are made on the understanding that they will be renewed unless some impediment arises (can. 488,1).

## By the will of the institute

The same canon goes on to say that the institute may, for reasonable and just motives, decide not to admit the religious to renewal of vows or to perpetual profession. The motive for non-admission need not be so strong as for dismissal (can. 647); it will usually be unsuitability for religious life shown in the behavior of the religious either morally or intellectually or in his character and temperament, or absence of the positive signs of a vocation required as a sufficient guarantee.

The law does not provide for an appeal, especially with suspensive force, but appeal against a decision can always be made to a higher authority in the institute or to the Holy See.

## III  health

Canon 637 says that ill health cannot be a reason for non-admission unless it be clearly proved that the religious, before profession, had fraudulently hidden or dissimulated the illness.

According to Church law and the terms of *Sedes sapientiae* (1956) and *Renovationis causam* (1969), the period of temporary vows is looked upon more in the light of a time of probation or trial, during which the religious and the institute get to know each other better and find out whether he is really suitable for religious life. An urgent question arises out of this. How can a religious family be obliged to admit to profession a person who is found to be suffering from a psychical disorder or any other that makes him unfitted for life in the institute? It seems logical that if the time of probation has revealed the existence of a malady either psychic or organic which makes him unsuitable, the institute should be free not to permit him to renew his vows.

The problem was resolved by the S. Congregation of Religious by the Decree of 12-8-70 suspending the prescription of can. 637 and permitting the non-admission to renewal of temporary vows or to perpetual vows of a religious suffering from a physical or mental malady that makes him unsuitable for religious life, both for his own sake and for the harm that would be done to the institute.[5]

The malady in question must be one of a nature that could do serious harm to the harmony, equilibrium and peace of the community or of the person himself, or both; it is a moral rather than a financial question, and harm is likely to result chiefly from mental disorders such as paranoia, hysteria, schizophrenia or permanent nervous depression. A person afflicted with such maladies will be unhappy in community and may be a cause of serious disturbance to others; any priest or doctor consulted by him should advise him to withdraw from religious life. In some cases non-admission may also be justified by a physical or organic malady, especially if accompanied by psychic or temperamental difficulties, even if the latter do not amount to an abnormal condition that would in itself justify non-admission.

The motive required by the Decree is unsuitability for religious life. Financial hardship caused by providing expensive cures would not be admissible as a motive; and the S. Congregation's decision of 5-2-25 remains in force: the institute is obliged to provide for one of its members who has lost his reason.

Mental illness is sufficient for non-admission even if it existed before the first profession; it cannot be supposed that the institute would have wished to burden itself with an unsuitable person.

To ensure that a right use of this power is made by superiors the Decree requires that the existence and consequences of the malady be established by serious consultation of doctors or specialists according to the case; the superior must also obtain the consent of his council.

Charity will always seek the true good of the person concerned and not only or chiefly the protection of the institute, which has a certain duty in equity if not in strict law toward one who entered it with the intention of remaining in it always. Illness must not simply be a pretext; nor must it be of a transitory and curable nature. All the circumstances must be taken into consideration. It would be more difficult to ask anyone to leave if his state of health had been known before his admission to first vows, or if he had not received adequate treatment for a cure. Before sending a person away, the institute must have done all in its power to find a cure.

The basic problem is that of a vocation for this institute; if circumstances show that the vocation is lacking, it is normal that the institute refuse the final and binding commitment. It would be no kindness to admit a person not fitted for it.

Nonetheless, charity and equity require that superiors should do all they can to make a return to the world easier, helping the man or woman to find an occupation and settle down in a way of life with proper provision for the future.

## 3. Exclaustration

Exclaustration may be defined as permission to remain outside the institute for a limited time, with a certain diminution or suspension of the bond with the institute.[6] The word has disagreeable overtones, and indeed it is often the first step toward total and complete separation.

A person who is exclaustrated remains bound by his vows and the obligations assumed at profession, except those which he cannot carry out in his new condition; in particular he is dispensed from the common life (cf. can. 639). He loses the right to wear the religious habit, though this is sometimes allowed for special reasons; but he remains a religious and must live as becomes a consecrated person.

During the period of exclaustration the religious loses active and passive voice; he can neither attend chapters nor vote in elections, nor be elected to any post or office in his own institute.

As regards the vows, the vow of chastity remains unchanged; the vow of obedience places him under the authority of the local Ordinary wherever he happens to be living, and the latter takes the place of his superior. If his religious superior sees anything undesirable in his behavior he must intervene and, if necessary, rescind the permission for exclaustration.

The vow of poverty remains in force with regard to what he has earned in the past; it belongs to the institute; but what he earns now, and any other property that may come to him, are for his own use. If he contracts debts or obligations he must answer for them personally, unless he is acting for the institute with the necessary authorization (can. 536). He is expected to earn his own living unless it is really impossible, in which case the institute will provide for him.

## Duration and causes

The indult is granted for a specified time, usually not more than two or three years, or as long as the motive for it exists, e.g. illness or the family's state of need. It does not, however, fix a compulsory date; superiors can, for just motives, recall a religious before the time is up, and he, on his part, may ask to come back sooner, in which case they are bound to receive him. When the period of exclaustration comes to an end the religious must return to his community.

The causes justifying the indult may concern the religious personally: mental health, difficulties in community life through a clash of characters or for other reasons, a desire to try the experiment of life in the world, and so on; or they may concern other persons: parents or other relatives in urgent need of assistance, work that lies outside the aims of the institute.

Sometimes exclaustration is suggested by the Holy See to someone who has asked for a dispensation from vows, to let him see what living in the world is like.

In the present practice of the S. Congregation of Religious, a new kind of action by the Holy See has been introduced, i.e. exclaustration *ad nutum S. Sedis.* It is usually imposed not by the institute but by the Holy See itself, and acceptance by the person is not necessary.[7] As the name implies, it is not granted for any specified time but for as long as the Holy See chooses. The reason for it is the impossibility or at least the grave difficulty of the common life for the religious himself or for others, even if he is not to blame for it. The institute which asked for this indult for one of its religious must provide for his maintenance insofar as he is incapable of it, but naturally he is expected to earn his own living to the best of his ability.

There is yet another form of indult called "qualified exclaustration" granted by the Holy See to religious priests who wish to give up the priestly state; its purpose is to give them time to reflect seriously. For a specified time they may live like laymen, maintaining celibacy but dispensed from all other obligations and rights derived from the priesthood or from religious life.

A comparison

There is a certain affinity between exclaustration and permission to live outside the house,[8] but their juridical effects are different.

Experimentation is sometimes judged by superiors as a sufficient reason for allowing absence from the house.[9]

An exclaustrated religious loses active and passive voice; those merely absent retain it. Leave of absence is the term used for one who is away for personal reasons such as deciding on his vocation; his situation is rather different from that of a religious who is absent for the purposes of the institute or for reasons not of his own choice and the institute may, within the limits of its power, treat them differently. It scarcely seems right that one who is away should share in important decisions of the community while not sharing its life, and some institutes have decided that all who are absent for personal reasons lose active and passive voice during their absence.

# 4. Secularization and dispensation from vows

Nature

Secularization is the cessation of the bonds and obligations contracted by religious profession with regard to the institute and the Church. By Can. 638 it carries with it the cessation of the vows, and therefore dispensation from them. The two acts are, however, distinct.

In pontifical institutes the Holy See alone can grant secularization to those who have made perpetual vows; the local Ordinary can grant it to those under perpetual or temporary vows in diocesan institutes. By the rescript *Cum admotae* 14, the superiors general of pontifical clerical institutes were given the faculty of dispensing from temporary vows; the Decree of 11-29-69 gave the superiors general of lay institutes of men or women the right to grant secularization to such religious, and this, as stated above, carries with it dispensation from their vows.[10]

According to the practice of the Holy See the indult does not take effect unless accepted within a given time from the date on which the person concerned is informed of its granting or its execution.[11] In view of the gravity of the act, due reflection and consideration are required, and even when the request has been made and granted the Holy See insists upon a further decision to make use of it.[12]

The power to dispense from vows is included in the Church's power to annul obligations toward itself and the vicarious power to release from obligations undertaken toward God. Secularization, according to can. 640, severs all the links resulting from religious profession, so that the religious man or woman returns to secular status, clerical or lay.

## Causes and remedies

At the present time we are faced by the situation of thousands of religious men and women leaving the religious life, a phenomenon totally unlooked-for only a short time ago and calling urgently for some explanation.

It was only to be expected that in the post-conciliar period some institutes and some individual religious should have difficulty in adapting themselves to a view of religious life that contained new aspects and made new demands. But the scale on which difficulties have arisen, and above all the widespread conclusion that the only remedy was to give up religious life, cannot be regarded as normal.

A certain number of requests for secularization can be explained fairly easily. A good many of those who have left were from the beginning unsuited to religious life and ought never to have been admitted; others became unsuited to it through a lack of fidelity which made them a dead weight in the institute and a hindrance to their fellow religious. Others again, who had managed fairly well in the former conditions, found that an examination in depth of religious life and its demands in the world of today resulted in asking of them more than they were prepared to give; they had put their hand to the plow (Lk. 9:62) but looked back for lack of generosity and courage.

To a religious who comes to the conclusion that he or she never had a vocation, or who lacks the will to fulfill the obligations assumed—either through habits acquired, the style of life adopted or relationships that have grown up—dispensation from vows appears as a liberation for himself and for others.

Trying to justify their action, some have recourse to the theory of a *temporary vocation,* which is nothing but a "tranquillizer" for their conscience. They try to make God responsible for their own change of attitude.

Various theories on the priesthood and the permanence of religious life are now current and play their part in inducing people to leave a state of life chosen in the past with great generosity (Paul VI, 4-9-71).

A more serious problem is raised by the harmful effect of current errors in ideology and sociology which distort the concept of religious life and encourage giving it up, sometimes by declaring it an obstacle to the development of the human person, showing it as lacking in dignity and strength, purposeless and useless, and a hindrance to those who wish to work for their fellow men.

In the petitions for secularization the same motives constantly recur: not finding in the religious life personal development and room for proper self-assertion; feeling suffocated by the structures; being unable to work according to one's personal charism; being in a state of tension and misunderstanding; finding in it the opposite of true witness.

Some, both men and women, complain of opposition and slowness in the process of updating, or a lack of understanding of what updating really is. Others, and not always wrongfully, say that changes have been too radical and that the secularizing tendency has lost sight of the inspiration of the founders; some experiments and changes certainly cut deep into the form of life embraced at profession.

The comment has been made that we are going through a period of purification for religious institutes, who are losing members much as a tree in a gale loses the fruit that is less firmly attached to it; true religious life, it is said, is now seen as more demanding than people used to think; candidates were too easily accepted, and this will not happen in the future. Unfortunately, among the fruit that is dropping off, much is good and can ill be spared.

Each institute should analyze the phenomenon within its own sphere and its own experience, and find out whether any complaints made by those who leave it are well founded. A really energetic effort to bring about the return to the Gospel and the primitive inspiration of the founders, to give spiritual meaning and life to the structures and create an atmosphere of mutual esteem, respect and love, together with effective updating of the forms of apostolic work, might obviate certain defections.

At times, faith in the values of religious life is shaken because faith itself is shaken and is going through a time of crisis; or it may be moral habits which are shaken and this results in a life-style that no longer has anything religious about it.[13]

## Religious priests

Secularization is granted definitively to a religious priest when he is admitted immediately and definitively to a diocese (can. 641 § 2). If the bishop wishes for an experimental period it is granted for three years which may be followed by another three, after which he becomes a permanent member of the diocesan clergy unless the bishop decides to the contrary.[14]

## Duties of the institute to those who have left

Since the aim and purpose of religious profession is spiritual and has no connection with money matters,[15] there is no injustice in the statement in can. 643: "Whoever leaves his institute, whether at the expiration of temporary vows or by virtue of an indult of secularization, or whoever is dismissed, cannot seek compensation for the services rendered by him to the institute." It defends the institute from unjustified demands.

Nonetheless, even when the religious leaves of his own free will, certain duties of charity remain. The same canon goes on to say that for a woman who brought no dowry or for whom the dowry returned to her[16] is insufficient, the institute should provide the means of returning to her home and a sum for her maintenance for a certain time, to be decided by mutual agreement or, in case of disagreement, by the local Ordinary.

Social conditions today make greater demands on equity than in former times. Pensions are provided under insurance plans for illness, disability and old age, and it is unthinkable that a religious who has worked for years in his institute should find himself destitute upon leaving it, especially if he cannot, or can only with difficulty, earn a living for himself. The situation is understood by the institutes,[17] which have various ways of meeting it without giving those who are in no need the right to demand in strict justice large sums of money or pensions that the institute cannot afford.[18] The situation of the institute must be considered as well as that of the person who has left. Hence the provision of appeal to the local bishop is wise.

Moral help may be needed as much as financial help by those who have to adapt themselves to a different way of life.[19] Charity to those who leave and charity to the institute and those who remain faithful, though differently expressed, are one and the same and cannot be separated.

## 5. Unlawful departure

An apostate from religion is one who, having made profession of perpetual vows, unlawfully leaves the religious house with the intention of not returning; or who, with the intention of withdrawing from religious obedience, though he left it lawfully does not return to it (can. 644 § 1). By this violation of the law he incurs various penalties (cf. can. 2385) which include excommunication — reserved to major superiors for clerical institutes and to the local Ordinary for others — incapacity to make legitimate acts, the loss of all the privileges of the institute and the loss of active and passive voice even after his return.[20] The major superior can add other penalties according to the gravity of the fault.

Two things must combine to constitute the offense: departure from the religious house or neglecting to return to it, and the explicit or implicit intention to withdraw from obedience or from life in community in a way that implies leaving the institute.[21] This intention is presumed if the religious lets a month pass without returning or telling the superior that he intends to return.

Neither the apostate nor the fugitive—who leaves without permission but intends to return—is released from his obligations and vows; he must return at once; his superiors will seek him as the good shepherd seeks the lost sheep, and welcome him if he returns. His behavior is not in itself a cause for dismissal, but if repeated appeals and warnings have no effect, dismissal may follow.

A fugitive loses *ipso facto* any office he may hold and if he is a priest incurs suspension reserved to major superiors, and other penalties according to the constitutions and the judgment of major superiors (can. 2386).

Going out of the house without permission or staying out longer than the time allowed does not make a person a fugitive; the offense consists in the intention of placing oneself for a time outside the control of obedience.

# 6. Dismissal from the institute

Dismissal is the severance of links with the institute and the loss of rights connected with it; consequently it means the departure of the religious from the institute and his return to secular status.

On account of its painful nature dismissal is not often put into practice; one who deserves it may be induced to ask for dispensation from his vows.[22]

The Code distinguishes between four kinds of dismissal and gives rules for each: the first (can. 646) is dismissal by the Code itself; the second and third (can. 646-652) are dealt with in administrative form; and the fourth is judicial (can. 654-667).

The religious who are *ipso facto* regarded as lawfully dismissed are those who have either publicly apostatized from the Catholic faith; or gone away with a person of the opposite sex; or attempted or contracted marriage, even the so-called civil marriage.

## Temporary vows

In the atmosphere which prevails since Vatican II it is rare for a religious under temporary vows to be dismissed; more often an indult of secularization will be obtained.[23] However, the procedure for dismissal is set out as follows in can. 647-648: The competent authority is the superior general of a pontifical institute or the abbot of an independent monastery, acting with the consent of his council given by secret vote; in monasteries of nuns it is the bishop; for nuns subject to Regulars it is the Regular superior, acting on a written report from the local superior and her council explaining the causes; in diocesan institutes it is the bishop, who should not act if the superiors do not know or if they have just cause to dissent.

The motives for dismissal must be grave, that is, proportionate to the bond which exists between the religious and the institute; want of religious spirit which gives scandal to others is a sufficient motive. It is assumed that the cause is culpable and that admonitions and corrections have had no effect; in other cases, e.g., inaptitude for studies or for the ministry, or ill health falling within the terms of the Decree of 12-8-70, non-admission at the expiry of vows would be the solution. Before dismissal the religious in question must always be informed of the motives for it and given full liberty to reply (can. 647 § 2, 3); he has the right to appeal within ten days to the Holy See, and action is suspended pending a reply.[24] Dismissal carries with it dispensation from vows; for priests, the obligations of his ordination remain and can. 641 and 648 are still in force.

## Perpetual vows

For religious under perpetual vows, exempt or not, the Code requires at least three grave offenses, two admonitions and failure to amend, according to the terms of can. 656-662, which specify that the three faults must be of the same kind or such that together they show incorrigible bad will; one fault will have the same effect if it is continuous and persisted in after two admonitions (can. 657). The admonition must be given by the immediate major superior or by another acting for him with certain knowledge of the facts, and accompanied by exhortations, corrections, penalties and any means that might obtain amendment (can. 659-661). The religious is considered incorrigible if after the second admonition he commits a new offense or perseveres in the old one, but six days at least must elapse before further steps are taken (can. 662).

When all this has been proved the superior general will discuss with his council whether or not the religious is to be dismissed; if the majority is in favor of dismissal,[25] in a diocesan institute the whole case is referred to the bishop of the place where the house is situated, and the decision is left to his judgment; in a pontifical institute the superior general himself issues the decree of dismissal; it does not take effect, however, until confirmed by the Holy See.

The religious has a right to set forth his reasons freely and his replies must be faithfully recorded in the acts (can. 650 § 3). This is a rule of natural law and respect for the human person, who has the right to defend himself. It must not appear a mere formality to be carried out when everything is already decided; the members of the council must have all the documentation before them, including the defense of the religious, before giving their final vote.

For women's institutes the Code has separate canons; in practice, however, the Holy See requires the same conditions for dismissing women as for dismissing men. In diocesan institutes the decision lies with the bishop; in pontifical institutes and in monasteries of nuns the Holy See issues the decree of dismissal on the report, respectively, of the superior general, the local Ordinary or the Regular superior as the case may be, accompanied by the relative acts and documents.

In an exempt clerical institute the dismissal of a religious under perpetual vows either solemn or simple, whether clerical or lay, is a matter for a judicial process as set forth in can. 654-667, all that has been said above concerning grave causes, the manner of making admonitions and the question of incorrigibility being applicable.

However, in practice it has been found almost impossible and has sometimes resulted in an invalid act. There is a strong movement today for dropping the judicial process and substituting the administrative form, which can adequately safeguard all the demands of justice.[26]

According to can. 653 and 668, in case of grave external scandal or the menace of very grave injury to the institute, a religious may be summarily dismissed from the institute by the major superior with the consent of his or her council; or even, if the danger is imminent and there is no time to refer to the major superior, by the immediate superior with the consent of the local council and the local Ordinary. For exempt religious the consent of the Ordinary is not required. The superiors will refer the matter without delay to the Holy See, which will give the final decision.[27] The dismissed religious must immediately take off the religious habit.

## The situation of dismissed religious

By the very fact of his dismissal, a religious under temporary vows is released from his vows (can. 648), whereas for one under perpetual vows the binding force of them remains unless the constitutions or the Holy See determine otherwise (can. 669 § 1). According to the practice of the Holy See, constitutions usually state that the dismissal of lay religious, Brothers or Sisters, carries with it the cessation or dispensation from their vows. Occasionally, but rarely, the same thing holds for priests in a clerical institute.[28]

If a dismissed religious remains bound by his vows, he is obliged to return to the institute; and if he shows for three years that he has really mended his ways, he must be taken back; if there are serious reasons for not doing this, the case must be referred to the Holy See (can. 672§1).[29] In practice this rule applies to priests and deacons and shows the Church's maternal solicitude for them and for their return.[30]

Can. 671 determines the situation of a priest or deacon dismissed from the institute: he is suspended until he has been absolved by the Holy See; when directed to do so he will reside in a diocese under the care of the bishop, and if he cannot provide for his own needs the institute will charitably come to his help. If his conduct is good he can ask to be absolved from suspension and begin to exercise the ministry little by little; after a sufficient time of trial he can ask for readmission to the institute.

1. Only the main points are referred to and new aspects arising from Vatican II and present-day conditions.

For further details a commentary on canons 632-672 may be consulted.

2. Prudence will suggest to superiors that all necessary inquiries be made. The superiors of those who wish to be transferred to another institute must look at the question objectively and in a supernatural spirit. It would not be reasonable to require previous dispensation from vows.

3. Some indults authorize an even longer time of trial.

4. Vows expire on the anniversary of the day they were made (cf. can. 34 § 3, 5).

5. Further explanations on this subject are given in an article by E. Gambari in *Vita consacrata* (1971), pp. 359-364.

6. Superiors general cannot grant exclaustration, but only absence from the house. Cf. Chapter VIII, section 3.

7. The causes must be very serious; a religious family cannot break off community life for one of its members unless it is the only remedy. Even if no blame attaches to it, and therefore no idea of a penalty, prudence and equity require that the religious be informed that this form of exclaustration is proposed, and the reasons for it, so that if he has any objections to make he can do so.

8. *Cum admotae* 15 and *Religionum laicalium* 4.

9. *Renovationis causam* art. 8 gives it as a legitimate cause.

10. Cf. E. Gambari, *Rivista delle Religiose* (1970), pp. 306-309, for an explanation of the working of this faculty, which is valid also for diocesan institutes.

11. In a few rare cases dispensation is imposed; it then has the effect of dismissal without the painful connotations of the latter.

12. The present practice of the Holy See is to allow ten days for acceptance after the notification is received; after that, the indult lapses.

13. In some cases the one asking for dispensation has incurred a penalty or censure as fugitive or apostate (can. 644 and 2385-2386); in such cases the indult absolves from the penalty.

14. Restrictions on the offices that a secularized religious priest may hold have been suspended (Decree of the S. Congregation of Religious of 2-2-72).

15. Cf. ch. I, section 1 above. Religious profession cannot be equated with a civil contract.

16. Cf. can. 551 § 1.

17. The same problem arises for those who give up the priesthood. The religious institutes and the bishops have been asked to examine the situation and deal with it. Charitable aid may be a duty for an institute or a diocese, so far as they can give it.

18. Sisters who leave often hold diplomas which enable them to find work, and institutes frequently take part in the insurance plans which place their members in the same condition as others.

19. In France and elsewhere associations have been formed for the purpose of helping those who have left the priesthood or religious life.

20. Of its nature this penalty is perpetual, but nowadays restitution of active and passive voice is granted more easily, especially if the matter was not public.

21. Unlawful departure often ends in a request for dispensation from vows, which is granted together with a faculty for remission of the penalties.

22. The case must be quite clear.

23. The sending away of those who have made promises or other commitments instead of vows is regulated by the constitutions (cf. *Renovationis causam* 6).

24. Decree of the S. Congregation of Religious of 7-20-23 (AAS 15, 1923) p. 457.

25. For dismissal the council acts collegially.

26. On 11-25-69 the S. C. of Religious approved for the Franciscan Friars Minor a procedure for the dismissal of religious under solemn vows which gives all the safeguards of judicial action (cf. *Regulae et Constitutiones Generales O.F.M.*, Rome, arts. 332-346).

27. Sending the religious away at once is equivalent to a provisional dismissal.

28. In such cases, which very seldom occur, the question of assistance for the dismissed priest arises.

According to can. 672 § 2, the case of priests whose vows have ceased and who have not found a bishop willing to take them must be submitted to the Holy See.

29. The institute is not obliged to take back priests who have been dismissed in force of can. 646 (cf. Commentary for interpretation of the Code, 7-30-34, AAS: 1934, p. 494).

30. Can. 670 regulates the situation of ordained clerics dismissed for particular offenses which call for more severe measures.

# Chapter XVII
# The religious vocation: fidelity

*Lumen gentium,* Chapter VI, and *Perfectae caritatis* both end with an appeal for fidelity, an appeal to institutes and to individual religious. In *Evangelica testificatio,* Paul VI sets forth all the substance of religious life and the urgency of renewal, and warns against possible deviations from the ideal.

Those who are drawn away by deviations do not look upon them as infidelities; it is important therefore to have a clear understanding of what fidelity means.

## 1. The individual religious

### Fidelity to the pledged word

Fidelity to the pledged word is in itself a human virtue highly and rightly esteemed, a matter for proper self-respect. "I give you my word" is a phrase expressing mutual trust and valued as such. To break one's word is betrayal.

But fidelity to religious vows is infinitely more than that. "Infinitely" is no exaggeration, for by a vow we pledge our word to God.

"Religious today, at a time when so many are in fact leaving the religious state...must constantly choose anew their way of life, their permanent commitment."[1] This entails asking themselves what a vocation is, what their response is and why they make it.

## Fidelity to religious consecration

In the previous chapter we remarked that many who leave the religious life declare that when they entered they did not understand what they were doing. They never understood the mission of the religious as the Council documents have shown it: an entering into the mystery of the Church, a sign of the indissoluble union of Christ and the Church.

A vocation is God's call to a particular man or a particular woman to carry out that mission with all it implies. To respond with a yes is to consent to being what God wants us to be. With our yes, there is no need to look elsewhere for the means to develop an authentic personality.

The response to God's call is a response of love to a particular mark of love. "You have not chosen me, but I have chosen you" (Jn 15:16). It is Christ who says, "Follow me." But we are free to accept or refuse. If the response is "they left their nets and followed him," the gift of self is total and irreversible. The juridical act of dispensation from vows remits a moral obligation, but how weak it appears when we look at the existential reality of religious profession and the bond it creates. The religious, like Our Lady, has said, "be it done to me as you say" and placed himself at Our Lord's disposal as an inseparable companion to cooperate in His redemptive work. Profession is not a point of arrival but a starting-point, and the new life that begins is a life of consecration. Marked out as belonging to God, the religious enters into salvation history. For the world, the sense of God is kept alive by the sight of those who have given up all for no other reason than to possess Him.

# 2. The institute

## Fidelity to the charism[2]

The fidelity of the individual religious is not the fidelity of a hermit. In his institute he has his part to play to ensure that renewal goes forward as the Council urges it, that is, in a constant return to original sources and a constant adaptation of them to current needs. The two lines of action are not parallel but convergent, or rather, it is a single line, coming from God to inspire men and returning to God to gather fresh energy and pour forth new light, strength and love on the world.[3]

The institute, as well as the person, needs to deepen its knowledge and understanding of its own nature, willed by the wisdom and love of God and expressed in a specific charism. Deeper knowledge will lead to an increasing appreciation of the gift and a clearer sight of the part religious life has to play in a secularized world where men are blindly groping for something higher than themselves.

The joys and sorrows of the ever-changing world, deeply felt by the Church, as *Gaudium et spes* tells us, are nowhere more deeply felt than in religious institutes, which have given themselves for the service and aid of mankind. The challenge before them today is to strengthen and develop religious life in the whole of its content, so that it brings each person to maturity and answers the expectations of God and of their fellow men; each religious family has its own sources and can bring out of its treasures old things and new (Mt 13:52).[4]

The charism must not be left to fossilize; it is an inexhaustible wellspring of spiritual and apostolic life (ES II,1). Texts endeavor to express it, but it cannot be contained within them; as a living thing it is ever at work in the institute and in the members. To the institute as to the individual, talents are entrusted which must be put to profit. The seed that becomes a tree is a symbol of what God expects from all alike.

More than the revision of rules and structures, needful though it is, the urgent need today for institutes and religious is to examine themselves, their mentality, their behavior, to bring it into line with all that consecration calls for and with the radicalism of the Gospel which admits of no half-measures.[5] Fidelity is not static but dynamic, and love is the irrestible force that gives meaning to a life in which God continually invites and man continually receives and responds (ET 47).

## Fidelity to love

The following of Christ begins as a response of love, the love which eagerly desires to go beyond the precept and chooses the counsel as a means of reaching out toward the measure of God's own love, which has no measure. The outward framework itself is seen as an expression of love, but it is transcended by the light and guidance of the Holy Spirit.[6] Personal responsibility, where the framework provides for it, as, for example, in prayer, cannot be taken lightly. Careless neglect of prayer would be a betrayal of love; deliberate neglect would be unthinkable.[7]

Love alone transforms a whole life, not once for all but in constantly renewed self-giving, for life itself is lived minute by minute, always moving onward. God asks more and more, and at every fresh step forward, joy increases.

## 3. Fulfillment

The paschal mystery is a continual passage through death[8] to life, foreshadowed by nature itself, and lived day by day until its meaning is revealed when the time comes to leave this world and God calls us to Himself. In the splendor of His light what we have seen "dimly, as in a mirror" will be lit up in the face-to-face encounter. As St. Paul tells us, our imperfect prophecies and knowledge will pass away, but when faith and hope are no longer needed, "love never ends."

Day by day, from the first *yes* of response to a vocation, the religious has walked in the footsteps of Jesus and Mary, from Bethlehem to Calvary, from the resurrection to the ascension and the assumption. It is to Our Lady's mediation that Vatican II entrusts the fidelity of all religious, "that they may go from strength to strength and bring forth in ever greater abundance the fruits of salvation" (PC 25); and Paul VI ends the Exhortation *Evangelica testificatio* with a prayer to her and an appeal to imitate her: "May the most blessed Mother of the Lord obtain for you in your daily journeying that lasting joy which Jesus alone can give. May your life, following her example, give witness to that maternal love which should animate all those who are associated in the apostolic mission of the Church" (ET 56).

1. B. O'Leary, Supplement to *The Way*, XVI (1972).

2. "For a living being, adaptation to its surrounding does not consist in abandoning its true identity" (ET 51).

There is a profound analogy between the critical danger threatening the priesthood and the existing situation in religious life.

3. E. Gambari, *Renewal in Religious Life* (Boston: St. Paul Editions, 1967), Part I, ch. II and ch. III treat at length of the principles and characteristics of renewal, especially pp. 28-30, 19-68 and 69-116.

4. "Your own sources of energy must spring up with renewed vigor and freshness.

"The interior driving force must continually revitalize the outward forms...but—a note of warning—an excessive desire for flexibility and creative spontaneity may lead to the disruption of a community" (ET 12, 32, 51).

5. The aim of the present work is to help religious to enter into the new spirit and follow its inward inspirations in the direction indicated.

6. Mt. 5:17.

7. Some sensation was caused in recent years by a book written by a nun who had left the convent. Some time later she wrote an article which appeared in the press, declaring that she would never have left if she had been faithful to prayer.

8. On the Christian attitude toward death see M. Bordoni, *Dimensioni antropologiche delle morte* and L. Boros, *The Moment of Truth*.

# APPENDIX I

## Documents of special interest to religious

11-30-63 M. P. *Pastorale munus* (AAS 56 [1964] p. 5-12). Faculties and privileges of bishops.

11-6-64 Papal Rescript *Cum admotae* (AAS 59 [1967] p. 374-378). Delegation of special faculties to superiors general of clerical institutes.

2-17-66 Apostolic Const. *Poenitemini* (AAS 58 [1966] p. 182-196). On the practice of penance.

5-31-66 Decree of the S. C. Rel. *Religionum laicalium* (AAS 59 [1967] p. 362-364). Special faculties for superiors general of pontifical lay institutes.

6-15-66 M. P. *De episcoporum muneribus* (AAS 58 [1966] p. 467-472). On the faculty of bishops to dispense from general laws.

8-6-66 M. P. *Ecclesiae Sanctae* (AAS 58 [1966] p. 769-782). For the application of the council decrees.

6-18-67 M. P. *Sacrum diaconatus ordinem* (AAS 59 [1967] p. 697-704).

8-15-67 Ap. Const. *Regiminis ecclesiae universae* (AAS 59 [1967] p. 885-928). For the reform of the Roman Curia.

1-6-69 Instr. of the S.C. Rel. *Renovationis causam* (AAS 61 [1969] p. 103-120). On the formation of religious.

8-15-69 Instr. of the S. C. Rel. *Venite seorsum* (AAS 61 [1969] p. 674-690). On the contemplative life and cloister for nuns.

11-27-69 Decree of the S. C. Rel. *Clericalia instituta* (AAS 61 [1969] p. 739-740). On the participation of lay members in the government of clerical institutes.

11-27-69 Decree of the S. C. Rel. *Cum superiores generales* (AAS 61 [1969] p. 738-739). On the secularization of those under temporary vows in lay institutes.

1-2-70   *Ordo professionis religiosae* (AAS 62 [1970] p. 553.

1-6-70   *Ratio fundamentalis institutionis sacerdotalis.* Basic norms for priestly training given by the S. C. for Catholic Education (AAS 62 [1970] p. 321-384).

6-4-70   Decr. S. C. Rel. *Ad instituenda experimenta* (AAS 62 [1970] p. 549-550). Suspension of various canons.

12-8-70   Decr. S. C. Rel. *Dum canonicarum legum* (AAS 63 [1971] p. 318-319). On confession for religious men and women.

2-1-71   Declaration by the S. C. for Catholic Education on co-education in schools other than primary conducted by religious (AAS 63 [1971] p. 250-251).

6-29-71   Apostolic Exhortation *Evangelica testificatio.* On the renewal of religious life (AAS 63 [1971] p. 497-526).

2-2-72   Decr. S. C. Rel. *Experimenta.* (AAS 64 [1972] p. 393-396). On the personal authority of the superior and the suspension of can. 642.

2-2-72   Allocution of Paul VI on secular institutes.

8-15-72   M. P. *Ministeria quaedam.* On the new discipline concerning the clergy and the "ministries."

8-15-72   M. P. *Ad pascendum* on the diaconate.

# APPENDIX II

### Modifications made in the canons either by suspension of the norms contained in them by way of experiment or by the granting of special faculties

can. 251    The S. C. Rel. restructured in *Regiminis ecclesiae universae* 71-74.

can. 452    The Ordinary can entrust parishes to religious. ES I, 33, 1.

can. 488,4    *Perfectae caritatis* 15,3 provides for institutes with parity between clerics and lay members.

can. 494,1    Approval of the Holy See no longer required for the erection of new provinces or the suppression of those that exist. Decr. *Ad instituenda experimenta* 1.

can. 497,1 and 498    Requirement of permission from the Holy See suspended as regards the opening or closing of an exempt religious house, except for monasteries *sui juris* of nuns. Decr. *Ad instituenda experimenta* 2.

can. 499,2    Nomination of Cardinal Protectors suspended. *Letter from Secr. of State* 4-28-64.

can. 500,1    Dependence on bishops specified in the Decree *Christus Dominus* 35,4; and in *Ecclesiae Sanctae* I, 25-28.

can. 501,1    Jurisdiction granted to all superiors general of pontifical clerical institutes, with the right of sub-delegation. *Cum admotae* 13.

can. 504    Perpetual profession the only condition for holding office; the superior general must be 35 years of age, other major superiors and the novice master not under 30. Decr. of 6-4-70, art. 3.

In many cases illegitimacy no longer an impediment to office of superior general. *Letter from Secr. of State* 2-27-67.

can. 505　The superior general of pontifical institutes can prolong the term of office of a local superior for a third three-year period with the consent of his council and after consulting the local Ordinary. *Cum admotae* 19 and *Religionum laicalium* 8.

can. 510　The quinquennial report is suspended. S. C. Rel. 3-13-67.

can. 516　The necessity of personal authority is clearly stated in the Decr. *Experimenta* 2-2-72.

can. 518-    The regulations concerning confession and con-
528      fessors are modified. Decr. *Dum canonicarum* 8-12-70. See Volume II ch. VI, Sec. 5.

can. 534　Pontifical institutes may apply to themselves the sums of money fixed by the Episcopal Conference of the region. *Cum admotae* 9 and *Religionum laicalium* 2.

Diocesan institutes may be authorized by the bishops up to the same amount. *Pastorale munus* 32.

can. 538-    See the book E. Gambari, *Updating of Religious
570      Formation.* (Boston: St. Paul Editions, 1969), pp. 141-147.

can. 552;    Canonical examination before novitiate, temporary
571,3     vows and perpetual vows suspended. A retreat of five days is sufficient. Decr. of 6-4-70, arts. 7 and 5.

can. 574　Bonds of other kinds may be substituted for vows. Period of temporary vows may be prolonged up to 9 years. *Renovationis causam* 34; 37.

can. 580　*Perfectae caritatis* 13 permits religious under simple vows to give up their patrimony.

can. 583,1　Permission to give up personal property. *Perfectae caritatis* 13 and *Ecclesiae Sanctae* II, 24.

can. 583,2　The superior general of a pontifical institute can authorize the alteration of a will. *Cum admotae* 17 and *Religionum laicalium* 6.

can. 595,1    Frequent confession, that is, once a fortnight. *Dum
and 3     canonicarum* I,3.

can. 596　Certain situations may justify the use of secular dress, but the consecration of religious must always be borne in mind. *Evangelica testificatio* 22.

can. 597　Regulars, except monks, may adopt the cloister of institutes of simple vows. Decr. of 6-4-70.

can. 600　Number of persons who may enter the enclosure increased. *Venite seorsum*, Norms, 7.

can. 600-    Faculty of the bishop in *Pastorale munus* 34.
601

can. 600-605   *Venite seorsum*, Norms 1-16, has partially updated the regulations.

can. 606   Superiors general of pontifical institutes can authorize absence from the house for more than six months. *Cum admotae* 15; *Religionum laicalium* 4.

can. 607   Prescription suspended; vigilance against possible abuses required. Decr. *Ad instituenda* 8.

can. 608   Given with greater precision in *Ecclesiae Sanctae* I,28-39.

can. 610   Adapted in *Instructio generalis de Liturgia Horarum* 2-2-71.

can. 610   Faculty for superiors of nuns to dispense from private recitation of Divine Office or commute it. *Religionum laicalium* 9.

can. 615   Exemption refers chiefly to the internal affairs of the institute. *Christus Dominus* 35,3.

can. 620   Bishops cannot dispense from laws concerning religious as such. Cf. M. P. *De episcoporum muneribus* 6-15-66, art. IX, 4.

can. 621   Obligation to keep to the norms of the Episcopal Conferences. *Ecclesiae Sanctae* I,27-1.

can. 622   Confirmed by *Ecclesiae Sanctae* I,27 -2.

can. 624   Cf. 621.

can. 632   The bishop authorizes transfer from one diocesan institute to another. *Pastorale munus* 38.

can. 637   Possibility of non-admission to renewal of vows or to perpetual profession in case of illness. *Dum canonicarum* II, 12-8-70.

can. 638   The superior general of a pontifical clerical institute dispenses from temporary vows. *Cum admotae* 14; the superior general of a lay institute permits religious under temporary vows to return to the world. Decr. of 11-27-69.

can. 642   Limitations concerning offices and benefices that may be held by ex-religious suspended. Decr. S. C. Rel. 2-2-72.

can. 875   Superiors general of pontifical clerical institutes grant jurisdiction for confessions. *Cum admotae* 13.

can. 876,1   Special jurisdiction no longer necessary for hearing confessions of nuns.

can. 2342   Suspension of penalties for breaking the rules of cloister for nuns. *Venite seorsum*, Norms, 16.

# Daughters of St. Paul

**In Massachusetts**
    50 St. Paul's Avenue, *Boston*, Mass. 02130
    172 Tremont Street, *Boston*, Mass. 02111
**In New York**
    78 Fort Place, *Staten Island,* N.Y. 10301
    625 East 187th Street, *Bronx*, N.Y. 10458
    525 Main Street, *Buffalo*, N.Y. 14203
**In Connecticut**
    202 Fairfield Avenue, *Bridgeport*, Conn. 06603
**In Ohio**
    2105 Ontario St. (at Prospect Ave.), *Cleveland*, Ohio 44115
**In Pennsylvania**
    1127 South Broad Street, *Philadelphia*, Pa. 19147
**In Florida**
    2700 Biscayne Blvd., *Miami*, Florida 33137
**In Louisiana**
    4403 Veterans Memorial Blvd., Metairie,
    *New Orleans*, La. 70002
    86 Bolton Avenue, *Alexandria*, La. 71301
**In Missouri**
    1001 Pine St., *St. Louis*, Mo. 63101
**In Texas**
    114 East Main Plaza, *San Antonio*, Texas 78205
**In California**
    1570 Fifth Avenue, *San Diego*, Calif. 92101
    278 17th Street, *Oakland*, Calif. 94612
    46 Geary Street, *San Francisco*, Calif. 94108
**In Canada**
    3022 Dufferin Street, *Toronto* 395, Ontario, Canada
**In England**
    57, Kensington Church Street, *London* W. 8, England
**In Australia**
    58, Abbotsford Rd., Homebush, N.S.W., *Sydney* 2140,
    Australia